Disturbing the Peace:

Writings by Colorado Attorneys

Colorado and Denver Bar Associations

Jacket and text design by Karen Bries-Long
Set in 11-point Schoolbook

ISBN: 0-9653567-1-X

Acknowledgements

Major thanks to Greg Rawlings for having this good idea; he also helped proof and wrote a story to include. We appreciate all the attorneys (plus several judges and several former judges) for their contributions to the book. Robert Baldwin helped us with some very necessary details in actually publishing the book. Doug McQuiston, Manuel Ramos, David Erickson and Richard Holme were kind enough to judge. Thanks to Ira Selkowitz of the Colorado Lawyers for the Arts (CoLA) for helping us with reprint legalities. Colorado Bar Association Executive Director Chuck Turner came up with the name and isn't over it yet. Thanks to Margaret Maupin of The Tattered Cover for her help and enthusiasm. For editing, proofing and cheerleading: Leona Martinez, Karen Bries-Long, Molly Osberg and Diane Hartman.

Excuses

Is it true that all lawyers want to be writers? Some would say all lawyers are writers, but that would be too generous. Still there are a goodly number who practice law by day and write an amazing array of fiction and nonfiction in their "spare time." A lot of it is good. Last year, we invited Colorado attorneys to send us their work. Some did—then we used a somewhat arbitrary process of selection, resulting in only a few altercations between judges (all in the abstract). We want to apologize for leaving some worthy writers out. It isn't our fault. We also want to apologize for mistakes that may have crept into the copy behind our backs. Again, it's not our fault.

Profits

Proceeds go to Colorado Lawyers for the Arts.

Contents

Fiction

Non-Fiction

Fiction

If We Had Been Dancing

by Manuel Ramos

I walked into the bar the same as I had a hundred times before and my thoughts were the same as a hundred times before.

This is all I have to do *after work? Drink beer, shoot the bull with the bar flies, flirt with Maggie, throw a dollar in the jukebox? What a life.*

Maggie winked and popped open a beer before I had made it to my stool. She slid it in front of me and said, "How's it hangin', Alvarez? Workin' hard or hardly workin'?" She laughed; the boys two stools over laughed and I grinned a little. That's what she always said and it bugged me but that's what happened at the Club Lido. A man had to put up with Maggie's clichés if he wanted to drink cold Bud in a bottle for two bucks.

In the background a one-hit wonder soul singer cried about his ba-a-a-by breaking his pore ole li'l heart and the boys two stools over told lawyer jokes.

I had nothing but respect for Maggie. She had grown up in the neighborhood around the bar and spent so much time in the Club Lido that when she started tending the bar no one thought much about it. Seemed like a natural place for her.

I peeled off my damp jacket and draped it over the stool next to me, then swept my hand through my hair to shake out some of the raindrops that hadn't yet run down the back of my neck. My sweater was wet, too, but I needed to keep that on. I sucked down half of the brew before I looked around the place. Same old dirty windows looking out on the same old rain-slicked street, same old grimy pool table, same old tired face staring back at me from the stained and cracked mirror behind the bar. Nothing had changed.

The door to the bar opened, letting in cold, moist air, but I ignored it and concentrated on my beer.

That's when the girl picked up my jacket and eased herself onto the stool next to me. My beer stopped halfway to my mouth.

She said, "This yours?"

I took it from her hand and dropped it between the bar rail and the floor. It was an old jacket without any sentimental value, and I wanted to look at her and not the jacket. She had a small, pinched face with a thin nose and thin lips that held a droopy cigarette. Black, very short hair hung across her forehead and dripped wetly down her neck. She looked like a duckling who had been thrown in the lake by the mama duck, before she knew how to tread water. She wore jeans, boots, a loose red scarf, a black tee-shirt and a denim vest that exposed skinny arms and a three-inch tattoo of Our Lady of Guadalupe crushing a snake with her bare foot. And when she looked at me she did it with a pair of brown eyes that were tinged with the gray smoke of her cigarette and the cobalt shadow of her soggy hair.

Maggie turned to her and asked, "What'll you have honey?"

The girl smiled, at the word honey I assumed, and said, "Jack, black. Plenty of ice."

She stubbed out her wet smoke and plucked

another one from a wrinkled pack she had dragged out of a bulky red leather purse that hung on her hip, the strap twisted across her narrow shoulders. She seemed to move to the beat of the music.

So I asked, “You like this song?”

She finished lighting her cigarette, carefully put the match in the ashtray, filled her lungs with smoke, let it all go in a big cloud of drama. She tapped the bar, then she turned to me.

“Yeah, I do as a matter of fact. Something about this song that makes me feel like a teenager again, know what I mean? A teenager getting ready for the prom, thinking that she’s about to lose her cherry, maybe. Know what I mean?”

It was my turn to take my time. I drank my beer, picked at the label with my fingernail, and then looked into the crazy house of those eyes. I said, “I never thought of it that way, actually. It’s more like this bitter-sweet poem about a man’s foolishness and the price he pays for being a man.”

She licked the wet edge of her glass with a tiny pink tongue, and did a move with her shoulders that could have been a dance step, if we had been on the dance floor, if we had been dancing. When she finished with the motions, she said, “A foolish man. It’s always a foolish man.”

Right then I knew that our dance had finished before it had even started. She had to be under the weight of a story that was guaranteed to bore me or make me laugh or maybe even make me feel pity for her but none of those responses was what she wanted. The truth of the matter was that I would never figure out what she was looking for, not if we had all the time in the world to sit in that bar and talk about it. Not if we went to her place and spent the night talking about it; not even if she told me all about it while we lay naked in her bed, smoking cigarettes. I would never know because what she carried around with her was not for me to know. It's a lesson I had learned in that bar so long ago that I had forgotten my teacher but I had never forgotten the lesson.

I shrugged and let it go. Maybe she wanted to get picked up. Maybe she only wanted a drink. Maybe she was waiting for the latest in a long line of foolish men, and maybe he was the kind of guy who would not appreciate another man talking to her about the implications of the sensual vocalizing streaming from the jukebox. It got all complicated right then and there, and I decided that I should have another beer. I waved my empty bottle at Maggie and she retrieved one from the cooler at the end of the bar. Almost simultaneously, the girl hollered, "Hey, another Jack, black. More ice."

One of the boys next to her said, "Put that on my tab, Maggie. Let me buy the little lady a drink."

I winced and waited for something, anything, because what the guy said just didn't seem right and a response of some kind had to be on its way.

The girl said, "Hey, I never pass up a free drink. Thanks, mister."

Then she turned to me.

"Your friends okay? Or are they maybe perverts who want to get me drunk and do something really nasty to a little thing like me?"

The boys laughed and she laughed and I laughed and I thought that at any minute the Club Lido would turn weird. But it was weird in that bar all the time, and I told myself that whatever I was watching had nothing to do with me.

I kept an eye on Maggie, who had proven to be a good gauge for weirdness and trouble. When something was about to break, she could sense it. Fifteen years of serving drinks to crowds of men in varying stages of inebriation will do that. She often had a bat in her hand at the same instant that a drunk decided to trash the place, and then he would either leave or she would open up his forehead with the bat. I had seen it, and I trusted her to figure out the girl.

Maggie did not offer any body language that told me anything about the girl. She served us our drinks and I tried to relax and enjoy my rest stop after work.

One of the boys said, "Hey now, that ain't us, sweetheart. Ask Maggie there. She'll vouch for us. We're okay. Right, Maggie?"

The bartender had her head back in the cooler, counting beer bottles, so none of us could see her face when she said, "A couple of teddy bears, honey. Real gentlemen. Just don't believe them when they say they want you to meet their mother." The boys laughed again, a bit nervously I thought.

The girl stood up from her stool and moved a little behind us. She had her hand in her purse. I offered her a cigarette from a pack I had sitting on the bar but she shook her head and persisted in digging in that purse. The boys went back to telling jokes, because it looked as if the girl would play with that purse for a long time. I had to make a decision. A glass of bourbon meant that it could turn into a longer night than I had anticipated at the Club Lido. I could leave, grab a burger on the way home, and get a good night of sleep. A loud clap of thunder shook the outside world and the lights in the bar flickered. Rain fell in sheets against the dirty windows and I no longer had to make a decision. There was no way I would run to my car in the downpour.

I tried to get Maggie's attention but she stared only at the girl, still standing behind us. Maggie looked sick, and I worried that maybe she had eaten too many of the microwave burritos that were Club Lido's specialty.

Maggie said, "Hey, honey, put that away. There's no need for that."

I turned and saw a very shiny handgun pointed in

the general direction of Maggie but whose sweep had to include me and the boys two stools over. I said, "Damn."

The boys stopped talking, and one of them raised his hands above his head. He apparently had some experience with the situation and so his buddy and I followed his lead.

Maggie said, "Honey, put that away. I mean it. This is stupid. There's no need."

The girl waved the gun at Maggie and Maggie stopped talking. The girl had not said a word for several minutes but she communicated very well, I thought.

She kept the gun pointed at all of us while she moved in the general direction of Maggie. She walked behind the bar, sneered at the two boys with their hands in the air, then she rested the barrel of her gun against Maggie's temple.

Her words came out in a whisper, and I almost didn't believe what I heard her say.

"*Cabrona*. I told you not to mess with me. Here I am, Maggie, just like I promised."

The boys looked at each other, then at Maggie, then at me. I raised my eyebrows at them although I didn't understand what I meant by that.

Maggie rotated her neck as if she were warming up for an exercise class. A tear slowly made its way down her cheek, leaving a trail through the makeup that she wore with pride. She said, "Honey, we can talk this out. What you think you're doing? Put that gun away and let's go home and talk about this. This is crazy, honey. Crazy."

The girl pressed the gun into Maggie's head and Maggie quit rotating her neck.

"*Cabrona! Cabrona, Cabrona!* I told you not to mess with me. You can't dump me, *vieja. Vieja cabrona!* You can't dump me."

Tears from those wild eyes raced down her face

and her thin lips quivered. I feared that her shaking might cause her to pull the trigger by accident.

One of the boys said, "What the hell is this? What's this dyke to you, Maggie?"

The girl pointed the gun at the boy, and he shut up, but it was too late. The shot sounded like a blast from a cannon. He twirled on his bar stool and flew across space until he landed on his back on the muddy floor.

He said, "Oh God. She shot me. She shot me."

His right hand gripped his left shoulder where blood oozed across his fingers. His friend's wide-open eyes gaped at the blood. Large tears formed at the corners of those eyes. There seemed to be a lot of crying and I was starting to feel a little emotional myself.

Maggie said, "Oh, hell, Coreen, you've done it now. You plan to shoot all of us? Kill me and these guys just because you can't take it that it's over between us? You are crazy. I knew it, and now you've proven it."

I didn't like the fact that Maggie appeared to be giving ideas to the girl about what she had to do next, but I didn't want to say anything. The last person who had intruded into what was obviously a lovers' spat had ended up whimpering on the floor while a pool of his blood slowly radiated around his upper torso. I did not want to join him.

The girl finally spoke: "I don't care about you, bitch. You think that's what this is about? You give yourself too much credit, hag. I want the money. Clean out the cash drawer and get the stuff from the back, in the safe. Then I'm out of here and you and your puta can live happily ever after for all I care."

Maggie shook her head as if she wanted to take the girl in her arms and soothe the bad feelings.

The girl screamed, "Do it! Get the *pinche* money! Get it now!"

She waved the gun in the air with herky-jerky spasms of her hands. I bobbed and weaved like a punch-drunk palooka to keep out of the line that a stray bullet might travel.

Maggie continued shaking her head, not ready to believe what was happening, but she opened the cash register drawer and scooped out a wad of bills. She was handing them over to the girl when the siren froze everyone. The money hung in midair between Maggie and the girl. The wounded boy did not groan, did not twist in his blood. His friend did not shake. And I did not lick my lips although my thirst had become a cotton football stuck in my throat since I had decided that I would stop at Club Lido for a couple of beers after work.

Maggie said, "Someone heard the shot. Called the cops. Now what?"

The girl looked stupidly at Maggie. She hesitated but the siren blared louder and she finally understood she had to do something. The money was forgotten. She hugged Maggie, the gun resting on Maggie's shoulder, and gave her a kiss that seemed too long under the circumstances.

Then she ran from behind the bar and avoided the boy she had shot. She passed within inches of me.
I was halfway off the stool, my feet flat on the floor. I thought about many things right then. I thought how here was a young, troubled girl, part of my raza, my people, with not much going for her except a pair of damn beautiful eyes. I thought that, except to the poor guy bleeding on the floor, she was more scared and hurt than dangerous. I thought how sometimes you have to give people a break, a second chance. I thought those things.

I tripped her as she ran to the door and she flew head first to the floor. The gun slid from her hand and clunked against a wall.

She looked up and saw the gun I had drawn from

the holster under my sweater. Her wonderful eyes begged Maggie but no help existed behind the bar.

I said, "You're under arrest. You have the right to remain silent. Anything you say . . . "

Manuel Ramos is the Director of Advocacy for Colorado Legal Services, the statewide legal aid program, and a part-time faculty member at The Metropolitan State College of Denver. His series of mystery novels featuring Denver lawyer Luis Montez was awarded the Colorado Book Award and nominated for the Edgar Award.

Silo Run

by Robert Baldwin

Arlan Blake stood as one man among many, waiting at the gate a half-mile from foundations of silos fixed in a field of wheat sprouts. Out of work, out of money, and nearly out of sorts, he huddled with the rest while the night wind swirled dust at their feet, while their hearts pumped the remnant of fire retardant out their arteries and back through their veins.

He shifted his feet in the cold and leaned his backside against the warm fender of a pickup rumbling from an idling engine. He could have told any one of the men, just as any one of them could have told him, that the fire retardant was only one of many chemicals bringing him the good luck and ability to make 20 years of mortgage payments, car payments, payments he found reason to be glad to make; and, after those 20 years, it brought him nearer eternity and payments he couldn't make.

He remembered all too well the day the manager called him into the main office at the chemical plant, though Blake lacked any memory of the fact charged upon him. The manager stared out the office window at the green surface of the Tittabawassee River. Beneath the window on a shelf sat a photograph of the man's wife and son eyeing him holding a walleye by the gills.

The manager cleared his throat. "Arlan, I have a problem."

Blake looked first at the manager, who refused to even glance at him, and then at the photograph. He considered his own wife and daughter, and their plans for his daughter to go away to Lake Superior College.

"The problem is this. Somehow a chemical was mislabeled in bags for a dairy supplement. Now those bags have been shipped across the state, and what was supposed to be supplement, but wasn't, was fed to dairy cattle." The manager eyeballed Blake. "You drink milk?"

A sinking sensation dropped through Blake's gut, and his arms prickled down to the tips of his fingers.

"So do I. So do most folks." The manager pointed to his heart. "That means we've got fire retardant in our blood, our muscles, our intestines, *our brains*. You know what makes it worse?"

Blake shook his head.

"It happened three years ago. And we've traced the mislabeling to a shipment you handled."

Blake felt the room spin a bit, almost tilt, and involuntarily his eyes followed those of the manager out the window to the view of the Tittabawassee River, the surface appearing unnaturally green, more tainted with an improbable color than that of any algae. For a moment he believed the water would carry him downstream, far away, and for the first time in 20 years, it occurred to him why the river appeared so green.

He heard the hollow sound of his voice from inside his throat. "How could something like that happen, and I didn't even know it?"

"Good goddamn question, Blake."

* * *

Newspapers ran stories without talking to him and cast him as a stooge. The chemical plant closed. The same month, the legislature refused to amend a law prohibiting the width of mobile home trailors on state highways, and the mobile home factory moved to another state permitting the width sought. Robots took jobs of men who, if they had considered it, stood for years on assembly lines like automatons anyway. Jobs became as scarce as a three-dollar bill.

Now Arlan Blake stood with the other men, hunched in the crowd in the dark before the gate a half-mile from the silo foundations. They shoved their hands in their pockets, turned their backs to gusts of wind, and felt lucky if they warmed their backsides from a fender heated by idling engine. This was supposed to be spring—but it was a spring too cold, with the cold of winter still in a man's heart like a shadow.

They waited until the night turned pale. They waited as wind rushed through the ditches, rattling cattails, dead from the past autumn. Headlights flashed and taillights glowed red from cars and pickups moving like ghosts up and down the road. With the sky growing light, iron clouds swept over the land, threatening a cold rain, and Blake caught the drive of voices over the throttle of engines.

"Too many men, too few jobs," said one.

"You believe them sons-a-bitches? Gonna make us run this half-mile against one another to get a job?" replied another.

The lit end of a cigarette moved like a torch in a third man's hand. "Well, if they don't hire the pin-prick who mixed fire suppressant with dairy feed over at the chemical plant, we ought to figure ourselves lucky."

Laughter stung Blake's ears. He moved away from the warm spot against the pickup's fender and pressed through the men up to the cold steel bars of the gate. In the distance, in the first edge of light, he could make out the wooden frame sitting on the silo foundations like a rough hewn crown. He wanted a piece of that crown. He remembered years before in high school, a bet he lined up on the outside of the track at the start of the 880-yard dash. Wearing his boots and a pair of overalls, he beat every one of the runners in that race. When the track coach asked him to join the team, he turned him down. "I don't have time. I've got a job at the chemical plant."

Now placing his bare hands on the steel bars, he wanted to pull them loose, throw down the gate, and run until his lungs burst. But the cold ran up his arms and into his shoulders, and he stuffed his hands back into his pockets to warm them up.

* * *

Wind blew fitfully, then lessened, then quit. Day broke across the land while the men grew edgy. At last, a pickup, the faded green of washed money, pulled up behind the other cars at the gate. From the cab stepped a man with a chest as broad as a bull, his face windbitten. He made his way through the crowd as the men pressed forward, pinning Blake against the gate.

"There's the foreman!" shouted one, pointing to the man with the broad chest and windbitten face.

The foreman climbed on top of the gate and yelled over the crowd. "First 110 men get jobs!"

"Open the damn gate!" hollered another.

"Let's go!"

Blake felt the air squished out of his lungs as the crowd surged up against him. The foreman jumped down from the gate, unlocked the padlock and chain, and the gate flew open as the men stampeded through the opening, down the road to the silos a half-mile away. Blake stumbled, found his footing and ran. He ran in his boots and overalls. He ran down the road with his arms and shoulders smacking against other men. He pumped his arms and legs. He jumped over a younger man who tripped, fell, and lay in the road covering his head with his hands as other men ran over him. Two more men went down. Still, Blake ran, his lungs emptying of air, burning, and his blood like a river thinning to its source. He stumbled in a pothole, slipped to the side of the road, and slowed to a flatfooted pace more like a plowhorse trying to trot than the boy who once raced along the 880 track of runners.

His heart pounded. Others passed him by. He reached the edge of the silos, sucked air through his mouth, lowered his head and set his jaw, and pushed his legs in a half-sprint he mustered from something left from 20 years before. He clenched his fists and passed three men. Up ahead the white construction trailer came into view. Already a group of men had formed a line from the door of the trailer. Now his legs nearly gave way. He fell into line with his chest on fire. He bent over at the waist and gagged. His mouth tasted like cotton. His gums stung.

No one argued. No one cut in line. Soon the foreman drove up. "Pliable as cooked custard, ain't ya?" he shouted at the men holding their chests, their guts, their sides, sucking air like the hiss of a tire pump. Blake wavered on his feet as a quick black light sparkled in his eyes. He caught himself, grabbed his knees to keep from fainting, then managed to count fewer than 70 men before him. Behind him, the line looked twice as long.

"A job," he muttered to himself under his breath. "I've got a job."

* * *

When he returned home, he found his wife and daughter at the kitchen table, leaning over loan and scholarship applications for college. Cramped, the kitchen held a gas stove older than his daughter, a Philco refrigerator humming like a jet on takeoff, and a two-hole sink devoid of any cupboard below it. His wife and daughter looked up at the same time, and they had the same eyes like night, the same black hair, and everyday he could swear his daughter was the girl his wife had been when he met her the day he ran and won the 880-yard dash in his boots. A spot in his chest warmed up thinking about it. Again, he pictured the calico dress, the ponytail, the smile of a girl about to become a woman, and his arms around her like luck couldn't do much better.

"Daddy," his daughter called out, in a voice not entirely her own. "Did you get the job?"

He walked behind his wife and rubbed her shoulders as both his wife and daughter looked up at him, their eyes hopeful. "I got the job."

His daughter clapped her hands together, gave him a hug, and danced out of the kitchen. He closed his eyes for a moment, feeling the soft shoulders of his wife beneath his hands.

* * *

That night, in the dark of their bedroom, his wife lay down next to him beneath the quilt she had made for their last Christmas. He felt her warm skin. "No pajamas tonight?"

She snuggled against him. "I thought maybe you'd like me like this."

He put his arms around her waist. "I do. Do you remember the dress you wore that first night?"

She let go a quiet laugh. "You mean the one I didn't wear? That old calico thing?"

"It wasn't old then."

She pushed the quilt back and raised up on her knees. The outline of her shoulders, her waist, and her hips showed like a shadow. "I remember seeing you win that race, and that night I was sitting like this in the woods behind old Joe Oster's farm. I undid each button. I thought you had stopped breathing."

He smiled in the dark, reaching out to touch her thigh. "I did stop breathing."

As if wearing the dress again, she undid each imaginary button from below her neck to her belly. "Is that how it was, Arlan?"

He pulled her to him, moisture in his eyes.

He arrived for his 12-hour shift at daybreak, drove down the half-mile lane to the silo foundations, and squinted in the long light of the early morning sun. Each day for 12 days he arrived as the nightlights hanging from the frame of the silos flicked off, the night crew trudged away, and the men of the day shift bent their backs in work. Gears of cement trucks meshed and whirred as cement poured down the sluice into a steel basket winched up the frame and dumped into wheelbarrows. One crew pushed the wheelbarrows about a circular track on top of the frame and poured concrete into the frame's mold. Another crew handled iron rebar, shoving the rods into slots in the frame around which the concrete rose inch-by-inch, leaving horizontal grooves on the wet outside walls of the silos.

He tore the flesh of his palms on the handles of a wheelbarrow, and like everyone else he sweated in the sun, froze in the rain and worked 12 hours without a break. Now and then he would turn to one of the other men, saying, "It's good to be working again," and whistling, he pushed the wheelbarrow like it was an old friend.

The silos rose into the sky like towers of a castle, the inside hollow as the barrel of a cannon. In autumn, he knew, where now the walls held only air and the echoes of men grunting with the weight of work, yellow grain would rise from the bottom to the top—grain so fine it could suck a man from the top to bottom, from life to death, like quicksand. It was an awful thing, he knew, to consider how grain could kill—the same grain that made bread and biscuits.

Each morning, he climbed the series of wooden ladders inside one of the silos to the top, pulling himself hand-over-hand up the wooden rungs of the ladder a little bit higher, stepping out on top to a view of the fields and woodlots spread below in shades of gray leafless trees, brown fields and here and there a strip of winter wheat shining green as the promise of spring.

On top, walking among the men, the steel, the concrete, and the wooden crown of a frame now 200 feet above the ground, he dreamed of walking across the sky with the world laid out as his own below.

"We're skywalkers!" one man would yell.

Blake felt the sinew and muscle tighten. He didn't care about fire retardant in his blood. It didn't matter if it had shortened his life. He was working, and he held power in his hands, his arms, his shoulders, his back, his legs. He lifted the hundred pounds of wet cement in the wheelbarrow and drove it furiously around the circular track on top of the silo's frame, sensing the strength to do that forever.

Robert Baldwin is a Denver attorney and founding member of Baldwin & Brown, P.C. His novella, "Door of Water," was a Denver best seller. His novel, "The Water Thief," is forthcoming from GreyCore Press in the fall of 2002 and was a finalist for the Ariadne Fiction Prize.

La Esfera

by Matthew J. Rita

On a rocky slope in a poor Andalusian village, a young boy looked up at the familiar sound of his mother's voice.

"Emilio!" the voice repeated. "Stay close to the house where I can see you."

Answering with an obedient "Sí, Mamá," Emilio skipped back toward the modest structure he had known as home for all of his seven years. The midday sun shone down on his small head of dark hair, making him easy to spot against the pale yellow and brown landscape. Seeing his mother's satisfied expression in the window, Emilio sat down to resume his play.

Life for María Ramirez was one of painful routine. Since her husband left for Barcelona, she had depended on her brother-in-law, Carlos, for support. "It is for Emilio," she would say to herself when Carlos arrived every two weeks with a small bag of pesetas. "It is for Emilio," she would repeat to herself as she humbly expressed her gratitude, all the while wondering if Carlos expected more.

María Ramirez gazed out at her son, who sat contentedly among the dried tufts of grass. "It is for Emilio," she sighed as she turned away from the window.

As his mother continued her stitching, Emilio held the

metallic sphere close to his face. His brown eyes absorbed every detail as he studied the intricate serpents and vines carved on its golden surface. To him, the object he cradled in his small hands seemed a wondrous gift from the parched earth. Carefully placing the sphere in his pocket, he rose to respond again to his mother's voice.

"¡Emilio, *ven aquí*!" she called. Moments later, the expectant face of her son appeared in the doorway. "*Mi hijo*, we are going down to the well soon. Wash up. There is still a little water left in the basin."

Emilio crossed the house's only room and stepped up onto an old fruit crate. Peering down into the basin, he contorted his face, finding pleasure in the varied expressions of his reflection.

Hearing no sounds of washing, María Ramirez looked up. "*¿Qué haces?*"

"*Nada, Mamá*," came the answer from the corner. Emilio splashed water onto his face and rubbed his hands together. With wet fingers, he dug the golden sphere out of his pocket and dipped a portion of it into the basin. Much to his delight, the water made the surface shine even more brightly. After more splashing and rubbing, Emilio soon had all of it shining.

Emilio returned the sphere to his pocket as his mother set down her sewing. He turned to see her standing before him with arms outstretched. Responding to her invitation, Emilio leapt from the crate into his mother's embrace.

Resting his head on her shoulder, she stroked her son's hair. "Emilio," she whispered in the half-sung, half-cried voice that he had heard often since his father went away. "Your mother loves you very much. Very, very much."

"*Te amo, también*," Emilio answered into the cloth of her dress. His mind left the exciting thoughts of the shining sphere in his pocket, settling instead on the tears he could sense running down his mother's face.

She lowered him to the ground and kissed his head.

"Fetch the buckets, please. I will get my kerchief." Emilio retrieved the buckets they would use to carry water back from the well. Soon they were heading down the winding road that led to the center of the village. María Ramirez stooped slightly as she walked, suggesting a burden of experiences beyond her years. Her feet shuffled along the ground, while her eyes remained fixed on the road ahead.

Emilio ambled along, following a random path that did not confine itself to the road. Swinging an empty bucket in one hand, the boy excitedly pointed with the other at all that caught his eye.

"*¡Mamá! ¡Mire el pájaro!*" he gleefully shouted as a bird flew from a thicket on one side of the road to an olive tree on the other. "*¡Buenos días, Señor Pájaro!*" Emilio sang. The bird watched the passing couple out of one eye, wary despite the height of its perch.

"Emilio," his mother softly chided, "you know that the birds cannot understand people."

"How do we know, Mamá?"

María Ramirez grinned and shook her head, knowing that she could not give her son a convincing answer to such a question. She looked down at Emilio's inquisitive face. "Well, *mi hijo*, if a bird ever talks to you, come and let me know. We shall invite him in for dinner."

Oblivious to his mother's gentle sarcasm, Emilio persisted. "But Mamá! The birds do talk to me! The one who sits in the tree near our house talks to me while I play."

"Oh? And what does he say to you, this talking bird?"

"All kinds of things," Emilio answered, raising his arms as high as the bucket would allow. "Even today this bird told me that Papá is coming home soon."

María Ramirez's looked away from her son as her mind turned to Felipe. It will be a year next month that he has been away, she thought. His departure to the north had been so hopeful: a promise of employment in Barcelona; after saving enough, he would send for her and Emilio. But no word had come—not after three months, not after six months. A new summer was upon them, and still no word.

"Do you think he could be right?" Emilio asked.

"Who, your father?"

"*¡No, el pájaro!* Do you think he is right that Papá will come to get us soon?"

"I hope so, *mi hijo*," she answered, and Emilio sensed more tears about to come.

The plaza was quiet when they reached it, the heat having driven many to seek shade. On one side of the square two burros stood tethered, waiting for their owners to emerge from a nearby tavern. The animals cocked their heads toward each other, as if sharing tales of journey's past.

The other side of the plaza was dominated by the old Guardia Civil building, which now housed the office of el Señor Alcalde. In the afternoon, its shadow fell on the drinking well behind it. The first parejas assigned to the area had determined early on that building their headquarters near the village water supply would help them maintain the public order.

As Emilio and his mother traversed the dusty square, the boy's attention was fixed on the burros. María Ramirez wondered if Emilio could hear them talking also, but she did not bother to ask him.

Approaching the well, the two saw a woman retrieving a bucket from the cool depths below the ground. She bent over the roughhewn stonework, the strands of muscle in her thin arms taut as she pulled the rope, and then finally her bucket, out of the hole. Setting it down beside another bucket she had already filled, the woman stopped to catch her breath. With one elbow resting on the edge of the well, she looked up as Emilio and his mother drew near.

"Buenos días," María Ramirez greeted the woman, recognizing her as the recently widowed Simona Perez.

"Ah, María," the woman nodded, straightening her frail form as best she could. "How are you and your son today?" She smiled at Emilio, the deep lines of her face reminding him of the carvings on his sphere. Reaching for his mother's hand, the boy listened as the two woman exchanged mutual sympathies.

"I am sorry for your loss, Simona. I know that your husband was a very special man to you."

"Gracias, María. We share a common sorrow. But you are young; there is still hope."

The two women stared at each other for a moment, neither quite sure what else to say. María Ramirez saw in Simona Perez's eyes a reflection of her own feelings, and perhaps, she feared, the picture of her own fate.

After a pause, the elder of the two women stooped to gather her buckets. Her posture worsened under the weight of her load, but her face maintained the same somber expression it had borne before. Taking a step to leave, Simona Perez hesitated. She looked first at Emilio, and then once again at his mother. "Remember, María, there is always hope."

"Yes, Simona," María Ramirez answered, gently squeezing Emilio's hand. "Hope."

Emilio watched as the widow trudged away slowly.

"Mamá, why is she so sad?"

"Oh," his mother explained as she began to tie one end of the well's rope to her bucket, "she has lost her husband. Now she is all alone in her house, no one to care for her."

"How will she live?"

María Ramirez began to lower the bucket into the darkness of the well.

"There are many kind people in our village, Emilio. Someone will watch over her."

It was true that their common poverty fostered an unspoken bond among the residents of the village. There would always be an extra piece of bread for a needy friend. Simona Perez would not die of hunger, María Ramirez thought, but from the grief that ate away at her heart.

After the first bucket had been filled and raised, María Ramirez took the second from Emilio and repeated the procedure. The boy looked on quietly, hands in his pockets. He grinned as he grasped the sphere tightly in his right hand. After hesitating a moment he withdrew it from its hiding place and looked at it once again in the light of day.

Glimpsing a sparkle out of the corner of her eye, María Ramirez turned her attention from the second bucket to her son. "*¿Emilio, qué tienes?*"

"I found it in the ground," he replied as he held it out for her to see.

Keeping one hand on the rope, María Ramirez took the sphere from him with the other. A look of amazement swept across her face. "In the ground? *¿Dónde*?"

"Behind the house, near the tree."

"Emilio, this looks like it is gold!" As she inspected it excitedly, her son was surprised to see her lips form a smile.

"It is very pretty, isn't it, Mamá?"

"And probably very valuable!" She kept her eyes fixed on the sphere, shaking her head in disbelief.

Emilio's joy in finding the sphere increased as he saw the happiness grow in his mother's face. She handed it back to him and hurriedly pulled up the second bucket of water.

"Put it back in your pocket, mi hijo. We are going to bring it to el Señor Alcalde as soon as I am done here."

Obeying, Emilio returned the sphere to its hiding place. He did not understand his mother's desire to conceal it. After seeing the effect it had on her, he wanted to show it to the whole world. He thought of Simona Perez, and how the sphere might make her smile—not just in her mouth, but in her eyes, too.

María Ramirez soon held the two buckets—now full—in her hands. Starting toward the front side of the building, she urged her son to follow. At the entrance she set down her load and knocked on the door. Turning to Emilio, she held out her hand for the sphere. "Give it to me. I will show it to el Señor Alcalde. Perhaps he will know if it is gold."

Sensing more anxious excitement than genuine pleasure, Emilio handed the sphere to his mother. He watched a cordial grin appear on her face as the door began to open.

"Ah, Señora Ramirez, and Emilio," the mayor greeted them. "What a pleasant surprise. What brings you to my office?"

Emilio looked up at the heavyset man, who was not much taller than his mother. The mayor's hands were clasped together in an almost reverent manner, and he rocked ever so slightly on his heels while he spoke. The boy could not see his eyes, as the light from the plaza reflected off the round lenses of his spectacles. His remaining features, however, suggested to Emilio that the mayor was a benevolent man. His bushy eyebrows and gray sideburns, as well as the roundness of his large nose, gave him a general look of softness which appealed to the boy.

"I was wondering if I could speak with you for a moment," María Ramirez explained.

"*Por supuesto, por supuesto*," the mayor beamed. He held the door open as María Ramirez led her son inside.

"*Por favor, siéntense*." The mayor gestured toward

a pair of wooden chairs facing his desk.

"No, I will not take much of your time, Señor Alcalde. I was wondering if you could look at this." María Ramirez produced the sphere for him.

"Well, what have we here?" The mayor examined the sphere in much the same way Emilio's mother had. Sheltered from the glare of the noon sun, Emilio could see his eyes grow wide.

"I was wondering if you might be able to tell me something about its value."

"Well, it certainly looks valuable, doesn't it?" chuckled the mayor, meeting María Ramirez's hopeful gaze for a brief moment. She returned a nervous smile. After further inspection, he spoke again. "As far as I can tell, at least the surface is made of gold." He held it very close to his eyes. "These carvings are very strange. But yes, I would say that this is a very valuable item, though I am not quite sure what it is." He handed it back to her gently. "May I ask you how you came to possess such an object?"

"Well, actually it is Emilio who came upon it. He found it while playing behind our house."

The man looked down at Emilio. "So, my little friend, you are the treasure hunter?" He patted the boy's head.

"Congratulations on your find."

"Yes, the treasure hunter," echoed María Ramirez.

"Señor Alcalde, I will not take any more of your time. Gracias."

He waved his hand as if to imply that there was no imposition. "My door is always open, Señora Ramirez. Again, though I am not an expert on such things, I am sure that your sphere is of some worth."

"Let us hope so," she replied.

Taking María Ramirez by the arm, the mayor led her to the door. "I have a cousin in Ubeda who works for a jeweler," he continued. "I could take you there tomorrow if you would like."

The mayor opened the door and Emilio slipped out. As his mother concluded the conversation, the boy turned his attention to the burros still tethered across the square. At the mayor's cry of "*¡Hasta mañana!*" Emilio looked back to see his mother waving.

The return trip was an easier one for María Ramirez, despite the full buckets of water she now carried. Thoughts of what the sphere might bring kept her mind off the soreness in her arms. Emilio, who could not quite manage the weight of a full bucket, walked alongside her with his head down. He was hurt that his mother would not let him carry the sphere. She had tucked it into the small purse she wore at her waist, telling him that it was too valuable for him to keep. When a small black bird pecking along the road ahead of them took to the air, Emilio showed no enthusiasm. He and his mother did not speak much on the way home, their minds occupied by the same—yet different—thoughts.

* * *

On a rocky slope in a poor Andalusian village, a young boy named Emilio felt something smooth just beneath the ground. Brushing away the soil, he ran his fingers along the object's convex surface. The exposed portion reminded him of the sphere he had found the day before.

"Emilio!" his mother called from the house. "Come, we are leaving soon! El Señor Alcalde will be waiting."

Emilio looked down thoughtfully. He patted the earth until the half-buried object before him was once again out of sight. Rising, he brushed his hands on his pants and began to skip back toward the house. "Coming, Mamá!"

* * *

Matt Rita is a litigation attorney in private practice. He and his wife, Liz, live in Denver with their three daughters. The original version of "La Esfera" received the Ellen A. King Memorial Prize for Writing. The author thanks Lisa Horton for helping to prepare the manuscript for this anthology.

The Tarpon Off the Wall

by Bruce Ducker

"It's always been out of place, darling."

He perched on the top step of the ladder, balancing himself with the mounted fish. She spoke the words with her back to him.

"A fish out of water."

"Out of place how?" He stood unsure what to do.

"Out of place with the rest of the room." He looked about. He'd not noticed until now. The room was furnished in a light chintz print, creams and lavenders. The writing desk was Queen Anne, the liquor cabinet an early Connecticut hanging cupboard.

"It's a den, Louise. It's where you'd put a tarpon."

"Is that what it is? I wonder why I repress the word. Perhaps because it sounds a bit sinister, like a feminine hygiene product."

Henry descended the three steps balancing the plaque and placed it behind his cartons. Of the three clusters of boxes, his was the smallest.

Louise let out a sigh. "If only you'd taken up bridge."

"Where would you prefer to have a fish if not in the den?"

Louise was inspecting a chinoiserie lacquer tray. "I'm sorry, darling?" He repeated his question.

"In the kitchen, I think. Au burre blanc. If I must have

one in the house at all." She went on quickly. "This came from those odd friends of your parents. For our wedding? The man who wore the white belt? I think it's Bengali."

"Yours by all means. If you want it." Henry could guess her intentions from the inflection of her voice. He hadn't been wrong yet. She placed the inlaid tray by the carton with the demitasse cups. Most of what had been in the breakfront, indeed most of the appointments of the room, sat in her cartons.

"We're not doing our share for dear old St. James," she said cheerfully as she approached the far book case. The books were his. One by one she read off titles and he indicated his stack or that for St. James. Louise's church, or so Henry considered it.

"He won't mind. He was martyred. Arrows I think."

"Killed by a mob."

"Still. Doesn't get much time for reading."

"How about these, darling?" Louise's choice of the word was prompted not by affection but by a disinclination towards his Christian name. She had never liked it, and particularly now, with the marriage all but dissolved save the court order, she felt that its use might signal a certain intimacy. Henry squinted. Louise was holding up tattered copies of *The Iliad* and *The Odyssey.*

"I've had those since college days."

"Exactly."

"No. I want to keep them. Someday I'll reread them."

She shrugged at the news and tossed the books without malice into a near carton.

"While you're up there, let me hand you a cloth. You can give those moldings a once-over."

He wasn't up there. She fetched a dust rag and he remounted the ladder. She continued to read titles as he worked. Every so often, when her tone betokened a lack of charity, he would cede a book to St. James. And each time, gratified, she would walk to the cartons by the door and place the volume on a neat pile.

He turned the cloth inside out. "It's curious. This house doesn't signify me at all. There's the mounted tarpon and that's it."

"Your books," she said.

"And my books. But my fly rods are in the basement, my shotguns and skis are in the garage. Did you ever notice, Louise, that with a few strokes we have eliminated any evidence that I ever lived here?"

"Now, now. No need to get morbid." They continued their tasks in silence. Occasionally she would call out a title and he would decide.

She opened the china cabinet and began winding bubble wrap about her Rosenthal plates. "Besides, the Realtor says the house will show better with our things out of it." He watched her consider small pieces—the dinner bell they'd never liked, the silver sugar basket. She was stingier to the church than he had been. On the top row were special pieces, beyond the pull, he felt sure, of her conscience: her mother's cordial set, the commemorative plates, and the special netsuke he had given her on their trip to Japan. It was, they had been told, a fertility symbol.

"Why in the world would you keep that fish?" Its glassy eye had arrested her as she made her way about the room.

"I don't know. That was a great week, a special fish."

She let it pass. He decided on a last phrase.

"Happier times."

"You prefer the company of men, darling. You should admit that about yourself. Nothing shameful." He promised himself he would not take the bait. "Now you'll have ample time for those trips."

He finished the moldings. Anticipating her next move, he slid the ladder over to the door jamb, climbed up and resumed dusting.

"The men from St. James will be here any moment. If you have something in the bedroom for them, you might pack it as well."

"They don't want my underwear, do they?"

"Anything at all. You might just take a look, I'd hate to call them back."

He descended, folded the dust cloth, and lay it on the ladder step, and went to see what he could find. The sight of his old, familiar clothes made him decide to move some of them out. A few sweaters, ties Louise had found too young for him, shirts he'd tired of. At the rear of the top drawer was a dress set. Louise had given it to him. He opened the velvet box. The cuff links were oversized and had to be forced through the buttonholes, so that whenever he put on a tuxedo they made him late. It was an expensive set, each piece faced in lapis and centered with a diamond chip. Whenever he wore it he would find himself looking down his shirt front and thinking of a casino ship floating beyond the three-mile limit. He closed the lid and slipped the box into his pocket.

"Any luck?"

"More than I would have guessed." He placed the clothing in a half-filled carton marked for the church and tucked the dress set underneath. His hand hit against an object, and he peeked in to see. It was the netsuke.

"That will be the men from St. James. Darling, do go see if there's beer in the refrigerator. I should offer them something."

Henry obliged. If he lingered long enough he would miss helping to load their truck.

"I'm afraid I don't have that much for you," Louise said to the two volunteers. "There's the love seat and hassock, and those boxes."

The men carried the furniture into their truck. They returned with a dolly to fetch the boxes.

"That's it?" They stood by the cartons in the bare room. The shelves were clean and empty and the wood floor glistened.

Louise eyed a dust ball as if it were a rodent. On the wall she saw an outline traced where the fish had hung. She knew Henry was skulking in the back of the house, he probably had turned on her kitchen television to watch some game.

"Not quite," she said. "Here, take this too." They loaded the dolly. It was fitted with a strap and winch, so they managed all the boxes in a single trip. They left. One man pushed the dolly, and under his arm the second carried the plaque Louise had given him, tarpon side out.

Bruce Ducker's work has won the Colorado Book Award and the Macallan Prize, and has been nominated for the American Library Award for Best Book and the Pulitzer. His sixth novel, "Bloodlines," appeared last year and was noticed by several unrelated observers.

Sports Analogies

by Cynthia T. Kennedy

The shades were drawn against the bright sun of autumnal noon. What sunlight broke through did so in shafts, which hit the walls and reflected from the glass-covered antique desk, creating a disorganized, shadowy light. The phone rang four times before the caller was routed to voicemail. All was quiet for a moment before the peace was interrupted by a number of metallic clangs as the postman forced bulging envelopes one by one through the hooded slot in the door. They fell with a soft thud onto the pile already on the floor, a pile of at least several days' accumulation. Then a key turned and the door opened. It immediately stuck on some of the envelopes, and there was a commotion as a manila envelope was kicked out of the way, releasing the log jam.

Rebecca entered and shut the door gingerly behind her, picking her way through the sea of envelopes lapping at her feet like angry little waves. The needs, desires and expectations of what seemed like a thousand souls pulsed from the pile. She felt the vertigo coming on already and made for the chair. Sinking into the soft leather, she swiveled away from the computer on the desk and toward the window. Shielding her eyes, she drew up the shade.

Outside stood a formidable oak tree bearing

leaves ranging in color from a bright pink/orange to a dark red. The intense noon sun made the translucent leaves glow, and the effect was lacy and feminine, like a colored crinoline. Odd apparel, thought Rebecca, for such a sturdy, stumping, knotty old trunk of a thing. Like me, she thought, swiveling her own formidable body back to the desk, a stump of a body, graced with . . . Her hands moved unconsciously to touch her hair, thick and flaxen, the kind of hair the sun can find a thousand colors in and the night can turn mysteriously dark. I've got good hair, she thought. There is that. But even as they lingered at her temples, her fingers started to throb and tingle, and the hands to go numb. Even the thought of turning on the computer had started the panic. The nausea came, then the ringing in the ears. "Oh, God," she said aloud and slid from the chair to the quieter, darker space under the desk. The wood cooled the skin of her face and she fell asleep.

When she awoke it was already dusk and the sun was just moving behind the hill beyond the oak, turning the old tree's crimson crown to fire. Rebecca got up, picked her way through the mail to the door, and left. She turned the key in the door and only briefly glanced at the metal strip, "Rebecca Jamison, Attorney at Law." Maybe she could handle it tomorrow.

The next day Rebecca had to shoulder the door to move the mass of mail, and she knew that, if she did not pull it together today, TODAY, the entirety of her life's effort, her legal education, her parent's sacrifice for her schooling, would be for naught. It had taken years to build up a practice, a reputation and yet, with a week of neglect, it would fall like a castle sucked down by the tide. She was a sole practitioner, but that was nothing to be ashamed of in this day of boutique practices. Rather, it was quite rare to have a woman sole practitioner with an exclusively commercial practice. For seven years she had worked to build her practice and had avoided the emotion of domestic relations, divorce and personal injury. So what was wrong?

It had started Monday. She had arrived at the office, as usual, at 8:30 a.m. and checked voicemail. Just the mechanical voice saying, "you have eight voicemail messages," made her cranky. The offended tone of the first caller ("I'd really appreciate a call back this time.") pushed her mood beyond cranky to irritated. The one call she took was an angry client. She had informed him by voicemail that they had lost a motion, just a motion, a stupid motion, not the case. "You told me it was a slam dunk," came the voice.

Rebecca would never have told anyone they would win a motion or a case, not with the caprices of the judges before whom she regularly practiced. Quite the opposite, she always calculated a five percent "caprice factor" that the judge was entirely asleep, absent or brain dead. But it was the "slam dunk" that really made her mad. It was a sore spot with Rebecca, who had never been a sports enthusiast. When she graduated law school and was given a prestigious position as the clerk to a federal judge, she'd had to spend weekends watching television just so she would understand those silly little analogies men make, such as: "No use engaging in Monday morning quarterbacking." When she became a trial lawyer in her own right it continued: "First down, Ms. Jamison, proceed." "He really gave you the ball on the tee that time, Ms. Jamison," (which she assumed had something to do with golf until she asked and was told T-ball was baseball for toddlers). "Let's level the playing field." And, of course, there were the references to "eagles" and "matches" and "knockouts" and "strikes" and all the rest. The American language is replete with them. Rebecca always thought their use was evidence of a lazy mind or of one who is so ill read with no other, more creative means of expression.

"Excuse me," said the message Rebecca left in

response, "it couldn't have been me. I don't use sports analogies." She hung up and did not answer the phone the rest of the day.

She had to appear in court on Tuesday, and she did. It was some poor farmers she was trying to help out through a reorganization bankruptcy. The creditor, Mr. Arnold, was the richest man in the county and had lent the farmers money years earlier and foreclosed on their land. He had refused to honor an option he gave the farmers to purchase the land back. Finally, Arnold had chased the farmers into bankruptcy, where he had engaged the nastiest opposition attorney in town. Everything Rebecca tried to do for the aging couple was challenged. Arnold even challenged whether the old folks, now in their 70s and farming for over 45 years, were farmers at all. Worst of all, they had drawn a tough judge who didn't seem to like farmers and definitely did not believe in reorganizations for farmers. The judge found that the folks were not farmers and Rebecca had had to appeal. It took years. It was aggravating, it was unjust; the case would never pay unless the farmers got their land back.

This hearing was Rebecca's motion, on behalf of her farmers (the appeals court had agreed they *were* farmers), to borrow funds. After years of appeals, it had been determined they did have the right to buy the farm back, but they had to come up with a $50,000 down payment within 30 days. Rebecca had found a funding source. She had filed the motion to approve the loan on an emergency basis. There was not even time to do the preliminary loan paperwork. When she got to court, Arnold was there, objecting, of course. The creditor and his counsel were claiming the motion could not be granted because of a technicality—a rule saying Rebecca had to send out a copy of the loan agreement with the motion. Well, there was no loan agreement, yet, just a verbal. There definitely was not time to send out another motion. It was now or never, and the creditor was hoping it was the deathblow.

The judge sank down into his chair, disappeared from eyesight, and then re-emerged, clenching his Bankruptcy Code, popping up dramatically like a skinny whale emerging from the ocean. "Ms. Jamison," he said, "the rules of this game are clear. The creditor is correct; read Rule 4001. You must attach a copy of the actual, complete agreement."

He was about to say, "Motion denied," when Rebecca said meekly, "Your Honor, may I have a moment?"

She moved to the podium overwhelmed with emotion. Not only was he going to deny the motion, he was going to blame her for not having attached a copy of an agreement that did not yet exist. How had she missed a rule? She knew her cases; she was a careful attorney. How had she missed the rule? Tears emerged from her eyes and no internal command could stop them. She stood before an embarrassed court, crying, not sobbing, just unable to stop the sheets of tears. She looked down at her copy of the Bankruptcy Code and paged to Rule 4001. The filmy text was in a tiny type and she could barely read the words. Then she calmed, read, and said quietly, "Your honor, Rule 4001, by its terms, applies to business reorganizations, not farmers."

The judge's already beady eyes grew narrower. The courtroom was silent for several minutes as the judge sank down below view. Rebecca concentrated on getting the tears to stop, but couldn't. There was a thundering pounding in her head that she knew would later be a migraine headache. It was an eternity. When finally the judge reemerged, it was to say, "Ms. Jamison is correct, motion granted." And it was over.

By the time she got back to the office, she could not deal with anything else. It was simply too much to go through, for anyone, even farmers. Win or lose, it was just too tough. So she didn't even check voicemail and the envelopes remained untouched. She took a painkiller for the migraine and fell asleep under the desk.

Wednesday, she sat at her desk for a couple of hours, benumbed. Finally, she was startled out of her trance by the phone.

"Rebecca, Jed Hawley here." Another farmer. "Damn, I know I told you I'd have some money on that bill of yours, but, damn, my financing fell through. Prize bull hit by lightining and the damn bank says I don't have the value in the herd without him. Sorry."

Rebecca hung up the phone without saying a word. She had no idea if she believed him or not, but it didn't matter. She would not be able to issue herself a paycheck this month. Then she dialed into voicemail, skipping over eighteen messages to which she had now not responded. Number nineteen was a message from the richest person she had ever met. Jason Marner had lived off trusts giving him over half a million dollars a year, but he had lost it all, gambled it on one big, hare-brained deal. He'd even borrowed a couple million more to invest; so he didn't just lose his trusts, he owed money. Rebecca filed a bankruptcy for him. He could not even pay the simple $500 fee for a Chapter 7 bankruptcy, but he could be as demanding as any paying client.

"Rebecca," the message said, "Jason here. Frank Reona called. Says he's going to challenge the bankruptcy. Says he can claim fraud. Says he'll make me look like James Bond and no judge'll be smart enough to figure it out when his mad dog lawyers get done with me. He wants me to promise to pay a million after the bankruptcy."

Rebecca had suggested Jason listen to what Reona wanted, but agree to nothing. What Reona wanted, of course, was outrageous. The threat he was making to get what he wanted, alleging fraud in the bankruptcy itself, was extortion. It was unethical. But Rebecca was out of moral outrage.

Why can't people have legal problems when they're flush? she wondered. That was the day she decided to give herself a break at noon and take a walk. She had not walked in years—just aimlessly walked through the city— but she walked now, breathing in the smells of autumn: drying tomato vines, marigolds in little gardens, and moist leaf-dust. As the day passed, she felt increasingly drugged by the deep intensity of the sun low on the horizon, which seemed to sharpen the contours of each home, each tree. And then there was the almost imperceptible lessening of density in the foliage, like all things living were drawing themselves in, tightening up. She wondered how many hours she would have to walk to lose the 70 pounds she'd put on since law school. In fact, law school, seven years ago, had been the last time she'd taken a walk, just taken a walk. Rebecca did not go back to the office that Wednesday afternoon.

Thursday, she walked in the morning and lost the afternoon to sleep. Now it was Friday. She felt relieved that there would be no new voicemail messages. The capacity of 24 messages had been exceeded. She wondered at what precise moment that had occurred. It seemed important. That moment had freed her somehow. Unless she erased a message, no one could impose, not through that medium. They would have to come in through the door, or the mail slot. No one ever came in through the door without calling first. She looked at the pile of mail. How would one start? Which envelope should she open first? Which client to apologize to first? Why should she apologize? Why should she have to apologize? Rebecca languidly realized that there was an element of anger in what she felt. It wouldn't be right to call people in this mood. She might insult them; she might tell them the truth. She was so tired of people and their problems. They all expected her not only to argue their position to the best of her ability (which is what she was trained to do), but to feel righteously indignant about their cause and to set their worlds right, to invoke vengeance on the other side, and to have it not cost anything. Clients were either sued or suing, but it didn't make any difference. They fought over land and property rights, onions, cows, computer software, water rights, money, patents and promises, but the subject matter was not significant. The one thing all clients had in common was their own indignation that they should have to pay either to defend themselves or to get something back, when they felt they had done nothing wrong. All clients disavowed any responsibility for their current situations, and nobody liked to pay to clean up their own messes.

I am, in reality, just a janitor, thought Rebecca, with a mop of tangled legal arguments and a bucket of water that started out clean enough but has grown slimy. I follow my clients around cleaning up their spills and I don't even like them. So, she decided she would work at the computer to finish a brief she was writing. If there was an aspect of law she liked, it was the solitude of that enterprise. It was law in the abstract, on paper, applied to assumed facts, uncomplicated by people and their expectations. At least she was engaged in work. Perhaps by Monday all would be set right.

Over the weekend she forgot the law. Rebecca walked. On Saturday, she even got in the car and drove to the hills where she really walked. The blood coursing through her veins felt new and the sun on hot pine needles gave off a scent that perfumed the whole of the forest. It infiltrated her hair like incense and she slept, dreaming of walking. She had read books about people walking across the country and thought she could understand wanting to do that, just to keep moving. On Sunday, she did the same thing over again. Her muscles even felt a bit tauter, just in the couple of days she had been getting out. What if all the poundage was really just padding she had built up at 10 pounds a year to insulate her from the clients she . . . She had to catch herself from using the word "hated?"

Monday morning brought a drizzling rain and Rebecca returned to her office with determination. Hanging her raincoat on the door hook, she carefully bent down and picked up an envelope. Walking to her desk, she started to open it with the letter-opener. She stared at the silver knife-blade of the opener and then drew it carefully, light as a feather, not penetrating, just floating a whisper above the skin, across her wrist. She dropped the envelope just as the phone rang. Rebecca stared at the black plastic device. It rang again. Here it was—her chance to join the real world again. She could pretend she'd been ill for a week, or on vacation, or injured. Maybe if she just "touched base" with the real world again, it would all slide into place. She laughed, having caught herself. It gave her the courage to put down the letter-opener and pick up the phone.

"This is Rebecca Jamison," she said curtly, in her best lawyer voice.

"Ms. Jamison, my name is Carmide, Michael Carmide. I represent Frank Reona. I understand our clients have come to an understanding."

Frank Reona was the very man who had taken Jason's trust funds, millions, his lands, his home, his condos, his bank accounts, even his furniture.

"An understanding?" she responded now, "Your client's million dollar understanding?"

"Exactly," came the reply.

"No deal," she said simply.

There was a pause at the other end of the line. "What do you mean no deal? Your client . . . "

"No deal. It would be unethical." She knew she had ventured well out of the territory of the counsel on the other end of the phone. It is unethical to threaten a criminal or administrative sanction to gain a personal advantage. In a bankruptcy, one gets a discharge (a forgiveness if you will) of one's debts. The threat to challenge the discharge, claiming fraud, should not be the basis for an agreement to pay the debt of one creditor. A debtor either deserves his discharge or not. But that was easy to say; the real threat was the cost, the attorney fees, and that it would take to go to court. Rebecca felt dirty even being on the phone with a lawyer who would allow his client to make such threats, but she was convinced he didn't comprehend the ethical issue. It never even dawned on him.

Instead, his rebuttal came clear and accusing, "Just who is calling the shots in this case?" he snarled.

"Excuse me?"

"You or your client? I want to know who is calling the shots?"

Rebecca hesitated. "Is that a sports analogy?" she asked.

"What?"

"Calling the shots. What sport? Would it be shot-put?"

"Basketball," came the voice in utter disbelief.

"So it's a sports analogy?"

"Well, sure," the voice was guarded.

"I don't like sports," she said, "there is no settlement and neither you nor your client may contact mine again. Good day," and she hung up.

The phone book lay on the desk and Rebecca reached for it calmly, deliberately. She thumbed through the Yellow Pages to "Insurance" fingered the entry "Financial Professional Liability" and dialed. A pleasant-voiced secretary answered and Rebecca said clearly and simply, "It is policy number 0011668. I've paid on it for years and years. I'm sending you the keys to my office. There will be a list of clients with case status on the computer." She paused and then continued, "You better send someone bright, and," she laughed, "if you can find someone, ethical. It's a commercial practice. Oh, you'll need a password to access the computer."

The shocked voice on the other end of the line said quietly, "Password?"

"Yes," said Rebecca, "write it down. The password is—" She hesitated, thinking, trying to find the right words to encapsulate what was happening. She would probably be put in a hospital or something, lose her license for sure, have to go to therapy. They'd call it exhaustion, or a nervous breakdown or something . . . if they found her.

She needed something free of rules, something solitudinous, something like flying a plane—she was scared of heights and didn't like mechanical things—something physical but not competitive, energetic but not in that burst of energy kind of way, something soothing, repetitious. Her mind was drifting through the sports magazines she had seen on occasion in doctors' offices and other waiting rooms. She tried to picture the covers (having never opened one) and thought hard about playing fields, balls, and uniforms. Then she had her picture: A fellow alone with water and pine trees, standing up to his waist in water, in the middle of the stream. That's where she felt she was. All on her own and up to her ass. She could almost feel the breeze in her hair, and smell the pine. Maybe she would actually like it.

"—Gone fishing," she said.

The voice replied, "Beg your pardon?"

"It's an analogy, a sports analogy," Rebecca replied, "Just write it down," and she hung up.

Cynthia Kennedy lives in Lafayette, Colo., with her husband, Jerry, and two adopted Nepali children, Sunita and Bishnu. Kennedy's creative work has appeared most recently in "Eureka Literary Magazine," "North Dakota Quarterly," "Oregon East," and "Touched by Adoption," an anthology.

My Future With Women

by Greg Rawlings

While relaxing on the veranda of my family's summer lodge, at about 6:30 on a drowsy summer evening, I gazed out the window at the river and witnessed Marge Fraley water skiing gracefully across the ruddy brown surface of the Ohio. Resplendent in a powder blue blouse with a short, darker blue summer skirt, with a fine crimson scarf twirled around her swanlike throat, she had black, high-heeled evening shoes tossed recklessly over her shoulder, tethered at the heels. As I watched her skimming toward her dock just down the river from our place, her husband's wood-hulled 19-foot Chris-Craft inboard-outboard roaring before her, my mother approached me from behind and tapped lightly on my shoulder. I looked up at her and smiled dreamily.

"She's nuts, you know, Billy," mother said, seeming to read my mind but speaking without any obvious trace of malice.

"I know," I said, trying my best to sound worldly, "but look at her go."

Mother walked away, shaking her head, either at my credulity or Marge's supposed madness. I was a rather naive 14 then and I didn't comprehend that a grown woman could be nuts, especially a grown woman who could water-ski down the Ohio in full party splendor, without so much as dampening her outfit. Later though, that winter, when the dank funk of December held thrall over the valley, Marge Fraley shot herself dead with her husband Daniel's .38.

"She should have just gone to Fort Lauderdale," my mother, a famously practical woman, told me. "That's what everybody else does when the winter gets too gloomy up here."

My mother, Ellen, was in her mid-30s by then. She'd married my father, Philip Wellman, the year after she graduated from Kenyon, and had me the year—almost to the day—after she married my father. She wasn't that much older than Marge Fraley, but she seemed terribly old and plain to me (which, in retrospect, she wasn't; in truth, she was considered one of the most beautiful women in the valley—tall, comely, sensibly blonde), while Marge Fraley, with her midnight black hair flashing in the river breeze, and a confident smile creasing her delicate oval face, epitomized all that was glamorous to me. I suppose this was not a good sign. At the very least, it augured ill for my future with women.

* * *

I graduated from Duke in the spring of 1981, with a bachelor's degree in history and a fellowship to attend graduate school in Madison, at the University of Wisconsin, a fine school if, admittedly, a notorious Ph.D. factory. While at Duke, I had become involved with a frivolous but enchanting girl from New York, a girl who bore a striking resemblance to the late, still lamented Marge Fraley: same wild flickering eyes, same lush black hair, same devil-may-care attitude toward all that life had to offer. I never saw her water ski, but I had seen her sail, which she managed effortlessly. I thought I loved her, and maybe I did.

We liked to drive down to the beach from

Durham, a trip of less than three hours, usually in my old convertible. Sometimes, we'd invite friends along—both of us were quite social—and sometimes we'd drive down by ourselves, singing Beatles songs or listening to the hillbilly music on the radio. She possessed a sweet soprano voice that drove me crazy, and the girl had no compunction about letting it loose at the drop of a hat.

I once sat on the steps of Duke's Perkins Library, that great Gothic pile next to the more famous chapel, and listened awestruck as she belted out a perfect a cappella rendition of "Here, There and Everywhere," for a trio of visiting Japanese economics professors. They smiled widely, bowed politely, clapped softly with small, delicate hands, for a moment or two, and finally wandered wide-eyed into the library.

"Americans," I heard one whisper.

"American women," another replied.

Her name was Melinda Tierney, and she wanted to be a big shot in the New York magazine world, although I personally thought Broadway a better bet. She knew who ran what magazine and who slept with whom so as to get the job. Her father was an advertising executive, Michael Tierney (you may have heard of him; he came up with a famous burger jingle in the late-1970s), who had encouraged her from childhood in her penthouse dreams. I had no doubt that she'd achieve what she sought. How could she fail? She looked enough like Marge Fraley and graduated *summa* at a fine enough school. Throw in her father's myriad connections and, with a little drive and patience, hello *Vanity Fair*, hello *WWD*; the glossy print world was hers for the asking. Dinners with Tina Brown, lunches with Hollywood power brokers at the bistros on the Upper East Side, late nights at Eurotrash-filled discos, inside stock tips, and finally a revealing autobiography; maybe the entire world was hers for the asking, and then the taking.

Well, the week after graduation, we decided to

drive down to the beach one last time, before she headed to Gotham (she already had an internship lined up at *Vogue*) and I headed to the land of cheese, beer and bratwurst.

It was a sentimental thing. We'd rented a room for the night—maybe our last, I knew—and had reservations at a seafood joint for that evening. I expected a day in the sun, body-surfing, maybe even rent a catamaran for a couple hours, have a few beers and then dinner. I also expected a fine, long night of making love, in our sea-scented room, overlooking the ocean, with the battering of the waves adding an inescapable romantic tinge to it all.

I wasn't too far wrong, but sometimes it's better to be way wrong or way right and avoid anything between those two poles. This was one of those times. We were at the bar of the restaurant that night, after a good day of passing the time in the abundant Carolina sunshine. Melinda's skin was darkly tanned, and this made her green eyes even more incongruous than usual, glimmering between her jet-black hair and dazzling smile. She looked like the kind of woman I could see myself spending the rest of my life with, someone with beauty and drive and charisma. She all but sparkled with inchoate power. As it was, I never even got to spend that night with her.

At our table in the bar, I saw her eyeing an older man with a thick head of blonde hair and a sailor's easy smile. He wore old khakis and boat shoes and a polo shirt that was frayed at the collar. In other words, he looked filthy rich. He also looked remarkably like her father, if a few years younger. He was drinking Mount Gay rum by the tumbler full, and sliding fresh oysters down his throat. The first moment I saw her looking at him the way she was looking at him, I knew the jig was up. There was something animal in her eyes and I recognized it for what it was. It was the exact same way I looked at her right before she took off her clothes at night, on the nights we spent together back at school. It was sex. She was going to sleep with that man, and sleep with him that very night, probably in the 12-meter racing boat he had docked at the adjacent marina. She was going to come up with some lame excuse and leave me alone. It was a horrible moment. I about vomited up my crab cakes then and there, aided and abetted by a few too many shots of 101-proof bourbon before dinner.

Instead, without saying a word, I rose from my chair and laid a fifty on the table. I bit my lip and walked away from her. She had caught me watching her and knew that I knew what was what. She sighed and stared down at her plate. I remember that there was a single fried shrimp, calabash-style, lying there on the plate in some smudged red cocktail sauce that smelled of horseradish; maybe there was also a wedge of lemon. I tossed her the hotel keys and walked out to the car. I never saw her again, although through mutual friends I heard that she ended up marrying the publisher of a New York weekly and fixing up an old barn-like house in rural Connecticut. She writes scathing editorials for her husband's magazine and occasionally appears as a talking head on the Sunday morning news shows. I always turn off the TV when her face appears. Even though it's still an awfully nice face to look at, there's something hard and mean in those glistening, hyper-attentive eyes.

I drove back to Durham that night and was almost arrested in a small town in eastern North Carolina for screaming "Damn You, Melinda Tierney!" a few times at the top of my lungs (I contemplated a serious echo effect, if I recall) as I drove around and around a traffic island in an otherwise peaceful hamlet. A lone cop pulled me over about a block after my outburst and asked, quite politely, "Son, what in hell's name is wrong with you?"

I gazed at him in utter peace with the universe.

"Just got dumped, good and proper," I answered him. He nodded his head sagely and motioned for me to drive on, which I did.

* * *

My first wife, Anna May Bell, was a girl I met in Madison; she was attending the law school there. Like me, she was a bright kid from the upper crust of the Great American Sticks, hailing from a coal town in western Pennsylvania, and was never quite as assured as she'd have liked you to believe.

I received my doctorate in 1986, and she finished law school that same year. A good school in the west had offered me a decent, entry-level position, a possibility of tenure and all that. Annie moved with me, and took the bar exam in Colorado.

We seemed to have a good life in Boulder, where I taught handsome, inattentive undergrads basic American and world history, and Annie toiled away in a boutique firm that specialized in environmental litigation. Neither of us made a lot of money, but Boulder is a fine place to pass the time, and the hiking and biking are free.

During our second year there, Annie had a chance to jump to a big, international firm in Denver, one that primarily represented "polluters." The money was double what her job in Boulder paid, and after much heated discussion, she took the position. That same year, the book version of my doctoral dissertation, "A History of the Idea of Freedom," was published by the Duke University Press, thanks to the influence of an old professor of mine. A prestigious New York publishing house bought the rights, and to my surprise (hell, to everyone's surprise), the book took off, going into 14 printings in hardback, and getting translated rather quickly into all the major European languages, as well as into Japanese. It lodged itself in the mid-reaches of the best-seller lists and stayed there, clinging like an old flame with a bad attitude, most of a year. And it secured my reputation in my field, something truly unusual for a professor yet to reach his 30th birthday. Colorado offered me tenure, Wisconsin offered me a sweetheart position as a summer lecturer, and even the Sorbonne sent me a letter asking what my plans were for the near future. My plans were actually quite simple. Teach history, write more books, love Annie, just in reverse order. With her signing bonus and my paperback advance, we purchased a Craftsman's-style bungalow in the area near Chautauqua Park in Boulder, in a neighborhood all but shadowed by the Flatirons—a rugged series of enormous ridges that rise from a grassy park like the flints the gods must have used to start the first fires; sharp, impossibly steep, of varying red and yellows and browns, often ornamented by the colorful ropes of climbers; these upshoots are my fondest memory of Colorado.

One night, about a year after Annie took her job in Denver, she came home, poured herself a drink, and sat down beside me on the lush sleeper sofa on our back porch. Ours was a large, screened-in porch, which rose above our backyard and opened into the kitchen, the living room, and our bedroom. From there, you could sit in peace and silence, perhaps sipping a gin and tonic, your workday behind you and a pleasant mountain evening awaiting you. Annie wore a loose silk blouse of soft peach and pink and pegged, ivory-hued linen slacks, with her auburn hair up in a loose bun. She kicked off her pumps and lit a cigarette. She kissed my cheek softly and blew a long blue plume of smoke toward the black mesh of the screen. It was autumn and a solitary Cedar Waxwing had just alighted on the birdbath near the apple tree in the backyard. I watched the dapper bird and sipped my drink. I glanced at Annie. We had been married for about four years. No children, not yet, not with our busy schedules and my increasingly active lecture docket, but I was hoping. I envisioned a tiny replica of Annie, with small white teeth and scrapes on her tiny knees, the beautiful daughter of my beautiful wife.

"Do you love me?" I asked, as I was wont to do. I loved to ask her if she loved me, and loved it even more when she answered yes. She had a voice as silken as her blouse. She wasn't a singer like Melinda had been, but she often walked around the house humming pleasantly. There is nothing quite so pleasant as the sound of a pretty woman humming.

"Yes," she said, "I do. But . . ." And here she paused and here my throat constricted as if I had been poisoned, and here my guts went terribly tight, and here I felt the weight of something indefinable bear down upon me.

"But what, Annie?" I ventured.

"I've been seeing someone else," she told me, voice so soft that I could barely hear what she was saying—that or the awful roaring in my ears was drowning out her words: "A partner at the firm. You don't know him." She sat back against a pillowy cushion and blew out more smoke.

I glanced at the yard and the Cedar Waxwing was gone. *What a beautiful bird, I thought, and now gone.*

"He wants me to transfer to the New York branch with him, at a substantial increase in salary, doing international environmental legal analysis," she continued. "It would be a big step up, career-wise, for me. It would be the big leagues."

I remembered the night when I learned that my book had reached the best-seller list in New York. Annie and I shared a bottle of good French champagne and went out for sushi. I don't think I'd ever been happier in my life. She wore a sun-yellow dress I'd given to her as a birthday present. We went dancing after dinner at a gay bar on 30th Street, and much later that wonderful luminous night we made love on the floor of our apartment in north Boulder, Annie's long, lean legs spread wide in a lazily inviting V, her half-closed eyes shimmering like emeralds, her small breasts tanned from where we'd been to the mountains and stretched out naked together on a huge flat boulder deep in the national forest.

"Of course, I won't ask for the house or any money," she said, with a look in her eyes of someone who has just granted a condemned man a last-second reprieve.

"That's good of you," I finally murmured, heart shrunken within me, eyes cast down at the dark wood of the floor.

She left that night, packing her things into the back of a sedan that had appeared a couple hours later as if by some dark magic. Classes were slated to begin the next week for me. I'd been given some plum graduate level seminars, and a large office in the old Arts and Sciences building. The chance for a name chair was not out of reach. Along with a slightly older female colleague of mine at CU, I was about the hottest thing in my field. A few years later, my brilliant colleague was awarded a MacArthur "genius" grant; by then, I had left the profession. By then, Boulder was merely a memory, one beautiful but dark, ineluctably dark, memory—a flimsy yellow dress tossed on a wooden floor, two bodies alive within each other, a cigarette burning in an antique ashtray, vermilion lipstick staining the slightly mashed filter, the ever-present Flatirons, success and failure, all on a grand scale.

* * *

Two years after the divorce, in the late summer of 1992, I learned that my parents had been killed in a car wreck on the road out to our summer place above the river. Their Cadillac had crashed head-on into a truck driven by a local contractor, a man they'd known for 30 years. He, too, died in the wreck. It had always been a dangerous road, especially in the context of all the drinking the summer people did. Rarely did you pass a car on that road and not have the driver lift a drink in salute; this was simply the way of the place.

The estate was considerable and complex. There were the two houses in Ohio, the condo in Florida, the ownership interest in the brokerage my father had founded, a rather large portfolio of stocks and bonds, insurance alone worth well over a million dollars, real estate in three different states. "I finally need a damn good lawyer and she's dumped me," I recall thinking. I also remembered a wild scream in a Carolina night and a kindly old cop and the Flatirons over Boulder, and I remembered a slender woman in her party clothes sliding gracefully across the surface of the river below the house where I then stood. Right then and there, on the morning of the funeral, I decided to move back into the rambling shingled house on the high banks of the wide, lazy, dirty, brown Ohio. I decided to move home.

That afternoon we held the funeral service and the burial at the vast tree-shaded cemetery in the center of the better part of my hometown. Hundreds of mourners were kind enough to come. My parents had been active in charities and with the First Presbyterian Church, were well known at the country club, and were both on the board of the small college in town, so they had cut a wide swath of acquaintance through the small community. A reporter from the town's paper was there, and so was a photographer; it was really quite the little event. I was shaking hands and hugging people until I thought I'd collapse, when I saw what appeared to be nothing so much as a ghost—the ghost of Marge Fraley, after all these years gone. The same black hair, the same quicksilver eyes, the same athletic body and adamant walk. I tugged on the sleeve of one of my mother's bridge partners, Phyllis Anderson, wife of state representative

Barney Anderson, and said, "Who, may I ask is that?" nodding at the tall, lean, graceful figure in the simple black dress who was walking between a line of stones and an old, lightning-scarred oak. I expected the woman to look at me like I was crazy and say, "William, son, there's nobody there, nobody at all, poor old dear." But she didn't. She whispered, "That's Angie Fraley. You might remember her poor mother, the one who took her own life back in '74, or was it '75 . . . Didn't they have the next camp up from yours?" I nodded yes, thanked Mrs. Anderson, and walked hurriedly toward the dark figure amid the white stones.

She was looking the other way, admiring a particularly handsome marble statue, a memorial for the town's fallen in the Civil War, when I tapped at her shoulder. As she turned around, I looked hard at her face. "Jesus Christ almighty," I muttered, stepping back from her. "You're the very image of your mother, and she was the most beautiful woman I've ever seen," I said, words tumbling from my mouth like young monkeys capering through a jungle canopy.

The girl blushed and then smiled. "You're William Wellman. I'm Angela Fraley. I'm awful sorry about your folks. They were good people. They helped me a lot after my mom died."

I nodded in agreement. Odd, I thought, that my folks never mentioned this girl to me. She appeared about ten years younger than me, somewhere in her early twenties. I was standing there, words suddenly all gone, when she touched my arm and said, "I loved your book. I have it at home, the one with your picture on the back with that old guy who did the narration for it on the PBS series."

"No way."

"Honest. I even ordered the videos."

"I'm amazed."

"Why? Don't I look bright enough?"

Angela Fraley, you shine like the northern star, I thought, the phrase "bright enough" does not even begin to do you justice.

"You look plenty bright," I said. I was nervous, and I stuck my hands into my pants pockets so she wouldn't see them trembling. I glanced over at the crowd, which was milling about in need of a field general. "I need to go say goodbye to some folks. Can I meet you later?"

"Will you autograph my book?" She emitted a halting, half-smile, becoming in one pleasant inquisition a kind of Midwestern Mona Lisa. Her eyes veritably glowed.

"Sure, I'd be glad to." With that, I touched her arm and walked back to the graveside. Still dizzied by her, I stared down into the two deep holes, dug side by side, facing southeast and, thus, the morning sun, as my parents had spelled out in their wills. Clods of crumbled earth blocked somewhat the hard shine of the brass on the caskets. I wondered again why my mother had never mentioned this gorgeous child, and recalled that she was not overly convinced of Marge's sanity, and that, as far as anyone could tell, she'd been right. As the last of the well-wishers shuffled away from the grave, I watched as Angela Fraley arranged a bouquet of lilies in front of a small tombstone beyond the great oak. It was her mother's place. Standing there in the cool of early fall in Ohio, I wondered what my future held, and whether this wide-eyed innocent was part of that future, and I realized that everything that had happened to me, my lovers, my career, my sadness, especially my sadness, was mere preparation for the time I would spend here, in this small town above the big river, with the raven-haired woman tending to her mother's grave.

She was my future with women, it seemed, in that she was the perfect culmination of my past.

Greg Rawlings is the lawyer/writer who originated "Disturbing the Peace." Hailing from an old Kentucky family, Greg lives in Denver with his wife Julia and daughter Hannah. His fiction was previously anthologized in "Forbidden Lines" (1988) before he turned to law. His essays and criticism regularly appear in the Denver Bar Association's The Docket.

An Excerpt From

Day One

by Connie Peterson

"The Court is in recess."

All stood at the command of the gavel. Eyes focused on the bench. The judge rose and turned to the door leading to his chambers. Casey watched the judge drag his black-robed, hulking frame from the courtroom. Was it his downcast look that pulled his shoulders forward in a slump? The judge's right hand was in a clenched fist.

Casey turned to his co-counsel. "Recess is 15 minutes. I'll be back in time for you to take a walk. Would you mind staying here and baby-sitting this stuff?" His right arm made a broad sweep toward fifteen boxes jammed with files and loose papers. The courtroom looked like an untidy law office.

Casey heard a soft echo as he spoke to his co-counsel. He loved the cathedral atmosphere of an empty courtroom. The pale November sun barely brightened the velvet burgundy drapes that framed the seven 15-foot windows. It was a grand room. Casey stroked the oak counsel table that matched the judge's bench and jury box.

Six Denver residents sat in that box just moments before. The bailiff now had the jury safely tucked in the jury room where they could wonder what they were supposed to do with all the detail thrown at them over the last four days.

Casey picked his way around the boxes strewn on the worn carpet and walked out of the courtroom down the marble-lined hall to the men's room. He was glad to be alone because it eliminated the temptation to talk shop.

Back in the hall, a woman clenched a child's forearm and was half-walking and half-dragging the child along in the hall. The sweaty, whimpering child looked tired. The woman looked like Bessie Smith after a 10K run. "Goddamn it, Crystal!" the woman cried. "We got to get to the court room to see Daddy when the sheriff brings him down. Now move it, or I'll beat your ass."

Casey winced. Why would you drag a child into the courthouse to see dad handcuffed? What kind of image is imprinted on the child?

Just then, a sheriff's deputy turned the corner in the hallway. He was with a giant in handcuffs and leg irons.

"Hey! Crystal, darlin' what's happenin'?" he yelled to the child. With a big innocent smile, the child broke from the woman and ran toward the man.

"Keep the kid back!" yelled the deputy.

"She's just a baby!" the prisoner barked. "What do you think she's gonna do?"

"Keep her back!"

"Crystal! Get back here," screamed the woman.

The child stopped in her tracks and began to wail.

"Christ, almighty!" said Casey.

"Fuck you," the woman said to him.

Casey just shook his head in disgust and walked to the courtroom. There was still plenty of recess time remaining for his co-counsel to take her break from the courtroom. The judge was due back on the bench at 3:30 p.m.

They had been in trial four days. Things seemed to be going well. The judge had ruled in their favor on all the important issues. Casey wondered if the jury was bored. They were "holed up" in the jury room waiting to come out and get this over with, he was sure. It wasn't an exciting case for the jury. Most jurors don't work up a lather over a breach of contract. But they seemed to be good sports. If nothing else, they gave the illusion that they were listening to the testimony. The only thing interesting in the case was the amount of money that was involved. He should win. It was pretty much a cut-and-dried case.

All the lawyers strolled back into the courtroom, including his co-counsel. Casey's client walked in and sat down next to him.

3:30 p.m. No judge.

One of the defense lawyers stood up, stretched and looked at Casey. "We got to be here. They come back when they please. Is that what you're going to do when you're on the federal bench, Casey?" he asked.

"Don't go there," replied Casey.

"Well, the word is that Judge Cartridge is retiring and you're going to make a run at it. Didn't you used to be friends with the Senator?"

"Oh, I don't know. We worked together at the Denver Country Club when we were in college. After he got religion, we didn't have much to say to each other." Casey answered, wanting to end this conversation. It was distracting his attention from the trial.

3:40 p.m. Still no judge.

At 3:45 p.m., Casey announced he was going to the judge's clerk to make sure everything was okay. "Sure it is," said the same lawyer, "he's just having trouble scheduling his golf game."

Casey left the courtroom through a door marked "Lawyers Only" into an inner hallway that separated the staff offices and the judges' chambers from the main hall. Stopping at the counter in the clerk's office, he asked her if everything was all right. She answered that she thought so—that Judge Johnson had left his chambers immediately after calling the recess, but he had not returned.

Casey went into the main hall and stood near the door. He had no desire to go back into the courtroom. He could see far down the hall. When the judge came back, Casey would see him coming and return to the courtroom.

He saw a woman sitting on a bench outside a divorce courtroom. She had her right hand across her eyes and nose and was crying softly. She was no doubt upset with her husband or ex-husband, and coming to court didn't make her feel any better. It hardly ever did. The courts were not designed to help her emotions. Probably, the judge had tried to enlighten her and her ex-husband on their legal positions. He probably tried to enter a conciliatory order in an attempt to make them work together to solve their problems without the aid of a court. She wanted the judge to tell her she was right and that her husband was a son-of-a-bitch. She never asked that judge if she should marry that son-of-a-bitch in the first place and have his babies, thought Casey, but now everything was the judge's fault.

Casey remembered the conversation in the courtroom and thought of Senator Wheat Field. It had been a long time. They had both been so young and so wild.

His thoughts were interrupted by his client standing at this side. Casey didn't see him come up and he was startled. "Well, Bob, what time is it?"

"4 p.m." answered the client. "What's going on? Is the judge sick?"

Casey told him that his clerk said he left chambers at the beginning of recess without explanation and had not returned. The jury and the judge's staff would be looking to go home at 5 p.m. This would put the case behind schedule and irritate the jury. Not a good turn for the plaintiff. The client also sensed this and also was irritated.

A puzzled looking bailiff came out in the hall. "How long will we wait for his honor?" asked Casey.

"5 p.m., I guess," answered the bailiff. He obviously didn't have a clue about the judge.

The client noticed the woman sitting on the bench, crying. "She's in a mess," he said to Casey. "Maybe she needs a date. I could use one." Casey snorted.

The door to the criminal courtroom opened and out came the same deputy sheriff and the same black prisoner. They continued down the hall without a word, both lost in their own thoughts.

Casey wondered about Crystal. The thought no sooner passed through his mind when the courtroom door opened again, and the woman came out with Crystal in tow. The woman was dragging the child along by the same forearm. The child was quiet now and let herself be led along.

Casey nodded at the woman. A mistake. She started to walk over to him, dragging Crystal along.

"You a lawyer?" she asked. When he nodded, she continued. "That was my man you seen coming out of the courtroom in custody. He needs a lawyer. Nobody got any money, though. Are you a street lawyer? You do criminal stuff?"

"I'm sure the judge will appoint the public defender for him," replied Casey without answering her questions.

"Public defender, shit!" she cursed. "He needs himself a street lawyer."

"What is he charged with?" he asked.

"He supposed to have poked Crystal here," she answered, giving the child a slight tug on her forearm. "But I know he didn't."

Casey recoiled. He could also sense his client's shock. He still wasn't jaded enough not to react to something like that. But he managed to simply say, "The public defender will do a good job. Good luck to you."

"And to poor Crystal," snapped the client.

The woman shot the client a dirty look and walked off with the child.

"God, what a happy place this is," sighed the client. "How can you make this your life? How can judges do it? How can they come here day after day and see this kind of stuff time and time again? Are they crazy or are they saints? Or just too stupid and too lazy to practice law?"

Casey smiled at the client. "Sometimes, a combination of all of the above, depending on the judge. Lawyers become judges for a variety of reasons. Some feel they can help people. Some feel they can help the legal system. Some don't feel at all. Some want to retire from the practice of law. For as many judges as there are, there are probably different reasons."

"Well, I heard that other lawyer talking to you about your being a judge. Why do you want to do it?" asked the client.

"To get away from clients like you." joked Casey. "Go talk to that poor, sobbing woman over there, and make her day."

They both looked at the bench. The woman was gone. Neither had seen her leave. What was her story? Casey wondered. He was sure it was a real tragedy to her, and it passed through his life like nothing. How can something be so important to one person and not even hardly a blip in another person's life? We all just kind of wander around the earth bumping into one another.

The courtroom door opened. Out came opposing counsel. "Where is the goddamned judge?" he asked, loudly. "I'm tired of waiting. What's going on? It's 4:30 p.m.! Why wait any longer? There's nothing that can be accomplished now. By the time we just get revved up, again, it will be time to quit. Let's ask the bailiff to send the jury home until tomorrow. It's no use, now."

Casey looked at his client, who nodded.

The bailiff was reluctant to make that decision himself. He telephoned the chief judge who gave her approval, after asking for an explanation that couldn't be given.

What was expected to be a successful day had ended badly. Casey turned to his client. "I have to take care of a case in night court. So, I'll see you tomorrow. We'll try to pick up where we left off." The client was clearly frustrated. Then they went their separate ways down the hall. We're all just bumping along, thought Casey.

Casey looked at his watch. 5:10 p.m. Night court started at 5:30 p.m. Judge Bludmann's a strange one, he thought. He was a judge in night court who heard only drug cases. The state had established a special drug court about three years ago. If your case was in drug court, it meant that you were under intensive supervision of the court. You had to return to court every two weeks and listen to the probation officer give a report on your progress during the last two weeks of your life. If you had done well, the judge congratulated you, and sometimes, you got the prize of having your probationary period reduced. If you did poorly, your probation could be lengthened or you could go to jail for awhile. If you really screwed up, you could go to prison.

Judge Marion V. Bludmann was known as a wizard for

success with the drug defendants. He was often the talk of the legal community. Some said he was magical. The defendants in his court seldom recidivated. Bludmann's theory was that a defendant should be given an early incentive to be cut loose from probation. To the dismay of the probation department, he would often terminate supervision by the probation department on the condition that the defendant would not in any way become the subject of law enforcement. He seemed to pick his candidates well because few found their way back into the criminal justice system. Those who did were not given a second chance, however, and were sentenced to long prison terms. Other judges who tried the same technique found themselves embarrassed by recidivism and gave up the procedure. When asked his secret, Bludmann would just turn his dark, vibrant eyes on the questioner, who would be seduced so far into the dark pools of Bludmann's eyes that he didn't hear the answer.

Casey couldn't explain why he was uneasy when he was anywhere near Bludmann's courtroom or Bludmann. Most people who had any dealings with Bludmann would say the same thing. Not that anyone Casey ever talked to had much contact with Bludmann. He knew nothing about the judge: where he came from, where he went to law school, who his friends were or his judicial philosophy other than his philosophy of turning certain defendants loose from probation, early. He wasn't even sure how long Bludmann had been a judge. He was known as a recluse who never socialized with anyone that Casey was aware of. Sometimes, he would be sighted late at night at a dark bar.

Casey was the first one in the dimly lit courtroom. He felt a slight shiver. He hoped he was not coming down with his first cold of the winter. The courtroom was of the same era as Judge Johnson's. The same vintage oak provided the imposing bench and jury box. The burgundy velvet drapes were probably cut from the same bolt as the drapes in Johnson's courtroom.

Bludmann held court very late into the night. The judge's explanation was that these were the hours of drug addicts, so you might as well hold court when they were awake. If you told the addict to be in court at 8 a.m., there was a greater chance he'd never show. Then what was accomplished?

Then his mind wandered to Judge Johnson. What would be his explanation for not returning to court after the mid-afternoon recess? Johnson's reputation was one of a conscientious judge. He always started his hearings and trials promptly and got his written ruling out quickly. He was intelligent and energetic enough. So, what would cause someone like Johnson to absent himself after the mid-afternoon recess without a word to his staff?

The courtroom door opened and Casey's client walked in. He could tell immediately that she was wasted.

"Caroline," Casey said as she sat down on the hard pew, next to him, "What do you think you're doing? You don't come to court drunk or stoned. I could tell you were stoned as soon as you walked in that door. The judge will see it, too, and if he does, you could be shipped off immediately to cool your butt in jail until he drags you back in here, tomorrow, to send you off to the department of corrections for violating your probation. This is nothing but stupid!"

Caroline began to cry. "I'm sorry. I guess I just relapsed."

"That's it?" Casey was stern. "You just relapsed? Caroline, you've got to get a grip. That's all there is to it. You're a young woman—a good looking, smart woman—but you're flushing your life down a rat hole of drugs. Other people have gotten a grip on themselves and you can do it, too. Sometimes, I just don't think you try."

"You don't know how hard I try," she said through her tears. "Like, if I wasn't still trying, I wouldn't have bothered to come here tonight."

Casey was apologetic. "You're right. It's just that I get frustrated. I'm sure you do, too, but you've relapsed three times before, and if Bludmann notices you're stoned tonight, he'll order an immediate drug test and when it comes back dirty, you'll spend the night in jail. Then, he'll have the sheriff bring you in tomorrow, and who knows what. Maybe D.O.C. This was just supposed to be routine review tonight, Caroline. Now, I'm going to have to work for my money."

"My money," she reminded him. "Or to be perfectly accurate, my father's money." She continued, "So what should I do? Leave?"

"No, that won't help. If you're not here, he'll issue a warrant for your arrest, and then what will you tell him when they drag you in here in cuffs after you're arrested on the warrant? What kind of cock 'n' bull story will you try to pull off, then? No, we might as well sit here, and give it our best shot now. Maybe he'll admire your courage."

"Maybe he'll admire my ass."

She continued to cry, but they stopped talking. The courtroom was filling up with drug defendants and their lawyers. Casey nodded to the attorneys whose eyes met his. Everyone looked tired. Casey felt weariness creeping in.

With three relapses, Caroline had been a C student in drug court. After the first relapse, Bludmann put her in jail for two days. Caroline hated it, but it didn't prevent her second relapse, which resulted in a 30-day jail sentence. She hated that even more, but it conditioned her for the 90 days she served after her third relapse. Now, here, she was totally wasted in court. This wasn't exactly showing respect. Casey thought there was a good chance that Bludmann might sentence her to DOC. The jail time would not have prepared her for prison. She could get her drugs there with no problem if she was willing or able to pay the price. Caroline would always have this monkey on her back.

The lights went up in the courtroom. The court reporter walked in and sat down at her machine. The bailiff entered and yelled for everyone to please rise and greet the Honorable Marion V. Bludmann. Everyone did, including Caroline with tears streaming down her face.

Casey was not paying close attention when the judge took the bench and called the first case; he was whispering to Caroline as he handed her his handkerchief so she could clean off her face. If she was not composed when her case was called, the judge would immediately be alerted that something was wrong. She had to act and talk straight.

Several cases were called by the bailiff. Nothing extraordinary happened in any of them. Everything was routine so far.

Casey hoped the judge would be lulled into a pattern.

He felt his stomach tighten when the bailiff called, "*People v. Caroline McNamara.*" He put his hand under Caroline's elbow to help her up and steady her. She was trembling but her face was still. The tears were gone. They walked to the podium which stood about 15 feet from Bludmann. Casey looked at the judge. Bludmann's face was flushed and his dark eyes were shining as he looked back. Casey felt himself being pulled into those dark eyes. His mouth was dry. He wondered if he could speak. He forced himself to look at the court reporter, a gray-haired woman in her 60s.

"Ross Casey appearing with Ms. McNamara, Your Honor," said Casey.

The judge stared at Caroline. It's over, thought Casey. She's gone. The judge continued to stare. Then, with a slight smile on his lips, he asked Caroline how she was feeling.

The timbre of the judge's voice was rich and musical. So much so, it startled Casey who looked up again, involuntarily, into the judge's dark eyes. Now the judge's slight smile was turned toward him. The judge sat tall in his chair. His curly, black hair, long enough in the back to hang below his collar, framed those dark eyes, full lips and a perfect aquiline nose. He looked vibrant and pulsating with life. Casey forced himself back to Caroline and the case.

Bludmann started to speak again, in that same rich voice. Caroline stared at the judge. Was she mesmerized or were the drugs at work?

"Ms. McNamara," the judge began, "your file indicates that on three prior occasions you relapsed and violated conditions of your probation." He stared at her again.

Here we fucking go! thought Casey.

The judge glanced at him. "Tonight, I think you are not being completely straight with the court, shall we say," said the judge. Casey's stomach tightened harder. Caroline gripped the edge of the podium and bit her bottom lip. Her eyes filled with tears. The judge continued, "Either the treatment provided by this court is too much of a challenge to you, or it is not enough. Either way, you and I are wasting our time. I'm tired of it, and I'm sure you are, too. So, let's stop."

"I always thought you had great potential, Ms. McNamara, but you disappointed me on a number of occasions. Now it will totally be your responsibility to succeed. I'm terminating your probation and releasing you from the supervision of this court. But if you ever appear before me again, expect the maximum sentence."

Casey and Caroline looked at each other in disbelief. Why now? This was so unusual that Casey thought maybe he hallucinated, but the court reporter's face told him it was true. She did not look pleased. Maybe she thought the judge was being too lenient. Maybe she thought he was letting Caroline off because she was a young, pretty good-looking woman. Caroline was crying openly now. The judge was starting to look disgusted, so Casey gave a hasty but sincere thanks to the judge and pushed Caroline out the door in an attempt to avoid any second thoughts by the judge.

Out in the hall, Caroline cried with relief. Then she started to jump up and down and waved her arms in the air over her head.

"Caroline!" said Casey "Take it easy. Don't you see that you've been set up, here? He's just put off the inevitable, as far as you're concerned. You can't stay off drugs. You'll get picked up again and charged and the judge will give you the maximum sentence. We've got to get together and think about this. We've got to come up with a plan so you don't end up here, again."

"Don't worry!" Caroline had a big smile on her face. "I don't need no plan. Don't you see? It's over. I *so* don't need to see Judge Blood Sucker anymore! That's what we call him on the street. Judge Blood Sucker. I'm out of here, man! I'm gone. This crap is over."

"Caroline, you need to get straight, and we need to talk. We need to make sure you're not back here," pleaded Casey.

"Oh, I won't be back here. I *so* won't get caught, again." Caroline smirked.

"Won't get caught, again? What's that supposed to

mean?"

"Simple. It means adios. Like I said, I'm out of here." Then she walked away.

But she was right. She would never return to the court again. The next time Casey would see Caroline McNamara, she would be dead.

Connie Peterson is senior counsel at Brownstein, Hyatt and Farber. She was a district judge (Second Judicial District) from 1985 to 2000 and also served as chief judge for seven years. Peterson's publications include a three-hour national television production by McNeil/Lehrer, titled "Education on Trial, Capital Crimes Benchbook," a book written to assist judges presiding over capital cases, which she co-authored and "Removal of Children From the State by the Custodial Parent."

SORENSEN'S CANE

by Robert Baldwin

In the dream he waited for spring, which never came, only winter laying the color of white all across the land. Waking, he shook away the dream and peered through the crack of his eyelids. But sight appeared no less imagined than the dream. All around him rose a colorless white as if the room stood in perpetual winter—a white floor, white walls, a white ceiling, and outside the world shone white with falling snow behind a frost-streaked window the color of his uncle's eyes the day before he died.

From down the hall he heard the voice of an old man, and the voice sounded strangely like that of his uncle. "Will it never be spring?"

Quickly he shut his eyes to the darkness that lay there. He tried to cover his ears with his hands and discovered his hands would not move. His heart quickened, an unfamiliar hot burn of panic rose within, and he remembered now where he was. Like a mouse burrowing into the dark hole of snow beneath a log, he tried desperately to squeeze himself back into the dream. But the voice of the old man down the hall persisted. "Spring! Give me yellow rays of sun in spring!"

* * *

Dr. Andujar's dark eyes appeared larger through the round lenses of her glasses as she read the neurology report on Jim Sorensen. The corners of her mouth tightened. Yes, an air embolism and a stroke. No, his arms and legs could not move. My God, a man like an insect. But an insect had no mind, and he did. She closed the medical chart, breathed sharply, and felt a tremor in her spine as she walked down the white walls of the hospital corridor. She frowned. She had been raised in the mountains of Peru, and she remembered her father's trim waist and barrel chest and those nights when she woke to his powerful grunts, her mother's rapid breath more a search for air, and each time, down the hall from them, she clutched her blanket, afraid the world would end.

Now, poised outside the door of Sorensen's room, holding the medical chart to her chest, she paused before she pushed through the door to see this man deprived of a man's body.

* * *

Sorensen woke from the fuzzy illumination of stick figures flicking behind his eyelids. His line of sight followed the white length of sheet covering his chest, his belly, his legs. Outside the snow continued to fall. He grew cold, very cold, and his ear caught the warm voice of a woman with a Spanish accent. "They found him lying on the floor of his garage holding the hose of an air compressor. He had a fresh cut on his finger. You can't be too careful, you know."

He heard another voice, deeper, but feminine still. "We can't locate any family. Before you go in, I want you to look at the latest tests."

Now footsteps receded down the hall with the voices blurring to a hum, indistinguishable from the sound of the fan in the wall blowing heat into the room. The heat blew around him but did not warm him and did not penetrate any faster than it could a cold stone.

* * *

Before becoming a doctor her name was only Maria Andujar, and she married young and came to America with a soccer player who first encouraged her to attend the university but then berated her failure to conceive a child. "You know how to make babies? You have to sleep with a man at least once in a while." She slapped him, he shoved his clothes into a duffel bag and swung out the door, and she never saw him again.

She took a job as a maid for a professor at the university and lived in his basement while keeping his house, cooking his meals, working her way through school. She was thankful he never made a pass at her. When she graduated from medical school, the professor placed his hand on her shoulder, let his half-moon glasses slide from his white eyebrows to the tip of his nose, and warned her about patients. "You can't care for them as you have for me. You can only do what you can to plant their life as you would a new tree. Sometimes that tree may be deformed and grow away from the sun."

She wanted to hold him as if he were her father. He only stood before her, within reach of her arms, with his hands in the pockets of his cardigan. Impulsively, she kissed him on the lips. "Don't worry," she said. "I know better than to fall in love with a patient."

One corner of the professor's mouth turned up. His white eyebrows twitched. "Maria, you are a young woman. Certain things you won't be able to prevent."

She laughed and walked out of the professor's house for the last time.

* * *

Sorensen would have laughed at his carelessness but the corners of his mouth felt frozen as if by a dentist's novocaine. Perfectly he saw the smooth image of the fender of the 1955 Ford pickup he had bought in Larkspur, Colorado, the cut on his finger from a metal burr beneath the edge of the fender he had just finished sanding, and the rush of air from the end of the hose across his fingers as he blew the sanding grit off the fender with the stream of air from the compressor. As if living that moment again, he felt dizzy, removed from his body, a distinct swelling within his head, and then nothing but blackness flashed into the white-walled room of the hospital.

Carelessness always killed quicker than others, and he wished he had remembered that before. Now he tried to move his hand to touch the numbness in his face, but his hand would not move. He willed his finger to move, but it did not. He told his toes to wiggle but they ignored him. He saw his chest rise and fall as he breathed, and the involuntary movement of his lungs over which he had no control caused him to look up to the ceiling by rolling his eyes. The white walls around him chased his eyelids shut. A simmer of electricity burned down his nerves as shadows formed behind his eyes, the shadows now the twin shapes of a man and woman walking away down the road, disappearing into the forest.

Sorensen remembered now that the dream haunted him not so much as a dream but as a picture of his imagination installed in his mind as an explanation. Growing up with his uncle on a farm, he recalled his uncle's nose like a fishhook, his ears like those of a mule. Each night he saw the dream in his sleep until he asked his uncle about it. "Ah," said the uncle. "Those two shadows walking away, they're your ma and your pa. That's who they are. And be glad about it, too."

His uncle refused to tell him anything more and took his knowledge with him to the grave. From then on the dream left him, until now as he lay in the hospital unable to move anything but his eyelids and his eyes. He considered the odd vantage point of white with his eyes open or darkness with them shut. The dim world of his closed eyes reminded him of the draw of the dark space of the closet in his uncle's bedroom. A magnetism lay within it like light leaking toward gravity in a black hole. He slipped into the closet and crouched beneath his uncle's clothes hanging above. Those clothes surrounded him with the hard smell of kerosene, manure from the barn, whisky, milkweed from the meadows, pipesmoke. He felt along the back wall with his hands, as if blind, and his hands touched a long object, round and cold like steel. He pulled it toward him, it struck against his chest, and he found himself staring down a narrow hole at the bottom of which a glint of light flashed in his eye. Frightened, he jumped back, the object fell to the floor, and a sound like thunder ripped through the house. He ran from the closet and saw his startled face in the shattered mirror at the other end of the room—the mirror flashing a thousand facets of light like the web of a spider.

His uncle dashed into the room and picked up the rifle from the floor. "What the Christmas-hell are you doing, boy? You could have killed somebody!" His uncle rubbed the wooden stock of the rifle before running his hand down the length of the barrel. "I keep her loaded," he said. "That way a man treats her with respect. Remember that, and don't blow your fool head off."

* * *

Dr. Andujar reached the end of the hall and pushed the door open. Inside, Sorensen lay motionless on the bed beneath a white sheet. His lips were purple. She covered him with a blanket. Her large dark eyes met his narrow blue ones. She smiled but he did not. He only blinked.

She put her warm hand on his. "I'm glad to see you are awake. How are you doing?"

He did not respond.

"I'm sorry. That was stupid."

Again Sorensen said nothing.

"Can you nod your head?" She saw no movement. She lifted his hand. "Can you move your fingers?"

Nothing happened.

A pang of unwanted heat suddenly crossed her forehead. "Let's try this. To say *yes*, blink your eyes once. Try that."

Sorensen blinked. Dr. Andujar smiled. "That's a start. What can we use for the word *no*?"

Sorensen blinked twice. Dr. Andujar impulsively stroked his short blond hair. His eyelids narrowed to slits like a cat. She withdrew her hand. "I'm sorry. I shouldn't have done that."

He blinked twice. She brushed his cheek with one of her fingers. He sensed her perfume, the perfume his wife wore the day they signed the divorce papers. He closed his eyes. When he did not open his eyes again, Dr. Andujar stood for a moment to watch the snow fall outside the window. Then she turned to leave, and Sorensen heard the quick click of her heels on the linoleum. It sounded like taps of a hammer on nails.

* * *

Imagination remained a reservoir left to him. He sped through his bank of memories. He pictured the sheriff taking him home at age 14 to his uncle after being caught joyriding in the sheriff's squad car. His uncle snapped the elastic of black suspenders over a belly the size of a small beer keg. "You want a car? Get a job and pay for one." So he did.

He worked for Junior Baker at the gas station in Sodus, Indiana. He pumped gas while Junior remade cars from rusted heaps into shining beauties. Between customers he hung around Junior like a pup around a big dog. Junior relented and soon Sorensen bumped, wet-sanded, and painted cars. Together they remade an Edsel, a 1966 Thunderbird, a V-12 Jaguar, a 1961 Lincoln Continental with suicide doors, a Packard, a 1965 Oldsmobile Delta 88 with a Rocket V-8, and a 1947 Dodge pickup. After he graduated from high school, they spent a month each winter in Colorado, New Mexico, Arizona, Nevada, and Utah looking for the right old car or pickup they could tow back to Indiana to rebuild.

Junior Baker would stand along a Western highway straight as a line of telephone poles, no trees in sight for miles, the wind in his hair, and bargain the price. Done, the owner walking away with cash, Junior stuck his thumbs into his jeans like he'd just made the best deal in the world. Back in Indiana, the car rebuilt and painted, Junior smiled again. "Looks better than a beautiful woman, don't she?"

Then came the black Chevy Deuce. Sorensen installed headers and duel exhausts, a Hurst fourspeed, chrome mags. The black paint shone with specks of silver metallic like rays of moonlight. It was his and his alone, until Junior borrowed it one night, got drunk with a red-headed woman, and drove in front of a train at the crossing at the end of town. "That wasn't careless," his uncle told him. "That was reckless. He might just as well put a gun to his head."

* * *

Dr. Andujar encouraged him to move his fingers, his hands, his forearms, and then his arms. Now he moved his toes and his legs. "You will walk," she said. "I know you will walk." At last he laughed, a slurred laugh like a man with senility might laugh, and the sound of it drove a flush of heat up his face in embarrassment.

She touched his arm. "You know what happened, don't you?"

His words stumbled out. "I'm not sure."

"We think you had an air embolism. That means there was an air bubble in your bloodstream, and the bubble floated free in your blood until it lodged in a narrow artery in your brain. When the air bubble got stuck, it was like a dam that blocked the flow of blood. Basically, you had a stroke."

"Only old men have strokes." He curled both forearms toward his chest.

Her eyes sparkled. She leaned over and kissed his cheek.

* * *

The night before Sorensen's wife told him she wanted a divorce, she kissed him precisely as Dr. Andujar had just kissed him. The premonition was more than disturbing, and when he recalled that kiss, the look in her eye, and how she edged to the other side of the bed and slept with her back to him, he dreamed she grew fat in her hips and belly with a child. But it was only a dream. Now, lying in the hospital bed, he shuddered and turned toward the violet sky receding into evening. The sky fell as cold as his wife's words, "I'm leaving." Her dark hair suddenly appeared as if painted by Lucifer. "I don't have to live like this. I don't have to smell the paint on your body. I don't have to live hand-to-mouth. I'm not going to have babies while you work on old cars and don't make any money. I'm not gonna be stuck here the rest of my life."

She slid out from under the blanket of the bed and slipped off her pajamas. When she flicked on the light, her hips glowed. Her waist narrowed like an hourglass. She clipped on a black bra, stepped into black panties, and pulled on silver lycra tights and a cropped top. Twirling around, she flung her hair to one side. "Take a good look. You ain't gonna see nothing like this for a long, long time."

* * *

Dr. Andujar stepped into the room and found Sorensen sitting up in bed. Surprised, she placed her hands to her mouth and hid a smile like a mother might smile. She hurried over to the bed and gently pressed her fingers against his shoulder. "You must lie down. You shouldn't be sitting up yet."

"Quit babying me." The slur was almost gone. "I'm going to walk today."

"I'll have some parallel bars brought in. You can walk with those."

"Screw the parallel bars. I'm going to walk without them."

She peered at him over the rims of her glasses. He slowly raised his hand and fingered the end of the stethoscope that hung from her neck down her chest. "That's a nice necklace you have there, doctor. When I walk out of here, can I take you to dinner and see how you look in pearls?"

Her eyes flashed. She held her chin up and looked him squarely in the eye. "You must be more of a gentleman than you've decided to be today."

He pursed his lips and tensed his muscles. "I'm going to walk."

He slid off the bed. His feet touched flat on the floor. He braced himself against the bed, set his jaw, and pushed forward. One leg followed, then another, then a third step, and he teetered before falling face first onto the floor. He groaned. She knelt beside him. "You okay?"

"No more thick than I ever was." He pushed himself into a kneeling position and tugged one leg up until his foot was flat again on the floor. He grabbed his other leg with both hands, drawing it forward and beneath himself, squatting on the floor more like a toad than a man. Slowly, gently, he pushed up, a bent spring uncoiling. He held his hands out for balance, wobbled, took three uneven steps to the door, then clung to the door knob and gasped for breath.

He called over his shoulder. "I'm walking right out this door!"

Dr. Andujar rushed across the room and held him steady.

"Here I go!" he yelled. He flung open the door and tottered down the hall, laughing and hollering and crying until he tripped and fell in front of the nurses' station. An old nurse peered over the counter as if he were Lazarus.

Dr. Andujar chased after him and put her small dark hand on his shoulder. Her Latin accent lilted from deep in her throat. "You are a lucky man, Jim Sorensen."

He rolled over like a log and looked up at her beaming face. "Yes," he said. "I am."

* * *

The next day she brought him a hickory cane. He held it up to the light, examined the fine whorls in the wood, and tapped it on the tiled floor of the hospital. She smiled at him. He frowned. "This is for an old man," he said.

She grabbed it from him and rapped it against his legs. "It will help you walk. When you no longer need it, you can break it in two." She handed it back to him. "Now get off that bed and walk."

He gripped the cane and steadied himself on the length of hickory. Taking first one step, then another, he hardly wobbled now, though one leg moved stiffly as if the knee were a rusty hinge, and the other leg dragged behind like a broken mop. He tugged at her arm and tapped the bottom of the cane on the floor. "Let's walk outside and get some cold air in our lungs."

She took his arm as far as the door. Once in the hallway, she simply walked alongside, an arm's length away. Outside, the sun shone bright against the snow, and the cold air turned their cheeks red. His left leg felt better with each step. But his right leg dragged behind.

Cumulus rose on the horizon, reminding him of the Rocky Mountains west of the Palmer Divide. He grimaced at the thought. That was where he bought the 1955 Ford pickup he was working on before the accident. He remembered Larkspur—Lodgepole pines at night, proud against the stars, and the air sharp in his lungs. Now he wanted to go back to the mountains and run up and down the long slopes and yell from the top of a mountain that he was alive.

He stopped his daydream and wrapped his arm around Maria. She gently removed his arm. "Please," she whispered. "Not here. Not at the hospital. You're my patient, remember."

When she looked up at him, he sank into the dark cream skin of her face, the eyes dark as Indiana loam, and the white teeth like pearls. Unable to bear it, he pointed at the puffy clouds. "Do they look like mountains to you?"

"Yes, they do."

"I'm going to run in the mountains."

* * *

That night he dreamed he ran like a mountain lion along the top ridge of a peak among blue lupine, purple asters and tiny wild daisies. Two figures stood near the peak in the distance like silhouettes, one taller than the other, one shorter and wider. Now it appeared as if the taller figure carried a long dark stick at his side. Suddenly, the stick raised to the man's shoulder, a distant boom sounded like the resonance of thunder from a far valley, and stones scattered about his feet. He stopped and crouched in the flowers. Behind him a man waved his arms. He recognized the man as his uncle, ran to him, and sprang within his uncle's belly, as if the lion became a child within the man, and when his uncle shouted at the two distant figures, they disappeared like smoke.

Then his uncle fell backward, turned pale, quivered, and his eyes rolled back into his head. Now Sorensen jumped from his uncle's belly as a child with a crippled leg and the cane. He stumbled through the flowers, beating the cane upon each rock he found, unable to break it into pieces no matter how hard he struck it—the cane like iron in his hands, stinging each time he smashed it against the side of the mountain.

In the morning he woke in yellow light. On the floor lay the cane, broken in pieces. He hobbled to the window, dragging his bad leg behind him. Outside, the clouds looked like mountains again. When Dr. Andujar walked into the room, his heart thumped like that of a lion.

Robert Baldwin is a Denver attorney and founding member of Baldwin & Brown, P.C. His novella, "Door of Water," was a Denver best seller. His novel, "The Water Thief," is forthcoming from GreyCore Press in the fall of 2002 and was a finalist for the Ariadne Fiction Prize.

The Grape Harvest

by Mark Apelman

The Gypsies arrived this morning, right on time. From the Château, I watched their rusty caravan bounce into the field next to the vineyard. Every year the grapes are ready at a different time, and every year Louchard's clan hits it dead on.

The women unfold plastic tables and chairs and rebuild the fire pits. The men go into the forest, come back with wood. In half an hour, it's a camp. Smoke rises from their fires. Children run through the field, arousing the dogs into a frenzy of barking.

I hate those mongrel Gypsy dogs. Two years ago, my best pointer bitch delivered seven mutts. I drove those pups to the village and left them in a box outside the cathedral. Now, while the Gypsies are here, I keep my hunting dogs locked in the kennel.

October in Médoc is prime hunting season, but I won't be using the dogs this year, and I have no wish to touch a gun, now or ever again. My daughter Caroline saw to that. I might as well sell every last dog. The guns are already gone. Camille threw each one in the river.

Sometimes I blame myself, sometimes I don't. It's too soon to know. I still go back and forth. I waver.

Jacques Louchard steps out from his trailer, stretches, surveys my property like he owns it. He lights a cigarette and yawns. I recognize this studied insolence. After all, it's for my benefit—the opening move in a negotiation we've turned into a ritual: the setting of the wage. Will the Gypsy come to me, or must I cross the road to his camp? Which of us is stronger? Who needs the other more?

Years past, this contest consumed me. Just last year, I waited for Louchard in the Château, refusing to cross over. At night I watched the fires in their camp, but the Gypsy did not cross. Downstairs Caroline played her piano, a grating irritation. In bed I woke Camille with my turning. She reached for my hand and pulled it under her face. "Relax, Henri, everything's fine." She heard the piano. "Listen to how pretty." But I was furious, drifting into sleep, then twisting and snapping awake. After breakfast, I stomped over to Louchard's camp. We negotiated a wage in his trailer, yelling loudly when we couldn't agree, delaying the picking for several hours and infuriating Fortin, my nervous little cellar-master. I hated Louchard that day. I wanted to kick his balls.

Today, the whole affair is a stupid, pointless game, and I decline to play.

I pull on my boots and go over to the Gypsy camp. The dogs rush me, lips curled back. I bend to pick up a stone and they retreat. I throw anyway, missing. Louchard—surprised to see me so soon?—takes a half step forward, yells the dogs away. "Henri," he says.

It's a move. Everything with Louchard is a move. He refuses to call me Monsieur Bascaux because he thinks it gives him an advantage, because he knows—secret of the Samurai—that anger weakens a man. But I'm not angry. "It's good to see you again, Louchard," I say, and I mean it.

I step toward him, we shake hands, and I find myself extending this touch longer than necessary, lingering in his grip, feeling the rough skin on the back of his hand. I wonder what secrets this man carries in his private heart. We're such mysteries, even to ourselves. You can live with someone for years, under the same roof, and have no clue. And, say you truly wanted to communicate, what would you use? Words? Bullets and blows might be better. More honest, anyway.

Louchard yells something in Romany to someone I can't see. He points to a chair and offers me a cigarette. We sit outside his trailer. "Everything is well with you and Camille?"

"Yes, of course," I say, nodding. "Fine. Everything is fine."

"The grapes look good this year, Henri, very good," he says. "You'll get rich from this harvest." He blows a mouthful of smoke at the fields where tomorrow and for the next three weeks the Gypsies will labor. Another move. These are not an occidental people.

Louchard is an impressive man. He has the look of a fighter. He must be sixty, but his hair and mustache are still black. He stands a full head taller than me. A woman I don't recognize brings two cups of Turkish coffee and a bowl of sugar on a wooden tray.

"For us, it was a hard year," the Gypsy says. "A very hard year. We lost Gaetan Peltier in Corsica. Now we have his widow—" he points to the woman walking away—"and three children. And since last year, everything costs so much more. This new EC does nothing for us, nothing at all. We barely survive on the wages we get."

I know the words by heart. An ancient ritual, honed by centuries of desert caravans, slow, circuitous negotiations over cups of sweet mint tea. Now it's my turn. I'll open my mouth, watch the words spill out: *Survival wasn't meant to be easy, Louchard. Wine's a hard business. And every year the California wines get better. They drive the prices down. And the costs*—a telling lift of the hand, face tilted skyward—*the costs keep going up.*

My mouth is a gaping hole, my words a foul excretion. *Ta geule, Henri. Shut your trap. You've done enough harm for one life.* "How much, Louchard? How much do you want? Spit it out."

The Gypsy cocks his head sideways and inspects me. He reminds me of a raven, trying to decipher some mystery of the universe with its stupid bird brain, like whether it's safe to peck out the deer's eyes, or did the car only stun it?

"Henri," says Louchard. "A good picker is hard to find. Such a person should be paid well, at least three hundred francs a day."

He'd be happy with half that. I know it, he knows I know.

On the road a car passes. The driver slows to stare at the Gypsy camp, then speeds off toward the village. From the woods a single shot rings out. Goddamn villagers, after pheasant or quail. I see them on the edge of the woods, shotguns hanging on their arms. I jump up and wave them away. "Not here, you pigs. Guns off my land!" They look for a second then scurry into the woods. I pick up a stone and fling it after them.

Louchard is staring at me. "$300's fine," I tell him. The Gypsy looks puzzled, but pleased.

"You've picked here for what? Ten years?" I feel compelled to add. "I admire your loyalty. Besides, the French are lazy. I could get Moroccans, but they're even lazier, if that's possible. And they steal."

Louchard laughs. He tosses his cigarette on the ground and stands up. "Henri, we're Gypsies, remember? Gypsies?" He pokes himself in the chest. "*We* steal."

I wave my hand, a gesture of dismissal and indifference. A light rain has started to fall. I wish I had my jacket. Can Caroline see me? I imagine her hovering above me—not cowering anymore—looking down—passing judgment? Still wanting my love? At night, sometimes, the faceless shapes weave and reel around my head. They chase me like the Furies. I wrestle them like Jacob. But I'm a modern man. I take this to be my own conscience. I don't take it as proof of guilt, although there may yet be some culpability here. Apparently it is not material that Caroline died by her own hand. It was not material to Camille. "This is on *your* hands," she said, her voice a hissing curse. But aren't people responsible for their own deeds? For the deeds of their own hands? She was almost 18 years old.

* * *

At night, flames illuminate the Gypsy camp. Flashes of steel in the flickering light. I sit in the dark, watching through the open window. Downstairs, Camille is writing letters. Writing, writing, writing, purging herself, creating a story she can live with, telling everyone she ever knew about the accident.

"Why don't you tell the truth?" I said, when she started these incessant letters.

"Do *you* know the truth, Henri? You tell me the truth."

"I don't care that you lied to the priest, but . . . " I shut up. We have been driven into separate worlds, torn apart, left alone with this hot and scalding thing. When we speak, the words explode. They burst from our mouths like cannonballs.

During the day, I stay busy, more or less. I talk wine with Fortin in the chai. I see to my financial affairs. After lunch, I drive to the village to pick up the mail. Sometimes I stop at the tavern for a beer. But at night, I miss Camille. I miss the time after supper when we sat together reading or watching television. I miss sleeping with her. In the Gypsy camp, someone is playing guitar. The rhythm carries into my bedroom. What if I walked over there? Belonged to their close-knit clan? Went with them after the harvest, to Spain or Corsica or wherever it is they go for the winter? Never came back?

* * *

I took her hunting once. She was a soft child, coddled, in my opinion, by Camille. She didn't like to get up early or go outside in the cold morning drizzle. We took two dogs and drove to the Gironde near Valeyrac. In the marshes and cattails we waded and crouched, and then the dogs pointed. I got ready to shoot. Caroline stood up to look.

"Get down! You'll spook them." And they did spook, two mallards, taking rise and flapping away. I took one hurried shot, missing everything. I thought perhaps I clipped a wing, but the dogs found nothing.

"Imbecile," I yelled. "I told you to stay low. What's the matter with you?" I was a puppet on the strings of rage, not speaking so much as being spoken.

Caroline started to cry. "I hate hunting. I'm cold."

It would be so easy to blame myself. I could wallow in self-pity. People would reward me with sympathy and forgiveness—relieved to keep intact their comforting notions of human causation. My other children might temper their condemnation. Even Camille might soften toward me. But I didn't get this far in life by bowing to convention, and I won't live by platitudes and lies.

* * *

I rise before dawn and go outside in the quiet, liminal time of day. The rain is gone. The air is so still, silence feels proper. I think to speak would be a sin. In the Gypsy camp, no sound at all. Even the dogs are asleep, sprawled around the fire pits. In the chai, lights are on. Fortin is already busy, scurrying around in his black jacket and wine-stained leather apron. The metal chutes are clean and gleaming. In a few hours they'll run purple, filling the oak vats with crushed grapes.

Fortin waves from across the chai. "Bonjour, Monsieur Bascaux. Everything's ready." The cellar-master rubs his head and waits for his compliment like a dog for a bone. I hate his servile manner, but I'll say this—Fortin knows wine. Even my enemies must concede Château Camille bottles some of the best wine in Médoc, and the credit for that goes to Fortin. I love these 30 hectares, but with Fortin, it's beyond that. Wine is his religion.

"Weather looks good," I say.

"A little too cold, Monsieur," he says. "But we can't wait."

"Bring out some table wine for the pickers." Fortin hates the Gypsies. He always forgets to bring them wine.

* * *

I'm reading *Le Monde* when Camille comes downstairs in her bathrobe. I fashion a smile and say, "Big day today."

"How can you think of business?"

"The grapes, Camille. They have to be picked. The Gypsies are here."

"You think I care about grapes?"

"Grapes pay for this house," I say, but then I slam my teeth shut, lock the words behind bars. Whole sentences appear in my mind—*What should I do, cancel the harvest? Let them rot on the vine? Wouldn't that be a fitting tribute*—but I don't speak them. I've learned this.

"I should've stopped you." She sits down across from me and hugs herself. I bought that robe for her birthday when we still lived in Paris. "I should've seen what you were doing to her," she says. "Do you even miss her?"

"Camille. Don't pick a fight."

"Do you?"

"Of course I miss her," I say, angry, full of affront, but I don't, not really. I wanted a boy, or at least a tougher girl. She was so easily hurt. My very presence seemed to wound her. Tone of voice, critical looks, sharp tongue—my words were poison darts, her skin was paper-thin. She made me feel like a monster. After Isabelle and Marianne finished school and went off to the university, I found it easier to avoid her.

* * *

I walk over to the fields to watch the harvest begin. It's cool for October, the sky a washed-out blue. Fortin is there, supervising. He runs the harvest like a Swiss railroad. He starts the picking on the south side, away from the woods, where the sun shines most.

In spring the grapes are hard as stone, tiny green pebbles you could not crush between your fingers. All summer they swell on the vine, distilling soil, sun, air, water. If there was blood on the ground, they'd use that, too. Now the fruit hangs full and heavy, deep blue grapes, firm in their skin, and the skin almost translucent. To see the harvest starting sends a shiver up my spine. My heart beats faster. This is the best wine in the world.

The work is hard. The grapes are heavy and close to the ground. Women, children and old men snip clumps of grapes into wooden baskets, yelling "Videz!" when they're full. The strongest men race through the rows, with open plastic buckets strapped on their backs. They collect the grapes and dump them in the vat behind the tractor, then head back into the vines to collect more. At the end of each row, a break: food and wine, coffee, a smoke. The Gypsies keep up a steady chatter as they work, shouting, throwing grapes, making faces behind his back when Fortin scolds them, but never slowing down.

I admire these Gypsies. For a thousand years they have wandered through nations, outcasts in every one. They are their own nation, like the Jews. Like the Jews, they survive by being smarter and faster than the French, and like the Jews, we have made them pay for it. But whoever calls them lazy, fortune-telling thieves has not seen them work these fields.

Louchard does not pick. He drives the tractor between the rows, hauling the vat where the men empty their plastic backpacks. He wears work boots and trousers that barely reach his ankles. He will not shave until the night of the harvest celebration, a superstitious ritual. He greets me with a nod, then continues to stare at a woman lagging behind the others. "Peltier's widow," he says, snapping his face in her direction. "She has to go faster."

"She looks tired," I say.

"You *have* changed," says the Gypsy. "I knew it yesterday." He spits, jumps down from the tractor. "I talked to Fortin," he says. "I'm sorry, Henri."

I say nothing. I will not meet his look.

The fastest pickers have already finished the row. They lounge on the grass, eating sausage and cheese, drinking table wine mixed with water from the plastic jugs strapped to the tractor. Peltier's widow is far back, still working.

I stare at the ground, eyes shut. *Impossible,* I think, *impossible.* From time to time, against my will, these feelings sweep over me. When I want to cry, I can't. But sometimes I cry without wanting to.

Louchard rests his hand on my shoulder for a moment, then climbs back on the tractor.

* * *

When she was 15, I took her to Spain. In the limestone caves at Altamira, 20,000 years ago, cavemen painted animals on the walls. I wanted to show her the savage existence of our first ancestors. Those hunters knew the rule of kill or be killed. I worried that if I didn't toughen her up, the world would eat her alive. Life would be a series of hurts.

In the Great Hall, saber-toothed tigers, bison, horses, deer. Silhouettes of human hands, the fingers spread apart and reaching for something. To me, those hands represented the human urge—the human right—to take. To grab. To hold.

"Papa, an elephant."

"That's a mammoth, not an elephant."

"Look, it has a red heart."

"That's so they know where to throw the spear. You couldn't afford to miss."

"But he's so beautiful." I saw the fight. She saw beauty. I saw the power of naming. She saw love.

"Beautiful, sure, but first they had to eat. What do you think, they went to the store?"

She looked dejected. Sorry for the mammoth, I suppose, sad to imagine it speared through the heart and dying. Every time she backed down, that awful wounded look in her eyes—it only made me push harder, sharpen the edge on my words. Her weakness made me attack, the way a lion chases anything that runs away. If only she'd stood up to me, fought back like Isabelle or Marianne, yelled, *"Ta geule, Papa, j'en ai marre de toi." Shut your fat trap, Dad, I'm sick of you.* But she was Caroline. She couldn't do that.

* * *

The vats fill up with grapes. Every day, Fortin measures the rising alcohol content, yeast fermenting sugar. Cautiously, he predicts a good year. One afternoon, coming back from the mail run, I see the Gypsies gathered around a woman on the ground. It's Peltier's widow. They carry her to their campsite and return to work. I stop the car and find Louchard. "Aren't you going to call a doctor?"

"She's fine, Henri. We won't charge you for her today."

"I'm calling the doctor. And from now on, let her work half-days. I'll pay her the same."

He gives me the raven look, then nods his assent.

The harvest falls into a rhythm, day after day of picking, Sundays free. The weather holds. Everyone has a role except me. Here at my own vineyard, I'm not needed.

* * *

The piano was her refuge—the one place she could forget me. I sit at her bench—trespasser in my own home—and press the keys. B flat. G. C sharp. I hold each note until the sound is gone. They last so long, fade so slowly, you can't say the precise moment when they stop.

Camille hears this, I'm sure, upstairs in her bedroom. Maybe, for a second, she thinks it's Caroline. Maybe I'm asking her to come down, to confront me, condemn me, forgive me, talk to me. Something. I play the notes till she appears, in her nightgown, hair spiked out with sleep. She squints and stares at me. What is she thinking? I have no idea. Such a strange expression on her face. She turns and goes back to bed.

I'm so restless. I think a drive might help, maybe a beer in the tavern. The road runs straight for six kilometers. I accelerate until the car shakes. But in the village I'm not ready to stop. With no destination, I turn south.

I like to drive. The motion and speed make me feel I'm achieving something. In Bordeaux I fill the tank and turn south.

The villages are poor, the countryside steep and rocky. Small terraces are cut into the hills. I drive all night through the dark winding hills of northern Spain. I'll take a room somewhere if I get tired, or sleep in the car. But I'm not tired. Near Santander, in the first pink light of dawn, I see that all along I *have* had a destination. The cave paintings are only a short distance away, near the ocean.

I turn onto the small side road as the sun lifts over the hills and light pours through the valley. At this early hour, before the tourists, Altamira is empty. Since I was here with Caroline, some of the caves have been closed, to protect the paintings from the humid air. Others remain open.

I find the Great Hall and sit in the semi-darkness. The animals are there, the straining human hands, the mammoth with the red heart. But all I see today are colors—paintings—a mammoth on the wall of a cave in Spain. It has a red heart on its side. Beyond that—mystery, story, human fabrication.

There was no note. If she meant to judge me, she left no written record. Just that sound ripping through the house, and the complete silence that followed. We knew. I knew, Camille knew. Perhaps we hoped for something else—village poachers, a burglar even—but we knew. Our eyes met—a second at most—we both looked away—but everything—the anguish, the censure and condemnation—it was all there in Camille's eyes in that first instant. In time, I hope, she will soften.

I sit in the cave until my legs hurt and I have to stand up. Outside the light stings my eyes. In the parking lot an old man is picking up trash, spearing cigarette packets and candy wrappers with a nail on the end of a long stick. He looks up, surprised to see anyone coming out at this early hour. "Buenos dias, Señor," says the man.

"Buenos dias," I say. I wish I remembered more Spanish. There's so much I'd like to say.

"Es muy bonito aquí," I say. *It's very pretty here.*

"Si. Muy bonito." I reach out my hand and he takes it.

* * *

On the last day the mood is light. Even Fortin seems happy, relieved, I think, to have the grapes safely inside. He jokes with the Gypsies, flirts with the young girls. By noon the last row has been picked. In the chai, the oak vats are full. I love the smell of fermenting grapes—so potent, sweet and rich.

At the harvest celebration dinner I feast them on lamprey à la Bordelaise, grilled entrecote with shallots, and fresh local champignons, salad, cheese, cognac, peaches in wine. I give each picker a bottle of the '74. I toast their good work and wish them luck until next year. "And one last word. I dedicate this harvest to my daughter, Caroline." I catch Camille's eye, and we look at each other.

* * *

With the Gypsies gone, the Château is lonely and still. A smoky autumn sadness fills the air. Already the vines are turning orange and red. Every time the wind blows, a thousand leaves fall to the ground, and overhead, the birds move south.

Soon, winter will bring the rain, and for six months the vines will hang dead beneath a grey and crushing sky. I stand at the water-streaked windows, forehead resting against the cool glass, looking out at the perfectly straight rows.

The Grape Harvest—Mark Apelman

Mark Apelman's stories and essays have appeared in numerous literary magazines, including "American Literary Review," "The Laurel Review" and "Pearl." He is associate fiction editor for the "High Plains Literary Review," and is a 1999 recipient of a Fiction Fellowship from the Colorado Council on the Arts. His story, "A Visitor's Guide to Berlin," won first place in International Quarterly's 1998 Crossing Boundaries Fiction Contest and was recently reprinted in "With Signs and Wonders: An International Anthology of Jewish Fabulist Fiction" (Invisible Cities Press, 2001). A 1986 graduate of the University of Michigan law school, he served in 1986-1987 as a law clerk to Chief Judge Richard P. Matsch of the U.S. District Court for the District of Colorado, and has been in private practice ever since. He lives in Denver with his wife, Mary Jo Young, M.D., and their two sons, Ben and Matt.

AN EXCERPT FROM

BLIND SPOT

by Stephanie Kane

In the domain of the Honorable Bertram J. Worrell, the twenty-foot molded ceilings muted the din of the masses to a genteel murmur and the chairs in the jury box were leather with brass tacks instead of the molded plastic of county court. District court was serious business: pilasters sprang from pink marble baseboard to be capped by gilded Ionic scrolls and the belts of the brawny deputies stationed at the door were so loaded with paraphernalia the men looked like human bombs. All talk came to a halt when the bailiff rapped his gavel and the judge mounted the bench, but once he was seated, the undertone resumed like a low-grade fever.

With appointed counsel roving the aisles, calling out names of clients they had not yet met, and prosecutors and defense attorneys negotiating last-minute concessions, the ambiance on days in which no trial was scheduled was more commercial than adversarial—a bazaar, if not a flea market. As the judge handled bond matters and pleas with the ruthless efficiency of an auctioneer, the courtroom emptied and refilled in a parade of jailhouse green and anxious-looking relatives. From the second row behind the swinging gate Jackie waited. Aaron's bail hearing was the last item on the morning docket, but she had no doubt Worrell would get to it long before any thought of a solitary sandwich in chambers entered his mind.

Bertram Worrell was a stickler for punctuality. Because his internal clock was set five minutes faster than Mountain Time, lawyers were well advised to advance their watches accordingly. The judge opened his own mail, had no use for law clerks or computer research, and wrote his decisions in longhand. Though his rulings were seldom appealed and almost never reversed, Worrell liked to say the only time he was certain he'd been right was when a higher power disagreed with him. When Jackie learned Aaron's case had been assigned to him, she'd told Pilar to break out the champagne.

Pratt was presenting a plea bargain for a drunk driver who'd killed a patrolman in an accident on Speer Boulevard. Worrell nodded impatiently, his round head bobbing on his reedy neck. His eyes were fixed but glazed, as if he were speed-reading the DA's statement somewhere on the rear wall of the chamber and was three lines ahead of him. This impression was confirmed when he cut Pratt off in mid-sentence and began questioning the defendant himself. As a flush crept from Pratt's collar to his ears, Jackie prayed the DA wouldn't delegate Aaron's case to one of his subordinates. Bail was only the first hand in the high-stakes poker game that would culminate in Aaron's trial.

At twenty minutes past eleven the doors swung open again and there was a sudden hush. A steady stream of reporters had filled the courtroom, and now they leaned forward as one. The steam radiators made the room unbearably stuffy and, sensing the barometric shift, the spectators roused themselves from their torpor. The sheriff's deputy escorting the single prisoner gave a self-conscious cough.

Catching Jackie's eye, Aaron raised his manacled wrists in acknowledgment and took his seat with the remaining men in the dock while two deputies stationed themselves at either end. As Jackie watched his gaze roam the courtroom, her misgivings about seeking her client's release returned. Denying bail would be more than a moral victory for the prosecution: at trial a jail-house pallor spoke louder than words, inviting the jury to send the prisoner back to the hole. Moreover, keeping Aaron in custody would have enabled her to force Pratt's hand by seeking an early trial, and Jackie had the nagging sense that her client was better off where she could keep her eye on him.

But seeking bail provided at least one advantage besides the freedom upon which Aaron insisted: to deny bail, the DA had to establish that the proof was evident and the presumption great that Aaron murdered Rae Malone. That meant a free peek at the prosecution's case—warts and all. Not a bad trade-off. In fact, a win-win situation for the defense no matter which way it came out.

Now, peering out over the gallery, the judge posed a rare rhetorical question.

"Are there any other matters to be heard before People vs. Best?"

Warfare in Worrell's court was nothing if not civilized.

The public defenders gathered their files and, comrades in arms, yielded the defense table to Jackie. Pratt's two assistants remained where they were, clearing the center of the prosecution table for their boss. Were all three planning to try Aaron, or had Pratt divided the work for the purpose of pretrial motions? Settling in the chair closest to the lectern, Jackie opened her briefcase and withdrew a yellow pad. As a deputy escorted Aaron to her side and unlocked his cuffs, she squeezed her client's arm. The gesture would not be lost on the reporters sitting directly behind them.

"Very well, then." Worrell scrutinized the file as if

seeing it for the first time, but Jackie knew he read the day's briefs when he arrived at his chambers two hours before the bailiffs punched in. "Ms. Flowers, I believe you filed this motion for—what is it?" He pretended to examine Pilar's paperwork more closely. "Ah, yes. *Bail.*"

Jackie rose but remained at her table. "That's correct, your honor." The burden was on the DA, and she wasn't about to let herself be suckered into counterpunching before her opponent entered the ring.

The judge fixed his beady eyes on Pratt.

"You're versed in the statutes, Mr. Pratt. I don't have to tell you"—but he would anyway, for the benefit of the stringers in the front row—"that Colorado law requires me to release Mr. Best on a suitable bond unless you convince me the proof is evident and the presumption great that he indeed committed the offense for which he is charged."

Pratt rose and strode confidently to the lectern.

"Yes, your honor. The abduction, murder, and decapitation of Rae Malone was a *heinous* crime, and we are quite satisfied—"

"Save the bombast for your opening statement—*if* the case gets that far. Proof, Mr. Pratt?"

"We have physical evidence linking Aaron Best to the crime scene. Specifically, a sheet from the room from which Ms. Malone was abducted, bearing DNA evidence establishing the defendant's presence."

"Which is evidence of what?"

"A sexual assault we believe occurred just prior to the abduction."

The courtroom was silent as Worrell took in this revelation with a slight frown.

"No eyewitnesses?" he asked.

"Well—of course not." Pratt turned slightly, playing to the crowd. His gaze lingered in one spot. Glancing over her shoulder, for the first time Jackie noticed Rae's husband, Rodger Malone. "In my experience, rapists and murderers restrict their audience to their victims. And physical evidence never lies."

"I see. How about the weapon, then?"

"Our investigation is ongoing . . ."

"Do I take it all you have at this point is a *bed-sheet*?"

Pratt clasped his hands behind his back. He'd gambled by calling the sexual encounter rape and upped the ante: with reporters—or was it Malone?—hanging on every word, the DA was trying to pressure the judge into denying bail by turning Aaron into Jack the Ripper. But Worrell wasn't buying, and now Dunc would have to play another card.

"And Mr. Best's history of violence against women," Pratt replied.

A nice fat headline for the early edition.

Jackie glanced at Aaron, who was doodling impassively on her yellow pad. Unless it established motive or some other element of the crime, his record was irrelevant both to the bail hearing and at trial. But she had to draw Pratt out.

"Mr. Pratt is referring to a scuffle in Mr. Best's home more than a year ago," Jackie replied, "a matter resolved by private counseling. It has no relevance to this case, and if the prosecution insists on making an issue of it, I will move to have it suppressed. If that and the bed-sheet are Mr. Pratt's *entire case*—"

"Not by a long shot! In addition to his record for domestic assault, Ms. Flowers's client almost killed a man in an unprovoked attack for which he *was* charged. This man is a threat to the public—"

What else hadn't Aaron told her?

Aaron had stopped doodling, but his eyes were glued to the pad. No matter what he was concealing, she had to act fast.

"And we will certainly move to suppress that incident as well!" Jackie strode to the lectern, giving Pratt no choice but to move aside. "Dirty linen, your honor, nothing more. A bedsheet showing evidence of a consensual sexual act"—let the *Rocky* and the *Post* print that tomorrow!—"establishes neither proof nor presumption of abduction and murder. As for prior *alleged* altercations in which my client may or may not have been involved, the sole purpose of bail is to ensure Mr. Best's presence at trial, and not punish him before conviction, either here or *in the press*—"

"I am quite aware of the law, Ms. Flowers . . ."

"He's a flight risk, your honor," Pratt broke in, "especially with a charge of this magnitude hanging over his head. Aaron Best—"

"—owns a business that's been in his family for two generations," Jackie smoothly continued. Because Aaron's family circumstances were relevant only to type and amount of bail, Pratt must be conceding he hadn't met his burden of proof on denial. "Mr. Best recently received the Entrepreneur of the Year Award from the Coalition for the Environment, runs his company with the assistance of his brother, lives with his wife and son in a bungalow near Washington Park—"

"He's separated from his wife," Pratt bellowed. "He isn't even in contact with his son!"

"That's quite enough from you both," the judge decided. "Ms. Flowers, when do you intend to file that motion to suppress?"

"As soon as I return to my office, your honor."

"I'm setting your motion to be heard in two weeks. What do you think would be the appropriate amount of bond?" He directed the question to her, ignoring Pratt.

Jackie skipped through the alternatives. Worrell would never release Aaron on personal recognizance, but if she started low, he'd bring it way down—"PR, your honor. Despite his awards, Mr. Best runs a modest—"

"One million dollars!" Pratt shot back.

"A hundred thousand." Worrell ruled. "Property or

cash."

"But, your honor—" Pratt blustered.

"Court adjourned."

Turning, Jackie saw Rodger Malone push his way through the crowd and out the door.

"—fantastic job." Aaron gripped her arm in excitement, grinning as if they'd just won the lottery. "Mark thought I should hire a guy to defend me, but I wanted you. I *knew* you could pull it off—"

Jackie heard a reporter call her name. For the first time since the hearing began, she looked her client square in the face. What did that artless front conceal? And if she was such a hero, why did she feel like she'd just been had? She detached herself from her client's grasp.

"Don't kid yourself, Aaron. Duncan Pratt's just warming up."

Stephanie Kane has practiced law since 1981. She was a partner in Holme Roberts & Owen and then did criminal defense work. She lectured on money laundering and white collar crime in Eastern Europe, has a black belt in karate and regularly beats the stuffing out of her husband, Federal Judge John Kane.

AN EXCERPT FROM

IN BROAD DAYLIGHT

by Harry MacLean

McElroy sat calmly in the Silverado, ignoring the group of men on the sidewalk to his right. He reached into the sack, pulled out the pack of Camels, tore it open, and extracted a cigarette. He stuck it in his mouth, but before lighting it, he started the engine. His yellow Bic lighter lay on the seat beside him, and he reached over to pick it up as he glanced at the men on the sidewalk. His motions were slow and deliberate.

When Trena got in the pickup, she noticed that men were still coming out of the tavern. Most of those inside, except Red Smith, came out. Many of them turned west up the hill, and several stood on the edge of the sidewalk and the street, between the Silverado and the car parked next to it. All the men were staring in their direction. She turned to Ken.

"What're they staring for?" she asked.

"I don't know," he replied.

Steve Peter and a few others moved closer to the rear of the Silverado on Trena's side. She noticed Peter's hands moving in the air. She rolled down the window to see if he wanted something, but no words were spoken. Then she saw a solitary figure walking toward her from the side or the front of the tavern. She recognized Del

Clement in his jeans, cowboy hat, and cowboy boots. Because Del was the only person moving, she turned her head and watched him as he crossed the street behind her. He walked to the cab of a dark red Ford pickup parked up the street a little way. He opened the door, reached inside, and pulled out a .30-30. Then he walked to the back of the Ford, closer to the Silverado. She saw him pull the lever down, snap it back up, raise the rifle to his right shoulder, and sight down the barrel.

"They've got *guns*!" she cried.

Ken didn't move.

Trena watched as Del squeezed the trigger, then she heard the crack of the shot and the sound of the rear window blowing apart. She turned to look at Ken and saw a huge hole in his cheek and the shattered rear window. She turned back to look at Del and saw his finger pull the trigger again and heard the explosion of a second shot. She looked at Ken and saw that he had been hit a second time.

"Oh, God! Oh, God! Oh, God!" Trena screamed. "Please stop shooting him!"

Someone jerked her door open, and a man yelled, "Get down, or they'll shoot you, too." A big man pulled her out of the truck onto the ground, and then another man, whom she knew but didn't recognize, grabbed her and hustled her up the street to the bank. As she went up the sidewalk, still screaming, she looked up and saw two women watching from a window in the bank. A few men noticed the spreading wetness on the inner thighs of her jeans.

* * *

When Steve Peter heard the first shot, his eyes were pulled to the shattering glass in the driver's door. As Trena began screaming, and her door opened, Steve decided he had better get down and out of the line of fire. He squatted between the trucks, not moving while the shots continued. Looking south, away from the shooting, he saw he was in a direct line with the west edge of the pool hall, and he figured that that would be the quickest way to get somewhere other than where he was, so he took off in a crouching lope down the side of a building. He circled west and north back to his pickup, which was parked across the street from the Sumy station, and drove home to tell his wife.

A twelve-year-old boy, who had gone inside Sumy's gas station a few minutes earlier to get a bottle of pop, was standing by the water cooler when he heard the shots. He looked out the front window and saw a man standing at the west edge of the post office with a rifle to his shoulder, firing across the street in the direction of the tavern. The boy bolted from the gas station and raced through alleys and across yards to his home. When he told his parents what he had seen, his father told him not to tell anyone.

When Cheryl heard the crack of the rifle, she saw the window shatter and McElroy's head bob down. An instant later, the second shot pushed his head further down, and she saw Trena open the door and jump out screaming. Blood and dirt streaked her arms and blouse. Jack Clement came over to where Trena was lying in the grass, picked her up, and rushed her toward the bank. (One law enforcement official would comment later that only a man with a father's faith in his son's marksmanship would walk into the line of fire like that.) Through the screen in the tavern door, Kermit saw Trena—looking like a frightened animal in search of a place to hide.

Most of the men standing around dropped down between the vehicles or took off up the hill in the direction of Sumy's gas station. The men already there stayed where they were, watching the scene unfold below. At the sound of the gunfire their eyes shifted a fraction to the left of the Silverado, and the shooters and their blazing guns came instantly into focus. The flash of the gray gunmetal, the smell of burned gunpowder, the sounds of splintering glass and a woman's screams of terror, would be forever seared in their memories.

* * *

After the men had followed McElroy and Trena out the front door, Red Smith caught up on collecting for the beer and pop and was chatting with Kermit at the south end of the bar. A few men had begun playing pool, and the talk was picking up a little when Red heard what he first thought were firecrackers going off.

"Get down," someone yelled. "Those are bullets flying!"

Red dived onto the floor behind the bar. He lay on the cement floor shaking, listening to the gunfire and praying that the bullets wouldn't start ripping into the tin building.

Kermit heard the first *boom!*, a pause, and then a second *boom!* He hit the floor beside Red, thinking that somebody had shot at McElroy and missed, and now McElroy was shooting back. *There might be a goddamn war starting and those high powers would blow right through the tin walls*, he thought. He heard three more shots: BOOM! . . .BOOM! . . . BOOM! In his mind he saw the levers on the rifles being cocked and the rifles being leveled and re-aimed between the shots. He figured the shooting lasted fifteen to twenty seconds.

Q was sitting at a table with several of his buddies when he heard the *blammy! blam! blam!* of the rifles. He dived under the pool table, where several others soon joined him.

When the shooting ended, the people in the bar stayed put for several minutes, unsure of what to do, but not wanting to be part of whatever was happening on the street.

"By God!" someone finally said after looking out the door. "It's over with now. He won't be bothering us no more."

A few men picked themselves up from the floor, wobbled to the bar, and ordered beers. Red, his hands shaking, got up and did his best to oblige.

The big Silverado engine was roaring, and somebody said, "Better shut it off."

"To hell with it," came the response. "Let it burn."

Q stood up, turned to his neighbor, and asked, "How long do you figure it will run like that?"

"Oh, maybe five or six minutes."

* * *

The heavy, dark head, its oily black hair slicked back, slammed down on the massive chest. The shock of the hit flowed down through the thick torso and the lower limbs until a booted foot rocked forward on the accelerator in a heavy thrust. The V-8 leapt into life and roared out in a full-throated angry protest. The engine wound up until, at full bore, its howl crashed through the town and ripped the still air like the bellowing of a mortally wounded beast. The howl rose to a terrible shriek, and smoke began pouring forth from the guts of the beast in thick black clouds. The head sat unmoving, like a huge black stone, but the heart continued to pump, and blood spurted from the holes in the neck and face, splattering everything around a bright, shiny crimson. The observers backed away slowly, mesmerized by the violence of the final throes. The heat of the struggle radiated outward in searing waves, turning the street into a huge blast furnace.

Finally, the beast's vital organs began to pop and

snap under the strain, and the observers could hear the sickening sound of guts tearing apart. In the crescendo of the shriek, its insides seized and locked together in a death grip of flesh and metal, and the horrible noise ceased. A final sigh escaped and fluids gushed onto the burning pavement with soft, gurgling sounds. Then silence filled the town.

Harry MacLean graduated from the DU College of Law in 1967. He has worked for the Securities and Exchange Commission, the Peace Corps, the state attorney general's office, and as a magistrate in Denver Juvenile Court and labor arbitrator. His first book, "In Broad Daylight," was published in 1989. It won an Edgar Award for Best True Crime, was on the New York Times *Bestseller List for 12 weeks, was a featured selection of the Book-of-the-Month Club, and was made into a TV movie. His second book, "Once Upon A Time, A True Story of Murder, Memory And The Law," was published in 1994. It was chosen as Notable Book of the Year by the* New York Times *Book Review and was a featured selection of the Book-of-the-Month Club.*

An Excerpt From

A Suggestion of Death

by Marianne Wesson

Never ask a witness a question unless you already know the answer. It's one of the first things they teach you in law school, but I already knew it anyway. Everybody knows it, from television. This advice is not really meant to apply to a discovery deposition, but even there you're at least supposed to know what it is you're trying to discover.

They also taught us that *A surprised lawyer is a bad lawyer*. Then there's another good one: *Don't get emotionally involved with a client.* Sterling principles, really, although I admit I never put much stock in the second. Even lawyers aren't so dull as to wish for lives devoid of surprise.

It was my law partner Tory Meadows who induced me to violate the first one, but although I broke it at Tory's behest, it wasn't on her behalf. It was for Mariah.

As for the last rule, I broke it on my own. I'd broken it at least once before. I suppose that makes me some kind of recidivist.

Our first meeting was unpromising. Inside the Hygiene Café the air was close and warm, a contrast to the windy March chill outside. Fog condensed onto my glasses as I stepped in. It was disorienting, and so was the slight but unmistakable lowering in volume of the ambient conversational buzz: the regulars turning to survey a newcomer. This breakfast spot was not on the tourist circuit.

A freckled waitress in red jeans smiled and came toward me, a menu in each hand. "You want breakfast or lunch?" she inquired.

"I'm supposed to meet someone," I said. "Mariah."

"Oh." She turned and looked at an older woman who was sorting checks behind the cash register. "Martha? You seen Mariah today?"

Martha shook her well-permed head without looking at me and took a deep drag off a cigarette that had been burning in an ashtray. "She works on Thursdays. She won't be coming in here."

I started to take a deep breath, then thought better of it. The fog that I had taken for steam had a large component of cigarette smoke too, I now saw. Smoking is not allowed in restaurants in Boulder, not even in bars, and like most Boulder types I have gotten used to smoke-free environments. But I gathered that the rules were different here in Hygiene, its name notwithstanding.

I smiled back at the waitress. "Suppose I just have coffee and a cinnamon roll. I hear you make really good ones."

"Betcha life," she agreed. I followed her through the first room of the café into a larger room at the back, empty except for one couple smoking and eating eggs and bacon at the same time. "Joe and sugar," she called out as we passed the service window. "Black?" she asked me as she gestured toward a worn Formica table with two tubular-steel-and-vinyl chairs.

"I'm sorry?"

"What are you sorry for? Do you want your coffee black?"

"Oh. No, cream, please. If you have it."

She smiled crookedly. "We have it."

"And if you see Mariah come in, will you tell her

I'm back here?"

"You heard Martha, didn't you? She won't be here."

"Well, just in case."

She shrugged indifferently. "I spose."

I couldn't believe I had neglected to bring anything to read; I never travel without a book or at least a magazine. *Abibliophobia*, Sam calls it. Fear of running out of reading material. He went to one of those schools that make you study Latin.

There weren't many other customers in this back room. The bacon and egg couple seemed absorbed in their breakfast and their smokes; they paid me no attention. I looked at the photographs of prize bovines and rodeo scenes on the walls for a few minutes, then gazed out the west-facing window. There was no opportunity for eavesdropping, because the room was too noisy. In the corner of the room an ice machine made loud *ka-whump* sounds, like it needed a visit to the small-engine repair shop I'd seen on the corner.

I could have used a tune-up myself. For days I had been suffering from Impostor Syndrome, certain that the confidence that had carried me through fifteen years of practicing law was in retrospect a delusion, that I did not have the slightest idea what I was doing, and never had. I believe it may have started with the dream, which would mean it really started when I agreed to be on the radio.

* * *

It was one of those anxiety dreams: I was back in law school, carrying a crushing load of casebooks in a backpack as I banged about through the dim corridors, trying to locate the room where my exam was to be held. I couldn't find it, even though I knew it would be the same room where the class had been meeting all semester. That knowledge didn't help because (here I could feel my armpits dripping and the blood buzzing through my arteries like a swarm of furious flies) I hadn't been to class all semester. Not once. I flew around a corner, but there was nothing there but the door to the law library, full of all the unobtainable answers to the examination I was certainly about to flunk. I couldn't even remember the *subject* of the exam, I realized with sickening clarity. It could be anything: torts, criminal law, civil procedure, contracts. Commercial paper. Regulated industries, first amendment, administrative law . . . .

I don't know why my dream self didn't just give up, didn't simply drag the hopeless pack of books back out to the parking lot, and drive the rattletrap Opel I had in those days away from the school and the law forever. But she didn't, and I pounded those corridors in a fever of anxiety and shame all night long. Then somehow, my waking mind must have suspended the memory of the dream. I didn't think about it all day.

It wasn't until the evening, when I was on the radio and the whispery voice asked its question (*What if it happens to a child?*), that the memory of the dream blew into my head like a chinook wind ahead of a cold front, and I knew I was about to be unmasked as the impostor I was.

But I was on the air and I had no time for dream analysis. And since simply saying "I don't know" is not good form when you are on the air, even if it's God's truth and in fact the only accurate answer, I used the skills I had. For despite the dream I had in fact passed all of my law school exams, graduated successfully, and even passed the bar exam, all many years ago. So I did know something useful. I knew how to make it *sound* as though I knew the answer, or that I *would* if it weren't such an ignorant and ill-formed question. And that's what I did. For which sin, utterly common in my profession, I am punished on various unpredictable nights by a recurrence of the dream.

Okay, sometimes I get ahead of myself; I never seem to know where to start. Let's go back to the radio show. The thing was, it never occurred to me that a radio appearance could be very difficult. Radio and I were old friends; I was into radio long before I knew anything about law. Twenty years ago, when I was in college in Poughkeepsie, New York, I used to deejay a folk music show: *The Flower Power Hour.* Folk music was old-hat by then; everyone else was into disco, *Saturday Night Fever* and all that, but I'd always had an unaccountable infatuation with the 1960s. I'd line up those big old vinyl platters on the turntable and fill in the spots between Leonard Cohen and Mimi Farina with innocent jokey patter left over from the sixties: Woodstock, and the Chicago Seven, and Senator Roman Hruska saying that even mediocre people deserved representation on the Supreme Court. At the time I imagined that being mediocre was about the worst fate a person could suffer.

I loved being on the radio because I had been told I had a sexy voice. Although our little collegiate broadcast station didn't have enough power to reach far beyond the campus, like an idiot I imagined lonely bachelors all over Poughkeepsie, and scattered through Cold Spring and Red Hook and Wappingers Falls, listening and imagining the slender, witty, lovely, but somehow melancholy girl talking away into the microphone on a Friday evening. At the time I weighed about two-ten, and probably hadn't had a date for eleven months. I believed that being fat was nearly as disgraceful as being mediocre, if perhaps not quite. My radio show comforted me immensely.

I don't know why I was always so hungry then, but the hunger left me without warning or explanation during my junior year. I lost eighty pounds and graduated from Vassar in a white size eight minidress; in the photographs my mother took, the dress barely covers my crotch. Almost everyone else in my class was wearing floppy polyester and pointed collars, including my roommate Susie (the Lock) Wheelock who graduated *magna cum laude* in philosophy, but I remained true to my chosen style. My final radio show was broadcast the night before graduation; the last song I played was *Fire and Rain*. "Goodnight, and peace," I whispered as Sweet Baby James hummed out the last measures. "This is Cinda Hayes, signing off. Hope your life just grooves along."

* * *

There was no student radio station at the University of Colorado, where I went to law school. Over time all the skinny hippies had turned into jocks: rock climbers, runners, swimmers. So I started running myself and now, in my forties, I get twitchy and weepy if I can't run for three days in a row, and I eat almost everything I want to. Like most prosperous cities today, Boulder is bursting with astonishing food—tender croissants spread out in glass cases, pearlescent smoked salmon in the grocery deli, cappuccinos and lattes with foam bubbles tiny as nanoseconds. I am almost prosperous enough to buy whatever treat catches my eye without hesitating over its cost. Unlike cars and boats and Manolo Blahnik shoes, food is so cheap in this country that even the best of it is affordable to a middle-class lawyer with a mortgage but no kids— if she doesn't like fish eggs, anyway, and I don't.

Business had been a little sparse lately, however, and the nest egg with which my law partner Tory Meadows and I had bankrolled our new law practice was beginning to dwindle a bit. Tory was getting snappish about the cost of copier paper and bicycle messenger services; the week before my radio appearance she had insisted on delivering a motion to the courthouse in Ft. Collins herself, on her motorcycle, despite the circumstance that her time is worth $150 an hour, and the messenger service would have charged us $15 for the delivery. But I think it was the footnote instead of the motorcycle trip that made me realize how slow things had gotten.

"What do you think of this motion?" she had asked me that afternoon, flapping a page in each hand to dry them as they emerged from our office inkjet printer.

"What is it?" I asked inattentively. I was looking over our billing records.

She shrugged. "Routine. Motion for return of items seized as evidence. In that violation of custody case I did in Ft. Collins."

I took the two-page document from her and looked it over. Probably she saw me trying unsuccessfully to suppress a smile.

"What?" she said.

"Nothing," I said back. "It looks great. Excellent."

"Give it up, Minnie. What's the smirk about?" Tory called me Minnie Mouse when she was annoyed at me, or wanted to annoy me. Together these circumstances accounted for about sixty percent of the time.

"What smirk?"

"It's the footnote, isn't it?"

"It's an excellent footnote," I said, squinting at it again. It described a skirmish between two Supreme Court justices concerning the proper view of how *another* footnote, in an earlier Supreme Court opinion, should be read.

"So?" she said.

I handed it back to her. "It's very impressive. But, without wishing to disparage the experience of being a judge of the Nineteenth Judicial District Court of Colorado, I doubt that any member of that worthy bench has ever seen a footnote in a two-page motion before. Not," I added hastily, "that there shouldn't be a first time for everything."

She turned away from me scornfully. "You talk like some professor, but you're one of the most anti-intellectual persons I have *ever* met, Minnie Mouse." Ten minutes later I heard the subdued roar of her Kawasaki as she turned it out of the alley behind Pearl Street, heading north toward Ft. Collins to file her motion. She had left without saying goodbye; I guess she was really fond of that footnote.

It was ridiculous. Ft. Collins is forty miles away, and even March days that start out sunny and mild can turn out very iffy in Colorado; March is the snowiest month here. I knew Tory's burning need to carry the motion to the courthouse herself by motorcycle had more to do with her own demons than with any need for us to economize. Tory had been kidnapped and hurt—hurt badly, I thought—by a thuggish police officer in 1989, in part because she knew something that might have proved the innocence of my client Jason Smiley. Jason was dead now, executed three years later because his innocence hadn't mattered enough. I thought I had come to terms with my failure to save his life, and Tory seemed to have recovered from her ordeal. But she wouldn't talk to me, or to her lover Linda, about what had happened to her that weekend. Linda and I agreed that this wasn't good, but it had been a long time since either one of us had brought the matter up with Tory. Constant motion was one way she kept her memories at bay.

Both the retreating whine of the bike's engine, and the footnote, made it clear we just weren't busy enough. Boulder had too many damn lawyers for us to sit around drinking lattés, decorating routine motions with footnotes, and waiting for clients to walk in; I needed to drum up a little action. So when Marta Tafoya, president of the Boulder County Bar Association, asked me later that week if I would take a turn hosting the legal advice call-in show on the local NPR affiliate, I said yes. I won't say I didn't worry at all about not knowing the answer to the inevitable landlord-tenant and marital dissolution questions. I've been a criminal lawyer most of my life; I only started handling civil cases when Tory and I began our partnership last year. But I did a quick brush-up from Continuing Legal Education outlines and thought I was ready. Other people did this kind of thing all the time, I told myself. I was smart; I had graduated in the top five in my law school class. Why shouldn't I be able to answer a few legal questions on the radio?

That was my conscious mind talking, there. Not the other part, the one that houses the ones that Stephen King calls the boys in the basement. Probably those boys were at work on the dream already.

It wasn't that I would be paid for appearing on the advice show; it's a volunteer service sponsored by the county bar association. But I had heard that sometimes people would listen to a lawyer on the radio show and decide that she sounded smart and easy to talk to, and later call the office and ask for an appointment. Marta had assured me I would be allowed, even expected, to strew mention of my name and our law firm, together with our specialties and location, liberally through the broadcast. And I had thought that being on radio again would be, as I would have said in my earlier radio days, a trip.

I arrived at the station about six in the evening, half an hour before the broadcast would begin. Dark had fallen, but the March evening air did not have too much bite as I walked across the parking lot to the drab warren of offices that housed KGNU. Fergus O'Shaughnessy, the station's programming manager, met me at the reception desk in a pair of spectacularly ragged overalls. He showed me to the glassed-in room we would use for the broadcast and introduced his assistants Shawna and Siobhan, a pair of University of Colorado students doing their internships. The place was like a Gaelic Woodstock; it made me quite nostalgic. Siobhan had a headful of ferociously red hair so spiky I made a whimsical mental note not to get too close, for safety reasons. She would be handling the technical end of the broadcast and providing introductions and transitions. Shawna, her shoulders under a Phish t-shirt at once slim and sturdy like a dancer's, would get coffee and water and provide general assistance. This was way more help than I was accustomed to having with anything, so I luxuriated in it as they spaced the mikes, checked the sound level, and coordinated with the telephone operator who would be answering the incoming calls and transferring them in to me and Siobhan through our headphones. I fiddled with the headset and leafed through the notes I had brought: a page of lawyer jokes in case things got slow, an index to the Colorado Revised Statutes, a list of legal resources to which I might refer a caller, the number of our nobly struggling local Legal Services office. I felt fine.

Six-thirty came, the red light went on, and I could hear a muted version of the perky music that always introduced the *Call A Lawyer Show*. After a few measures it faded away, and Siobhan began to speak. She had a great voice, I noticed, throaty but melodious; she was reading from the short written bio Fergus had asked me to bring.

"Our host tonight, in cooperation with the Boulder County Bar Association, is Cinda Hayes. Cinda is a graduate of the University of Colorado Law School, former Assistant District Attorney here in Boulder, and after that Director of the Boulder County Rape Crisis Team. She now practices law with the firm Hayes and Meadows, right here in Boulder, located on Pearl Street above Pour La France. Hayes and Meadows specializes in employment discrimination and personal injury litigation, especially intimate torts." Here Siobhan gave me a puzzled sideways look. The phrase was from my bio, and

I suddenly regretted it. It had looked good on the page, but sounded weird when she said it. "We're lucky to have her with us tonight, and we encourage you to call in with your legal questions," Siobhan continued. "Ah, there's a caller already. Hello, this is KGNU *Call a Lawyer*."

The first caller had put up her house to bond her brother out of jail on a drug charge. He'd disappeared and she was about to lose the house. She had no idea where he was, and he owed her five hundred dollars she had given him for the lawyer besides. He'd always been like that: rotten. And another thing, his dirtbag lawyer refused to tell her anything, even though he had to know where his client was. Can they do that? she asked.

Can they do that? How many times had I been asked that question in one form or another? It sounded like the name of a country-folk song, of the sort that Robert Earl Keen could have written in a funny version, or Michelle Shocked in one of her seriously bitter moods. I tried to be honest with the caller (*unless you have the money to pay off the bond amount, there's nothing you can do to keep them from taking your house*), while halfheartedly defending the tattered honor of my profession (*your brother's lawyer is not allowed to disclose any confidences that he may have learned*), and offering a small amount of useful information (*you are allowed to bid on your own house at the sheriff's sale, and if you are the high bidder, you can buy it back*).

I sighed as she hung up, realizing that what I had really wanted to tell her was *Gosh, you need a lawyer*. I often had the same impulse with my own clients, and sometimes wondered what they would say if I yielded to it.

But . . . aren't you a lawyer?

Siobhan was motioning to me: hel-*lo*. Another caller.

"This is Cinda Hayes. Did you have a legal question?" I leaned into the mike.

Barely suppressed chuckles in the headphone. "I was, like, wondering. For a legal reason. Like, what is an intimate tort? Exactly?" Big snort. It sounded like a teenage boy, probably with a confederate on the extension. Shit. I'd never been a junior high school teacher. I didn't know how to handle this stuff. The Socratic method—answering a question with another—occurred to me because I had seen so many of my law professors use it to stall for time when they didn't know how to handle a student's comment.

"Why?" I asked. "Do you think you may have been the victim of one?"

More snorting, followed by some puffing. "Puhhh! I don't *think* so."

Of course, the Socratic method didn't always work. I repaired to the more traditional lecture method. "A tort is a civil wrong—it may be a crime, but not necessarily," I explained. "The law uses some quaint terms, like we call a person who commits a tort a *tortfeasor*. An intimate tort is simply a tort committed by a tortfeasor who is in a close relationship with the victim. Does that answer your question, sir?"

"Pfhhh!" he snickered again. "Tartfreezer?"

"*Fee*sor. Tort*feasor*. One who commits a tort." I was getting tired of this conversation. "Sir? Does that answer your legal question?"

"OK," he said faintly, and hung up. I looked at Siobhan for guidance; she moved in smoothly, her well-modulated voice exuding competence..

"Do intimate torts pose any special legal issues, Ms. Hayes?" she asked, sounding profoundly interested.

"Well," I said with relief, "for many years, there were very few lawsuits based on these kinds of wrongs. Courts would say they were barred by family immunity, or victims just wouldn't want to sue the person who harmed them because they were too embarrassed. But family immunity has been abolished mostly, and victims have realized that civil suits can be a way to fight back. There's no reason why a victim of an acquaintance rape, or a woman who is beaten by her husband, can't sue for damages. My partner and I have handled several of those kinds of cases. They pose some special challenges, but we've been pretty successful with them."

I looked back at her, and she shook her head minutely. Still no caller. She pointed to my page of lawyer jokes.

"Now," I said in my best seductive radio voice, "for all of you who love to hate lawyers, a little joke. Do you know what lawyers use for contraception? No? They use . . . their *personalities*. Another one? What do you get when you cross a lawyer with The Godfather?"

Siobhan cut in. "Let's let them think about that one. Here's another caller, Ms. Hayes. Hello? This is *Call-A-Lawyer* with Cinda Hayes."

I could barely hear her at first, so soft was her voice, and like too many women she made every sentence into a question. "Those intimate torts you talked about? How long do you have to file them? You know what I mean? There's a name for it? But I can't remember . . . ."

"Statute of limitations," I broke in. "That's what we call the deadline for filing a lawsuit. It isn't always the same, even for intimate torts. Depends on the nature of the claim, and possibly even on the intentions of the tortfeasor. One year to six years in Colorado, depending."

"Well, what if someone hurts you on purpose?" the small voice persisted. "How long then?"

"Ah, those are the shorter limitation periods. One or two years, depending."

"I see," she said. "Depending on—like, on what?"

I realized I wasn't really sure. *Tell her you don't know, you big fake.* I coughed delicately. "Well, it's complicated, actually. Probably too much so for a radio show."

One of the advantages of a really fine legal education is that you develop an unerring sense of when someone is about to ask you a question that you can't answer. Because I could hear the youth in her childish diction, I knew what Ms. Whisper's next question would be in the dread instant before she said it.

"OK, then here's another thing? What if it happens to a child?"

That was when the memory of the dream broke over me like a wave, the hopeless chase around the echoing corridors looking for a test I was certain to fail. Worse, the dream had now acquired a soundtrack, an acerbic voice-over: *That's a good question, phonus balonus. And you don't know the answer, do you?*

The thing was, I sort of knew the answer. Sort of. I knew that in some places the statute of limitations doesn't start to run until a child reaches majority. And I also knew that in some places that's *not* the rule. So I knew quite a bit actually, but I didn't know the really rather small detail about whether Colorado was one of the first kind of place, or the second. This, too, was a result of having had a first-rate legal education. Even though I had gone to law school at the University of Colorado, my professors made a point of not teaching "local" law. We used to joke about it as students, dizzy from the relentless theorizing of our seminars: The really good law schools, we assured each other, will teach you in a way that is not limited to the law of a particular jurisdiction. And the *truly* elite schools, like this one, will teach you in a way that is not tied to the law of a particular planet.

If I'd had a few minutes I could have looked it up, but I didn't, and the unwelcome memory of the nightmare was expanding inside my head, crowding out everything else. It was fed by my terror of not knowing, but there was also the quaver of desperation in the caller's voice. I knew she wasn't calling out of curiosity. The headset started to feel hot and sticky on my ears, and I realized my hands were unsteady.

"Well, you know that's also a rather complex question." I gestured ferociously to Siobhan. "I wonder if our caller could leave her telephone number with the operator, and I could telephone her in a day or two so we could discuss these particular questions further without taking up more air time."

"Yes, why don't you do that," said Siobhan quickly into her mike. "I'll transfer you back to the operator. Thanks for calling. And now a news break from National Public Radio news. We'll be back at fifteen minutes after the hour for more of *Call-A-Lawyer* with Cinda Hayes of Boulder."

More peppy music. "Whew," I said, pulling off my headphones and wondering whether Siobhan saw right through me. "This is not easy."

"You're doing great," said Siobhan. "Just talk a little more slowly, if you can. Otherwise, you're fine. Water?" She gestured to an ancient-looking metal carafe.

"Sure," I said doubtfully, hoping the water was newer than the container. She started to pour a stream of it into a paper cup. "Shall I go back to the lawyer jokes when we come back?"

"Yeah, finish the one about when a lawyer is lying. Then if we don't have any callers, I'll ask you some questions myself. I prepared a few." She smiled brilliantly and handed me the paper cup. I peered at the water inside; it looked all right.

"Do you think that last caller will leave her number?" I asked.

"DK," replied Siobhan, running her hands over her alarming hair, seemingly unaware of the danger of a puncture wound.

"DK?" I repeated.

"Sorry," she said with a smile. "Don't know. I don't know if she'll leave her number. That sounded like kind of a complex question she was asking."

"Um, yeah. Really not of general interest, I

thought. Better to call her later."

"Sure," she smiled guilelessly. "Back on the air in five seconds."

I put the headphones back on and took a last sip from the cup.

Siobhan got me through the rest of the half-hour. I finished the lawyer joke (*an offer you can't understand*), a new caller had a zoning problem, a man asked about child custody evaluations. Someone wanted to discuss the Rodney King cases. Finally, it was over.

Fergus shook my hand and invited me to come back soon. I stumbled across the parking lot to my Subaru, still preoccupied with the desperate dream and the feelings it had uncaged, then remembered I had left behind my briefcase and turned back. Shawna met me with it at the door. "You did great," she said as she handed over the battered leather pouch, gesturing toward a folded slip of paper tucked into the outside pocket. "I put that one caller's phone number in there. She gave the operator a little more information, too, and said she'd really appreciate a call back."

"Thanks," I said. "Thanks for everything, Shawna."

"No prob," she said kindly.

Back in my car I unfolded the slip of paper. *Wants to know*, the operator had written, *what if stat. of lim. is about to run but she can't exactly remember what tort feesor (?) did to hurt her. Because she was very young. But is sure something happened. Please call. 405-7522. Mariah.*

Marianne Wesson, known to her friends as Mimi, has taught at the University of Colorado Law School since 1976. Her first novel, "Render Up the Body," was a finalist for the Colorado Book Award. Her novels have been translated into seven languages and sold in more than a dozen countries.

Bootleggers

by Kenneth L. Levinson

The explosion ripped through the dance club at 10:15 p.m. that cold February night. Joe Stone of the Denver Police was saying something—I never heard what—when the roar of the blast halted him in mid-sentence. Instantly, a pillar of thick black smoke erupted from the basement staircase, laden with the pungent odor of cordite.

Before anyone else could react, Stone jumped to his feet and began waving his leather badge case in the air. Over the din made by the dozens of terrified patrons, he shouted, "I'm a police officer. Everyone stay calm!"

The other undercover cops joined him, doing their best to calm the panicky crowd. If I hadn't been so furious at Stone, I might have admired his presence of mind. But I was too angry for that. Thanks to his pigheadedness, my weeks of planning had, quite literally, gone up in smoke.

My legal assistant and I had been spending our Saturday nights at Bootleggers, one of the new "theme" singles bars in LoDo, at 18th and Blake. We were making slow progress, but we were finally getting close to what we needed.

Until Stone interfered.

Just before 9 p.m., Maurice and I had snagged our

customary booth in the rear of the dining room, passing ourselves off as two older-than-usual customers with nothing better to do on a Saturday night than go out partying. We were finishing our first round of drinks when I felt a rough hand on my shoulder. It was Stone, in faded blue jeans and a Denver Nuggets sweatshirt.

His prominent jaw jutted out aggressively. He spat in a low, loathing voice, "Adam Larsen! What are you doing here?"

It took me a few seconds to recognize him. I had never seen Stone out of uniform. He was the Achilles heel of the Denver Police, the worst of the "shoot first and ask questions later" cops—all brawn and not enough brains.

"This is a public place," I said, "and I'm over 21, Officer. I—."

"Shut up!" he hissed. "I'm under cover."

I gestured for him to join us. He hesitated, flitting his eyes cautiously around the room. Then he jerked his head toward my legal assistant. "Move your hulk over, White."

Maurice, who had played middle linebacker for the Broncos for four years, glowered at Stone, but slid his 235 pounds aside. As Stone eased into the booth, his eyes bore in on me. "What are you two doing here?"

"We're here on business."

"So am I. And your business had better have nothing to do with *my* business!"

I shrugged. "One of my clients had a 20-year-old daughter. She became romantically involved with a drug dealer, although she didn't know what he was. When she found out, she tried to end the relationship. That proved fatal. She was found dead in an alley in Capitol Hill, of a massive overdose of crack cocaine. You probably know the gory details. Apparently, he does things with a flair."

"The Collardine girl," Stone said grimly.

"And I have been hired to deal with her killer."

Stone's eyes narrowed. "Deal with him how?"

"I'm going to collect money damages on behalf of my client."

His lips curled into a smirk. "You're going to sue a drug dealer for damages?"

I met his steely black eyes. "I didn't say anything about suing anyone, Stone."

"The two of you are going to gather up your things and get the hell out of here," he informed us. When neither of us moved, he barked, "Now!"

Calmly, I sipped scotch and water. "Wouldn't you like to know what we've learned so far?"

He eyed me, as though I was trying to lure him into a poker game with a stacked deck. His gaze shifted to Maurice and then back to me.

"What have you got?" he asked warily.

I surveyed the room, to make sure that no unfriendly ears were eavesdropping. The motif at Bootleggers was that of a 1920s speakeasy. Above our table were two "Wanted" posters, featuring Al Capone and Lucky Luciano.

"This establishment," I explained, "is owned by three men who, at least to the general public, appear to have nothing in common. For your information, they're all here tonight."

His eyes widened. "They are?"

I nodded. "I assume you know their names. If you were to turn left through the doorway along that far wall you'd find Ernest Meeker at the pool table, happily hustling the customers. They sometimes refer to him as 'Second-Story Meeker.' He served six years in Cañon City for burglary."

"Go on," Stone urged. "I'm listening."

"In the far corner of this room, sitting with his back to us, is Jackie Grant, a former middleweight WBC champion. He's known as 'Piledriver Grant.'"

Stone grunted. "What about the third one?"

"Upstairs, in the business office, is Parker Christianson. He was a shady lawyer in California until they disbarred him. Now he pretends to be a bailbondsman." With my eyes, I indicated a thin-waisted blonde in skintight slacks and a low-cut blouse that she abundantly filled. "That waitress is named Margot Franklin. She's been divorced three times. The bartender's name is Jimmy Washburn. He's—"

"What about the dead girl?" Stone interrupted.

"She was evidently killed by Second-Story Meeker, Piledriver Grant or Parker Christianson. The burglar, the boxer or the bailbondsman. Three B's."

He fixed his eyes on me. "So which one is it?"

I shrugged. "I have no idea."

Stone flashed with anger. "You mean after all this buildup, you—"

The blonde waitress placed a congenial hand on Maurice's left shoulder. Women were always doing that to him. "Another round, Sugar?"

He nodded and asked Stone, "What are you drinking?"

"Beer. Coors."

"You got it," Margot said. She leaned over to take our empty drink glasses—giving Maurice an almost unavoidable glimpse of cleavage.

A clean-cut busboy with wire-rimmed glasses appeared out of nowhere. He offered, "I'll get those, Margot."

"Thanks." Gesturing toward the bar, she told him, "Jimmy's been looking for you. He says he's just served up the last of the bar scotch. He needs you to bring up a couple of bottles. It's—"

"I know," he cut in. "Highland Mist."

She glided away, her hips swaying sensuously. The busboy began wiping our table with a damp rag. Abruptly, he blurted, "The deal's going down tonight, Sergeant. He's got over a hundred grand in his storage locker. The perp is the b—"

"Not now!" Stone snapped, gesturing meaningfully at Maurice and me.

The color drained from the busboy's face. "You mean they're not—"

"Hell, no, they're not cops! Meet me in the john in 15 minutes."

"But I thought—"

"I know what you thought. You could have blown the whole setup! Fifteen minutes."

The busboy walked shakily away, descending the stairs to the basement.

Stone turned to me. "What's down there?"

"The restrooms and two storage rooms. One for liquor and one's refrigerated, for storing food. There's also an employees' lounge."

"What's in the lounge?"

"Nothing much. A table, some chairs and a few metal lockers."

"Lockers?"

"Yeah. Like they have in high schools."

"Do the owners—"

"No. Theirs are upstairs, in the business office."

Maurice snapped his fingers. "That must be where the hundred grand is!"

"Probably not," I replied. "There's a safe up there. I'd—"

Stone asked, "A safe? Where?"

The anger I had been trying to restrain finally boiled over. I jerked my head toward the stairs, where the busboy had disappeared. "That was stupid, Stone. Vintage you!"

"What was?"

"The busboy. Why didn't you let him tell you—"

"With *you* sitting here? No way!"

"Stone, you're an idiot! What if something happens to him before—"

He snorted derisively. "You've been reading too many detective stories, Larsen. I'll meet him in the john and—"

Whatever Stone said after that was drowned out by the roar of the blast. Once it became clear that a bomb had gone off, Stone jumped to his feet.

"I'm a police officer!" he shouted. "Everyone stay calm!"

In the confusion that followed, I glanced at my wrist watch.

It was 10:15 p.m.

* * *

A few minutes past midnight, a uniformed patrolman led me up to the business office on the second floor of Bootleggers. Stone was seated behind the cheap metal desk.

He aimed a finger at me. "What were you doing here tonight?"

I lowered myself onto a rickety chair. "I told you. To collect—"

"I don't believe you, Larsen."

I shrugged. "Is the busboy dead?"

"Yeah, he's dead. Now, what were you—"

"What triggered the bomb?"

"Some sort of transmitter. Remote controlled."

"I wondered why your men insisted on searching me." I glanced pointedly at my wrist watch. "It's—"

"Forget it," he interrupted. "Nobody leaves until we find that transmitter."

"Dozens of people managed to get out of this place before—"

"Nobody leaves, Larsen! Even if we have to stay here all night!"

For the first time in all the years I had known and hated him, Stone looked worried.

"All right," I said in a deflated tone, "Calm down. What about the three owners of this place? Have you searched them?"

"Of course! The detectives have questioned all of them, together and separately. Nothing." Stone studied me for a while. "I'll tell you what I'll do, Larsen. In a couple of minutes, they're going to be brought up here. You stay and listen to what they have to say."

I lifted my brows. "You mean you want me to help you?"

"Of course not. I want to keep my eye on you. When they get here, you say nothing. You *do* nothing. You just sit here and watch. Understood?"

I glared at him. "You figure that if they get the idea that I'm associated with the police, my chances of accomplishing anything here in the future will be nonexistent."

He met my stare. "I'm glad we understand each other."

"Oh, we do," I said coldly. "It means that if I intend to accomplish anything for my client, I'll have to do it tonight."

Before he could respond, the door opened and another uniformed officer marched into the office. I recognized him as Dan McKeever, a likeable cop with a narrow, angular face.

"We've searched the last of the patrons, Sergeant. No transmitter. They're clamoring to go home."

"Let them clamor."

I asked McKeever, "How big is this device you're looking for?"

"The techs say it probably looks like a garage door opener."

Pointing to the row of metal lockers along the wall, he told Stone, "I've been through them with a fine tooth comb. It's not there. Neither is the money."

Stone sighed. "Bring those three up here."

McKeever left us. Soon, heavy footsteps came tramping up the stairs. The three suspects entered first, followed by McKeever. I slipped quietly to the back of the room, trying to look as unpoliceman-like as I could.

Parker Christianson, the disbarred lawyer, was the first to speak. Gesturing with smooth, manicured hands, he intoned, "Sergeant, let me assure you of my fullest cooperation and assistance in—"

Stone wasn't impressed. "Which one of you planted that bomb?"

The ex-lawyer bristled in his cheap suit, like an irate peacock. "I am shocked by the implications of that question."

"Tough. What were you doing when the bomb went off?"

"I've already told the officers everything—"

Stone slapped the desk with an open palm. "You can answer my questions here or downtown at the Justice Center."

Christianson said slowly and defiantly, "I was here, in this room, poring over some paperwork."

"Paperwork for Bootleggers?"

"No. I'm a licensed bailbondsman, and I have a forfeiture hearing first thing Monday morning. I was preparing for that."

Stone muttered skeptically, "Right. On a Saturday night."

Christianson shrugged. "It's the truth. When I heard the explosion, I ran downstairs."

Stone scrutinized Second-Story Meeker, a bony specimen with jet black skin and a thick Afro haircut. "What about you?"

"I was playing pool in the Prohibition Room," Meeker said. "First thing I noticed was when I heard the boom."

"Did you know the busboy who was killed?"

"Rudy? Sure. Everybody knew Rudy." Beads of

sweat were accumulating on Meeker's black forehead. His hands were trembling.

Stone asked, "What did you know about him?"

"Nothing much. Nobody had it in for him, or anything like that. At least, nobody I know of."

"Yeah? Well, somebody did." Stone turned to Piledriver Grant, the ex-fighter, whose most prominent feature was a flat, wide nose which bore the marks of having been broken half a dozen times. "What were you doing when the bomb went off?"

Grant spoke in a slow, slurred voice. His head bobbed up and down on a thick neck that was almost as wide as his stocky shoulders. "I was listening to my ex-wife carp about me being behind on her alimony. Like I got nothing better to worry about!"

"What did you do when the bomb went off?"

"I made for the door, like everyone else. I ain't no hero. But before I could get out, I heard someone holler that the fire was out and to relax. So I relaxed. After a while, a couple of cops said they wanted to search me. They didn't find nothing."

"I was searched, too," Parker Christianson protested. "And I am considering instituting legal action!"

Stone shrugged. "You won't be the first."

"Nor the last," Christianson agreed in a moderate tone, obviously disappointed that his threat had gone nowhere. "What were your men looking for?"

Stone answered the question with a question of his own, gesturing toward the metal safe in the corner of the office. "What's in there?"

"Probably the family jewels," Piledriver Grant wisecracked.

Stone glared at the pugilist. "If this was Chicago or Detroit, I'd—"

Grant shook his head back and forth, like an angry bull. "Yeah? Well, it ain't, and I've got you by 30 pounds." He eyed Stone. "At least."

"Open the safe," Stone growled.

The disbarred lawyer spoke up. "Do you have a search warrant?"

"Do you want to wait while I get one?" Stone asked. "A man was murdered here tonight. We have probable cause to—"

Grant told Second-Story Meeker, "Open it. We've got nothing to hide."

Meeker nodded, indicating he understood Grant's message that there was nothing incriminating inside. Meeker stooped down, using his body to shield his hands as he whirled the dial. It took his trembling fingers three tries to open the safe.

Stone kneeled in front of the safe and reached inside. All he found was a fat manilla file marked "IOUs."

There was no transmitter.

And no $100,000.

Meeker was reaching for the black desk phone. At first, I thought he was going to hit Stone with it, and I took an involuntary step forward. Instead, Meeker touch-toned a three digit number.

"Who is this?" he asked. "Margot? Oh, good. Bring me up a scotch and water. Make it a double."

Now I understood why Meeker was so shaky.

He needed a drink.

"Jack Daniels on the rocks for me," Parker Christianson called out festively.

Piledriver Grant added, "I'll have beer."

Stone jumped to his feet. He reached for the phone, but the ex-boxer lurched forward. "It ain't after hours and we ain't under age."

"I believe he's correct, officer," Christianson opined. He added snidely, "Would you care for anything?"

Stone glowered at him. "No."

Meeker suddenly noticed me, leaning nondescriptly against the back wall. "How about you? Are you a cop?"

I shook my head emphatically. "I'm a customer. Someone set off a bomb while I was trying to score with one of the waitresses. I plan to complain to the management."

He gave me a hearty laugh. "Put it in the suggestion box."

With a friendly nod, I said, "I'll do that. What kind of scotch are you drinking?"

He regarded me for a moment. "What kind are you paying for?"

I shrugged. "Whatever you serve the masses."

Piledriver Grant came over and cuffed me roughly on the shoulder. "Meeker, I like this guy. Give him a drink. Scotch, you say?"

"And water."

Meeker spoke into the telephone. "Another scotch and water."

Stone asked no one in particular, "Who hired the busboy?"

Parker Christianson spoke up. "I did."

"When did you hire him?"

The bailbondsman scratched his ear pensively. "I cannot recall."

"Give me your best guess."

"A couple of months ago, I suppose. If you'll let me get into the desk, I might locate his job application."

Stone stepped aside and watched while Christianson thumbed through rows of file folders. A knock sounded on the door and Margo glided into the room. Without needing to ask, she delivered the glasses to their proper recipients.

Meeker gulped down his drink. "Bring me another one, honey."

When she handed me the tumbler, Margot stared quizzically at me, obviously wondering what I was doing upstairs. I smiled disarmingly and handed her a five-dollar bill.

"Thanks, Sugar!"

Something suddenly occurred to me, and I decided I needed to get downstairs to check it out. It was a long shot, but it just might pan out. I noted with relief that Christianson was still searching through the desk, and Stone was standing with his back to me. Silently, I edged my way toward the exit. The knob made no sound as I rotated it clockwise. I was already half way out of the room when Stone happened to glance up.

"Larsen, where the hell are you—"

I pulled the door closed behind me.

* * *

Half an hour later, Stone zigzagged his way through the maze of overturned tables and chairs. The three owners of Bootleggers were close behind, being herded by McKeever and another uniformed officer. Maurice and I sat perched on adjoining stools at the bar, each of us nursing a mixed drink. At the end of the bar, Margot's blonde head rested sleepily on the polished wood surface. The bartender, who had a bodybuilder's physique and shoulder-length Fabio hair, was entertaining himself by stacking shot glasses into little pyramids.

Stone looked haggard and weary. "Why did you leave—"

"I needed to use the men's room," I lied. "I still do. But your merry men refuse to let me go downstairs."

"Me, too," Maurice chimed in, squirming uncomfortably on the bar stool.

"Tough!" Stone snarled. "The basement is off limits."

I swivelled slowly and deliberately. "Let him use the men's room, Stone. Don't make a second foolish mistake tonight."

Catching the edge in my voice, Stone regarded me for a full 15 seconds. Then he jerked his head toward the staircase. "Go on, White. Larsen, you stay here."

Maurice and I avoided exchanging glances. If Stone got even an inkling that we were up to something, he'd stop us dead in our tracks. Maurice carelessly grabbed his ski parka and headed toward the stairs that led down to the basement.

I asked Stone, "I take it, you haven't found the missing *object*?"

"You know damn well that I haven't!"

I glanced meaningfully at my wristwatch. "You're running out of time, Stone." Trying to make it sound casual, I commented, "Incidentally, Maurice and I have a brief due on Monday in Federal court. We'd like to use tomorrow morning to—"

"Tough! You stay put."

Again, I gazed at my wrist watch, this time for a full ten seconds. "Tick tock, tick tock . . ."

Stone looked agonized. "It has to be here! One of those three scumbags killed that busboy."

I heaved an elaborate sigh. "All right. I suppose I'm going to have to solve another case for you." I added, "If, that is, you'll agree to let us go home."

He worked his jaw three times before asking, "You know which one of those three did it?"

I smiled. "Have you thought about where the transmitter was when the bomb went off?"

"Of course, I have! It could have been anywhere."

"Not anywhere," I asserted. "The murderer would want to be at a nice, safe distance. Otherwise, he might blow himself up—or get trampled in the ensuing chaos. He also had to know when to set it off."

Stone eyed me suspiciously. "Keep talking."

I pointed toward the glass in front of me. "I'm having scotch and water. Would you care to join me?"

His face colored and he grabbed my shirt, pulling

me to my feet. "Why you—"

"Let go of me, Stone!"

He held on. We stood, glaring at each other. Through the corner of my eye, I spotted Maurice emerging from the basement. He was wearing his ski parka, with the zipper pulled all the way up. Stone saw him, too, and released me.

Maurice shivered. "Boy, it's cold down there!"

"Is everything okay?" I asked.

He nodded with satisfaction. "Just peachy."

I made a show of straightening my shirt. "I have a proposition for you, Stone. You want your murder solved. I want my law clerk to go home and get some sleep. Let him leave, and I'll solve your case for you."

"Yeah? Well, I have a deal of my own. You give me whatever information you're withholding, and I won't arrest you. Or get you disbarred!"

I shrugged. "Make all the threats you want. Those are my terms." Calmly and deliberately, I took a sip of scotch and water. "Tick tock, tick tock!"

"Stop that!" he flared.

"Whatever you say."

With a philosophical shrug, I returned to my place on the bar stool. During the long silence that followed, Stone's hands slowly began to fidget. Finally, he jerked his head toward the door. "All right, White. Get the hell out of here!"

Relief glittered in Maurice's eyes.

Fortunately, Stone didn't notice.

I watched Maurice lumber out of Bootleggers. Even taking into account the padding of his ski parka, his muscular torso was much bulkier than usual.

Stone demanded, "All right, who is it? The boxer, the burglar or the bailbondsman?" He gestured to McKeever, who led the trio over to the bar to join us. "Mr. Larsen here has something to say."

The three B's stared at me. None of them looked

very friendly.

I turned to Stone. "You still don't get it, do you? The killer had to know when to set off the bomb." I raised my glass. "Margot, my drink could use freshening."

Without bothering to lift her head off the bar, she called out, "Jimmy, give him another drink. Hell, give him the whole bottle!"

The bartender replenished my scotch and water.

I raised the glass. "This is my third one since the explosion, Stone. Highland Mist."

His eyes bore into me. "Okay, so you're a lush. Which one of them killed my informant?"

"Ask Margot. She can tell you who set off that bomb."

She lifted her head, taking a sudden interest in our conversation.

I remarked, "Tell me something, Stone. How did the murderer know when to push the button to set off the bomb? Mr. Meeker was in the next room, playing pool." I shifted my eyes to Meeker. "Right?"

He nodded firmly. "That's right."

"And Mr. Grant had his back to us."

"Yeah!" the former boxer agreed.

Parker Christianson saw all eyes focus on him. He whined, "I was upstairs in the office. I can prove it!"

I told Stone, "Unless you can shake their alibis, all three of your suspects are eliminated." Once again, I made a show of sipping my Highland Mist. "As Margot can attest, I normally drink Johnny Walker Black."

Stone wouldn't have gotten it even then, but a look of realization suddenly energized Margot's face—as though she had been jolted by a bolt of lightning.

"Hey, Jimmy, you told me to tell Rudy we were all out of bar scotch!"

I raised my drink to her, in a silent salute. "Excellent, Margot. You've solved the mystery. There's your answer, Stone: Not the boxer, not the bailbondsman, and not the burglar. In this case, 'B' is for Bartender. Right, Jimmy?"

The bartender cursed at me. Then he made a dash for the front door. I leaped off my bar stool, catching up with him three feet from the exit. It wasn't a proper shoulder tackle like Maurice would have made, but it held him until McKeever and the other officers could catch up with us.

* * *

Fuming, Stone paced in front of the bar, while McKeever searched me for the third time. Jimmy Washburn, now in handcuffs and under the careful scrutiny of two uniformed officers, watched sullenly. A rectangular device sat on the bar, having been found buried in the ice compartment where he hid it after the explosion.

I said, "Look, Stone, you've found the transmitter. You're going to find Washburn's fingerprints all over it. Why is McKeever searching me again?"

"You know damn well why, Larsen! The busboy said there was $100,000 in cash in a storage locker. What did you do with that money?"

"Search me," I said with an elaborate shrug. "Oh, you just did that, didn't you?"

McKeever had to bite his lip to avoid laughing.

Stone wasn't amused. "I want that money, Larsen, and I want it now! It belongs to—"

"To who?" I demanded. Turning, I addressed the bartender. "Jimmy, did you have any illegal drug money in your locker downstairs?"

Washburn glared at me and maintained a stony silence.

I told Stone, "The busboy is dead. You can't prove there was ever any money."

"Oh, yeah? I heard what he said! I can testify—"

"Sorry. Anything he told you is hearsay. Not admissible in a court of law. And Jimmy certainly isn't claiming that someone stole any drug money from him. Are you, Jimmy?"

His eyes smoldered with fury. "No."

Stone snapped his fingers. "White! That's why you were in such a hurry for him to leave. McKeever, get a search warrant. I want—"

I sighed wearily. "I know, I know. The ever-faithful Inspector Javert, endlessly tracking Jean Valjean. I told you I came here to collect damages for my client. As an added benefit, I solved your murder for you. Isn't that enough for one night?"

Stone sputtered, "That money belongs to—"

With an air of finality, I said, "Good night, Stone. Good night, McKeever."

As I strolled out of Bootleggers, I could hear Stone muttering, "One of these days, Larsen! One of these days . . . "

Kenneth L. Levinson is senior partner of Balaban & Levinson, P.C., emphasizing civil litigation, real estate and insurance. His first Adam Larsen novel, "A Shadow In The Night," is scheduled for release in September/October, 2001 by The Fiction Works (www.fictionworks.com).

Merry Christmas, Santa Claus

by Wick Downing

Long Beach was a lousy place to practice law in 1990. The problem was the judges, the defense lawyers thought. They had to send messages to the voters about how tough they were on crime. A guillotine on top of Signal Hill would have been perfect for their image. They could roll heads into the harbor.

But the lawyers were the real problem, the judges thought. We acted at law, rather than practiced it. We modeled our lives after lawyer novels, and "LA Law."

I was born in Long Beach in 1930, in the reflected glitter of Hollywood, and was caught up in the silliness too. My secretary-receptionist-investigator-paralegal was an exotic Oneida Indian from Wisconsin, for example. Her real name was Wisconsin Summer, but people called her "Whiskey" because she used to drink so much of the stuff. And my office was in the Seafarer Hotel, an old relic on the ocean side of Ocean Boulevard. Lawyers didn't have offices in hotels in real life, did they?

They did in Long Beach.

That morning, I swung into my act by checking the "business locator" stand to make sure my name was still on it. It was. "Jack S. Bard, Attorney, Suite 670." A few minutes after nine I walked into my office.

"Morning, Whiskey."

She quit drinking when the State of California sent her to prison for murder, where she learned enough law to get out. "Hi, boss." Whiskey was in her 40s, but her body stayed in its 20s. That morning, she'd wrapped it in red. "Remember Mr. Strand?"

I glanced at the thin, neatly dressed fellow sitting on the couch. "Hi, Lester," I said, dredging up his name. Late 30s, frightened eyes, a clown's smile pasted across his face. I didn't remember him as much as his old man. He'd been a mean bastard, and Lester looked like he'd been whipped a few times. "I'll see you in a couple of minutes, okay?"

The reception area was Whiskey's domain. The furniture glistened, and her desk was neat as a pin. My office was my domain, and it was a mess. I still don't know if that was part of my act or not, but it was the way I liked it. I kicked off my shoes, loosened my tie, took off my coat and hung it on the hook above the light switch, then padded out to the small conference room where we keep the coffee maker. I poured a cup for Whiskey and took it to her, a ceremony I wouldn't miss for an earthquake.

"Come on back, Lester." He tagged along behind me, then waited while I cleared some files off a chair. "Sit down. What can I do for you?"

He glanced around, then reached in his coat pocket. "I am so emb-b-barrassed, Mr. Bard," he said, handing me a three-page criminal complaint.

I could see why. He'd been charged with indecent exposure to a child under the age of 15, and a prior offense. By charging the prior, the misdemeanor became a felony. He could go to prison. "The trial's tomorrow."

I said, looking at the Notice to Set for Trial, "Why did you wait so long to come see me?"

"I . . . I don't know."

Guys like Lester never know, I thought. But there was nothing on my calendar that Whiskey couldn't reschedule.

"I'll need $10,000," I told him, hoping the fee was too much. "If we don't go to trial, like if you plead guilty to a lesser offense, you'll get half of it back."

He wrote me a check. I didn't think it would bounce.

Lester was all that was left of a once-prominent family. His grandfather had made a fortune in ship parts, and Lester had worked in the business. But his father, who'd been a great client because he was such a mean son of a bitch, sold it. Then the old man was killed in a car wreck that left his wife an invalid. Lester still lived at home as far as I knew, with his crippled mother.

He looked like a statue as he sat there. I asked him about the prior offense first, trying to loosen him up. It happened at a Christmas open house he said, given by his bank. His mother had died the week before, and when he told me that, I thought he would cry. He'd loved her deeply, he said, and her death had left him alone in a large house. She'd been a spiritual woman, he told me, who had thrilled to the true meaning of Christmas. The party engulfed Lester in cynicism. He got quite drunk.

A 12-foot Christmas tree, decorated with wax candles that burned with tiny flames, stood in the lobby. Boisterous people, most of whom were obese, pranced around with drinks in their hands. The conversations were about money, luxurious vacations and expensive gifts. Lester wanted to scream. Do we celebrate Christmas by gorging our bodies with food, then giving ourselves presents we don't need? His mother had always given what she could to charities. Lester knew he should not have come, but before leaving, he wanted to make a statement. He urinated on the candles, putting them out.

"You did what?"

In the process, he exposed his privates to persons under the age of 15.

Maybe there was more to Lester than met the eye.

His action was a statement, right? Freedom of speech? Like burning a flag? When he told me he'd sobered up in jail and pleaded guilty, I wondered if his plea could be withdrawn.

I asked him about the present offense, and he handed me a police report with statements of witnesses attached. According to them, Lester had run through the neighborhood one Sunday morning in nothing but an open bathrobe.

He flaunted his privates at a 13-year-old boy and a 12-year-old girl, and was photographed by a passing motorist with a camera. When questioned by Detective Wink Barret, the suspect said he wanted to teach the children a lesson. Wink saw several "girlie" magazines, and with the consent of the suspect, took a representative selection for evidence.

Evidence of what?

I asked Lester for his version. He'd been dozing on the living room sofa when a Frisbee hit the porch light and broke it, he said. He saw the children involved and recognized them because they often trampled through his flower beds. Something triggered in him and he gave chase. However, he tripped over the Frisbee and tumbled to the lawn. Having wrestled in college, he rolled to his feet and sped after them. But unknown to him, his robe had opened. "I wanted to teach them manners, Mr. Bard. Not . . ."

'The dirty magazines?" I asked.

"A detective knocked on my door. and I invited him in. The magazines were on the couch. He acted as though the situation was a mistake, and they might help him clear it up, so I gave them to him."

"What about the Frisbee? There's nothing in the report about that."

"I showed it to him, but it didn't interest him." He'd rather not muddy the water, if he has a clean case. "Did he advise you of your rights?"

"Yes. Off a card. A formality, he explained, a ritual he must go through before he could help me."

* * *

Stan Pillar had signed the complaint against Lester. Stan was to prosecutors what Dirty Harry was to cops. Most people loved him for his fervor, and he might be governor some day, but I hated him. I was one of the few in California who thought we needed the Bill of Rights.

"If it isn't old Jack S. Bard," Stan said when I walked in his office. He liked to make the "S" sound like "ass." In his early 40s, with carefully coiffed hair that he brushed under a blow-dryer, his muscles bulged under a silk shirt. I sat down. "Make yourself at home," he said.

"Lester Strand, Stan. How come he's yours? When did you get promoted to the petty felony desk?"

"You've got the weeny wagger?" he asked.

"An hour ago. I need a continuance."

"Sorry, Jack S. All my witness have been subpoena'd." That meant we'd go to trial. The judges didn't grant continuances unless the prosecutors told them it was okay.

"Then cut him some slack," I said. "Let him plead to something easy."

"For example? Impersonating a human?"

"How about disorderly conduct? Or the charge, if you dismiss the prior. Why pop him with a felony?"

"Can't, Jack S," he said. "Two in six months. Escalating, obviously. "He's dangerous."

"To whom? He shouldn't have copped to that first one. If he'd had a lawyer then, I wouldn't be here now."

"He'd have gone down. The mayor's wife saw him. He needs to register, too. The public has a right to know where guys like him are."

I got up. No use wasting my time.

"You're not leaving? Can't you stay for dinner?"

Back in my office, I hung the "Closed" sign on the door and laid the case out to Whiskey. She punched some buttons so the answering machine would take over in case someone called, which wasn't likely. Then she went out to see what she could find.

I took a nap.

* * *

"All rise," the bailiff said. "The Superior Court in and for the County of Los Angeles is in session."

Judge Mac Toner swept into the courtroom and sat down. "Be seated, please," he magnanimously allowed. Stan Pillar and Wink Barrett had the table near the jury box; Lester and I the table farthest away. The prospective jurors were in chairs behind the rail. A fourth-grade civics class was there, too. They sat in the rows in back.

"The clerk will call the roll of the prospective jurors."

I looked for people who understood what reasonable doubt meant.

Engineers didn't get it because in their world, a thing was, or it wasn't. School teachers did, for some reason. But the best jurors were archeologists, who approached a case from a unique perspective. They wondered about the factors that generated the law, not just the facts. They made up .006 percent of the population.

Long Beach jurors inclined toward the mentality of engineers. You could forget about reasonable doubt. None of them believed in the presumption of innocence, either. What we had in Long Beach was the presumption of guilt, because no one believed cops went around arresting innocent people.

The jury we selected was the typical posse of cattlemen after a rustler: five mothers, three retirees, two engineers, a janitor . . . but one archeologist. If Lester could get his eyes off the floor and quit looking guilty as hell, I thought we might hang it, which would at least give me time to get ready.

After lunch, with the witnesses in the hall waiting to testify, Pillar gave his opening statement. He sounded like Oliver Cromwell inciting zealots in England to puritanical excess. The Puritans on the jury ate it up. When told my client had exposed himself to children, the mothers glared at him. When the retirees learned one victim was a girl, they were aghast.

The janitor stared at Lester like he was a spot on the floor that wouldn't come out. And when Pillar brought up the photographs, the engineers nodded, as though to say, "Makes good sense."

But the archeologist folded his arms and waited.

"Mr. Bard, do you wish to give your open now, or later?"

Studies showed that most jurors made up their minds from the opening statements. But when I tried cases in the '50s, the defense always waited to tell the prosecutor what they had. Whiskey had given me some ammunition to shoot with, and I didn't want Stan to know what it was. "Later, your Honor."

"Call your first witness, Mr. Pillar."

Pillar set the stage through the eyes of the motorist with the photographs. The pictures were like snapshots by someone who saw a deer in his yard. By the time he found the camera, the animal was in the distance, running. But the blurs were recognizably people, and the photographs were enough for the witness to explain what he'd seen. My client chasing kids, his bathrobe flapping like a flag, his male organ waving in front for the world to see.

I took him on cross-examination. He remembered my client yelling at "those poor children," and yes, it could have been in anger. Also, at some point, he gave up the chase and appeared embarrassed. He wrapped the robe around him and hurried off.

The kids had two months to talk over the case, so I knew they'd be together in their tale. Beatrice Tum, 12, testified first. She had long legs, long blond hair, budding breasts and a watchful expression.

"We were just walking down the street, on the way to the beach, when that man came running out of his house!" She saw immediately that he didn't have on any underwear! Yes, she saw his penis, she testified, blushing prettily. "I didn't know what he would do if he caught me." Her tone suggested she feared the worst.

Whiskey had learned that Beatrice had an enormous interest in the opposite sex, and was as virginal as a crib girl. But on cross-examination, I couldn't take her down that path. The jury would convict Lester to teach me a lesson. But she denied stomping in his garden, and claimed no one broke his porch light with a Frisbee. No one even had a Frisbee, she said.

Thirteen-year-old Bly Givvens testified next. What a cute little elf.

With red hair, freckles, and eyes that alternated between angelic innocence and pure mischief, he looked like a Norman Rockwell poster boy. But Whiskey had found out that Bly had won the Long Beach Annhauser Tivoli Frisbee Shoot Out the summer before for his age class.

On direct examination, he said he was "kind of scared" when Lester came flying out the door. "It was like he wanted us to see his thing, you know?"

On cross, I showed him the Frisbee Lester had found on his porch. "This is yours, isn't it?" I asked.

"No sir."

On the bottom, in a logo like a splash of gang grafitti, was "Bly." I showed him the logo. "Are you sure?"

"Oh." He looked at it carefully. "I guess it is."

I had him testify about the Frisbee contests he'd been in. In the process, he told the jurors that he had 10 or 11 Frisbees and lost them sometimes. The one I showed him must be one he'd lost, because he didn't have one that day. He only took them to the beach when he could play catch with his dog, and his dog was at the vet's. So I asked him for his veterinarian's name and when he gave it, Whiskey wrote it down.

Pillar called Wink Barrett as his final witness. I knew Stan wanted to put the dirty magazines into evidence and asked permission to approach the side bar. "Clearly admissible to prove *mens rea* and motive," Stan said, righteously. "Absolutely clear. No question."

"Judge, they have some relevance to those things, but you can say that about anything. The color of the sky. It's blue, like the color of many of our laws. But my client isn't being tried for reading dirty magazines. That's what he'll be convicted of, though, if the jurors see the centerfolds!"

Good old Mac let them in.

On cross, I asked Wink how long he'd subscribed to *Penthouse* magazine?

Stan screamed like a stuck hog, and I thought Mac might throw the gavel at me. Pillar passed the magazines to the jury and rested his case.

While they gazed at the thighs and breasts and genitalia of women in erotic poses, I was supposed to give my opening statement. "Can you hear me folks?" I asked. "Or is this like telling a person who's been pushed out of an airplane to concentrate on a chess problem?"

A couple of smiles. I suggested one or two of them might know someone who subscribed to such magazines, and asked if the person was a sexual monster? Pillar thought about it, which I saw in his readiness to stand up, but he didn't object.

I told them our evidence would show a quiet man who was a target for neighborhood kids. They trampled his flower beds. But even though he was the designated creep, he'd been a wrestler in college 20 years ago.

On this particular Sunday morning, kids broke the porch light with a Frisbee. It was too much. He charged after them in his bathrobe, but tripped on the Frisbee and tumbled to his lawn. Leaping to his feet he forgot everything in his anger to catch them, including the fact he didn't have a stitch on under his bathrobe, or that it opened up.

"We don't deny what these kids saw. But it takes more than that to commit the crime. It takes intent on Mr. Strand's part to expose himself, and you'll find out he had no such intent."

Two of the mothers quit looking at Lester with such righteous disdain. I started thinking we had a chance. Defense lawyers often get deluded by their own oratory.

"Call your first witness, Mr. Bard."

Lester was all I had. He'd just heard me tell the jury what had happened, but could he repeat it?

No. He sat in the witness box and stared at something no one else could see. Then he trotted out a whole new set of mannerisms. Pausing after each question and stuttering with each answer, everything sounded like a lie. I didn't even believe him when he spelled his name for the record. I hurried him through the incident, hoping the jury would remember me instead of him.

"Lester, have you ever seen Beatrice Tum before?"

He thought about it. "Y-yes," he said, and blushed.

"What about Bly Givvens?"

"D-uh, are you referring to the young man who t-uh, testified earlier?"

"Yes, Lester." Who did he think I was talking about? Batman?

"Yes sir, Mr. Bard. I believe I have."

All he had to do was tell the jury how the two angelic hooligans had swept through his garden like a herd of locusts, but he couldn't get it out!

I saved what I thought was a high note to end it

on. "Can you identify this?" I showed him the Frisbee, marked as Defense Exhibit "A."

"What, that is, what is it?" he asked.

"You tell me."

"Oh. Yes. It's a Frisbee and I, uh, have seen it previously."

"When?"

"I believe, um, the day my porch light was broken."

Stan had a field day on cross. Lester agreed that when his porch light was busted, there was enough glass on the porch to cut his foot off at the ankle. Yet, his foot hadn't even been scratched. And certainly Lester knew the Frisbee was evidence. But he didn't give it to Officer Barrett, did he? Lester and I had talked about that, of course. He knew he should tell the jury that he'd tried, but the officer didn't want it. Instead, he said he didn't know!

"When those children romped in your flower beds Mr. Strand, did you ever complain to the police about them?"

Of course not. Lester wouldn't make trouble for anyone.

When Stan showed him the magazines, he instantly turned every color in the rainbow, a panty thief caught in the act.

Pillar then asked another question I'd warned Lester about, telling him not to answer until I could object. "You've never done anything like this before have you Mr. Strand?"

"Oh, no," Lester blurted. "Never."

"Objection!"

But the question had already been answered, and Mac wouldn't grant my motion to strike. Pillar had the right, on rebuttal, to show Lester had lied. He could prove up the other offense.

Court adjourned for the day. At home that night, I

crawled into a bottle of cognac. But at 11 p.m., the telephone rang. I'd been watching a nice, quiet movie to help me sleep. "Duel of the Chain Saw Killers."

"What is going on?" Whiskey demanded. "Is there an airplane in your living room?"

"No." I turned the volume down and was surprised at how loud my voice was. "What's up?"

During a recess in court that day, Whiskey heard a kid in the civics class talk to the teacher. He told her he'd seen Tums and Givvens in Lester's flower bed. The teacher didn't know what to do, but Whiskey did.

She gave the kid a subpoena.

She'd also talked to Givvens's veterinarian. Bly's dog had not been in his hospital the day of the incident. Whiskey gave him a subpoena, too.

And in a photograph taken by the motorist, Whiskey saw what might have been a dog. She showed it to the guy, and what do you know—it was a dog.

The motorist remembered the pup, too. It belonged to the boy with the freckles.

"You gave him a subpoena?" I asked.

"Of course."

I could hardly wait for court to start the next morning. But Lester was missing. I telephoned his house and sent Whiskey out to look, but he wasn't there. The law in California was clear on the subject. If the defendant didn't show up after the trial had started, it went on without him.

I told the judge I had more evidence.

Pillar tried to keep the boy in the civics class off the stand. He wasn't on my witness list, and he'd been in court in violation of the order to sequester witnesses. But I had a case and Mac had to let him testify.

The kid knew the older kids would stomp all over him later, but he was beautiful.When he was done, the jury knew Givvens and Tum had mangled Lester's flower bed at least three times, and lied when they said they hadn't.

The veterinarian wasn't that easy. He couldn't remember if the Givvens's dog had been in his hospital or not. Bly's parents glared at him as he testified, of course. I showed the man his own records, and he agreed there was nothing to show the dog had been there, but said dogs often are left overnight for checkups and, especially for good customers, no record would be kept. "If the boy said his dog was there, he probably was."

I called the motorist who had taken the pictures to the stand. That little spot in the photograph I showed him? A dog, he said. It belonged to the boy with the freckles.

I rested my case.

Pillar put the mayor's wife on in rebuttal. She told the jury of her shock when Lester Strand put out Christmas tree candles by peeing on them.

"Merry Christmas, Santa Claus!" he'd yelled. Some of the jurors laughed!

We argued the case and the jury had it before lunch. But where was Lester?

I drove out to his house. His car was gone and the doors were locked, so I pinned a note on the screen, telling him he wasn't helping himself and that the judge could have him arrested. He should call as soon as he got my message. Then I went back to my office and waited for the telephone to ring.

It did, just before 4 p.m. The jury had a verdict.

Stan was in a good mood, so I knew he thought he'd won.

"We'll let Jack S. serve the sentence," he said, grinning at the judge.

But when the jurors filed into their seats, they laughed and joked with each other, and shrugged at Stan. "Not guilty." I thanked them profusely for their service, and Stan, the politician, did too. But he wouldn't go to the Applejack for a toast. Neither would Wink.

I stopped by the office after 7 p.m., in the bag. Whiskey was there. She handed me a slip of paper with a telephone number. "Wink wants you to call."

I did. "You lose after all, counselor," Wink said.

"What do you mean?"

"I just come back from your boy's house, which ought to be worth a fortune to somebody. One of those big old rambling wrecks, know what I mean? But oceanside."

"What are you talking about?"

"The mailman saw him, 4:15 this afternoon. Got one of those nice old glass front doors and there was Lester, hanging from a rope, near the staircase."

I couldn't feel anything. "Suicide?" I asked stupidly.

"That would definitely be my best guess."

I could see Wink's face, wearing one of those satisfied expressions Long Beach cops are born with.

A moth was on the window, silhouetted against the pale blue ocean sky. I couldn't tell if he was on the inside trying to get out or on the outside, trying to get in.

The dumb shit. He probably didn't know either.

Wick Downing comes from a long line of lawyers who lived and practiced in the Denver area. He attended the University of Wyoming and graduated from the University of Denver and DU Law. He has been both a prosecution and defense attorney in California and Colorado. He's a novelist. He has nine books published, eight of which are under his real name (Warwick Downing) and one under his chosen name (Wick). His latest book is "Leonardo's Hand" (Houghton Mifflin Co.).

Death of a Hero

by Esteban A. Martinez

I'm in my apartment, sitting at the table with my cousin Adam. He's a student at the community college where I teach. I'm helping him write a research paper about starving Somalians. We're looking at some photographs from *Life*. Photographs of starving children. Skeletons with skin stretched over their bones. The subject makes me seethe with anger, makes me want to hit someone, anyone, in this godless world. Adam is the opposite. I can see in his eyes that he'll never hit anyone, that he wants to touch the people in the photographs, to hold them, to feed them and that he sees God everywhere, in everything. I sometimes become irritated by him because he always prays, gives thanks. We've been best friends since we were children.

My phone rings. I think of not answering. I don't have an answering machine, and it keeps ringing. Its on it's fifteenth ring by the time I answer it.

It's Laura, my sister, and her voice sounds like she's crying or has been crying.

"Santiago, Kootie's in the hospital. She might die."

Kootie's real name is Chantel. She's a beautiful three-year old with big brown eyes, full lips and an intelligent mind. In fact, she owns an IQ of 152 according to some shrink at her school. She came from my other sister, Robin.

I replay Laura's words in my head and don't feel anything. Maybe I'm in shock. I wait for her to say something else. Then she starts bawling and her voice sounds the way it did when she was a kid, lost and afraid. I haven't heard that voice for a long time. It does something to me, makes me feel like a child. I'm startled and speak fast.

"Stop. You're not making sense. Stop crying."

She starts hiccupping, and I become nervous, anxious.

I tell her to shut up.

The line goes quiet for about three seconds. Then the adult Laura speaks.

In control.

"Somebody burned Kootie's head with a hot frying pan. She's in critical condition. We're at Denver General. Robin and Tony are being questioned by the police and social services. Robin has burns, too. On her neck and chin."

Then the child returns, sort of whimpers.

"Santi.' Come down here. Hurry."

I don't say goodbye. I hang up and call my Dad. I tell him the story, tell him I'll meet him at the hospital, that I'm leaving. Then I hang up the phone again and sit on the kitchen floor. I've forgotten about Adam until he touches my shoulder.

* * *

The road is bumpy. The hospital is 10 miles from where I live. Adam sits next to me, silent. I'm thinking of clues, clues I never should've ignored, clues hinting that Robin's husband, Tony, beats her, that he abuses his kids.

I hope Tony burned Kootie's head on purpose so that he'll do some time.

I curse an old woman driving a Cadillac in front of

me. She's going too damn slow. I pass her and call her a name. Adam says my name.

"What?" I say.

"I was just remembering you."

"What do you mean?"

"I was thinking of when we were kids."

Adam always calls to my attention his left-field thoughts, thoughts that have nothing to do with the present. I look away from the road and stare at him with irritation.

"Why were you thinking about that?"

"You're so different."

"So."

"Back then you seemed so . . . so complete. I used to want to be you."

I'm thinking about what he's just said. Is he saying I'm not complete now?

I ask him. He thinks for about a full minute.

"No, that's not what I mean. What I mean is that . . . that you're different."

I'm upset about why were driving to the hospital, about Kootie, and give him another irritated look.

"Not now," I say. "Pray to your god."

Then I begin thinking of Robin, of how she used to be.

* * *

A small town near Rapid City, South Dakota. A pond about a mile behind our house. Eight years old. Looking for turtles and salamanders. Robin, 11, sits in mud at the edge of the pond, makes sure I don't kill anything. Laura, 13, plays with the pussy willows behind us. Time doesn't exist until a clump of mud splatters against my face.

I look at Laura, follow her gaze to Robin, who is staring at two boys I hate, Shane and Carol Stubblefield.

Shane is in Laura's grade and Carol is in my grade. I hate Carol because he calls me 'Cocheese' in school and I hate Shane because he told the kids at Laura's school that he fucked her. I'm not certain what 'fuck' means, but it doesn't sound good, especially because it made Laura cry.

I'm not afraid of Carol. I've beaten him to a pulp plenty of times, but Shane scares the shit out of me. Unlike his little brother, he doesn't have soft round features. He has a pointy chin, sharp little teeth and rat-pink eyes. And he's taller than any other kids his age that I know.

I want to tell my sisters to run, *run like hell.*

But when I open my mouth, Robin gives me a look that says shut up. I obey because I fear Robin more than I do Shane. Not only can she beat me in a fight, she can also make my life miserable by ignoring me.

Shane snorts and spits a mucous glob in my direction. Then he grins with his sharp little teeth.

"What are you shit-eating 'Injuns' doin' here? This is OUR pond."

I look from him to Robin. I want her to give us the order to run. I keep thinking, *please tell us to run, please.*

Instead, she scoots closer to the water and digs her hand into the muck, makes a small pile of it. Then she looks at Shane and speaks calm, matter-of-factly.

"We're not Indians, we're Mexicans."

Staring at Robin, Shane takes a few steps toward me.

"I don't care shithead. Din't you hear me? This is *our* pond."

My heart races. I'm terrified. And I'm angry because I'm terrified. I look at Robin who is rising slowly. She motions me to her and calls Laura over.

Laura walks to Robin and cries.

Robin holds her hand.

Another mud clump sails through the air.

It lands on Laura's head.

Everyone except the toads and crickets are quiet for about five seconds. Then Laura sort of moans Robin's name, and Robin screams a war cry.

Robin and I spend a lot of time with our father in bars. Have done so since we were toddlers. He's an alcoholic, a damn good pool player, and he likes to show us off. He never takes Laura. Damn near every word we've learned in the bars, Robin includes in her war cry:

"Damn, fuck, sonofabitch, cocksucker, cuntface, shithead, bastard, motherfucker, asshole!"

Shane's eyes become wide.

Robin bends over, lifts some of the pond muck she's piled, runs to Shane and smears his face with it.

Along with Shane, Laura and I stare at Robin in disbelief.

Backing away from Shane and readying herself for his move, Robin looks like one of those all-star wrestlers I watch on Saturday nights.

Despite her confidence, the odds are against her. Shane stands at least four inches taller than she does.

Carol looks utterly confused. Slowly, he's backing away from his brother and Robin. I want to laugh, because I know he's afraid.

Shane's face twists into a rattish snarl.

Robin tenses.

Then Shane kicks her in the crotch.

Robin doubles over. Laura screams.

Carol runs to Robin and kicks her in the face.

I charge, fists swinging.

Shane picks me up and throws me into the pond.

The water is warm from the sun.

I don't know what to do; I feel afraid. I look around and see that Laura is pointing and crying.

"Help her, Santiago! Help her!"

I look where she's pointing and see Robin

wrapped around Shane's leg biting his thigh. He's screaming.

She won't let go even though Carol is kicking at her.

I feel some rocks under my feet, rocks bigger than my hands, bend over and pull a fist-sized one from the murky pond. Then I rush Carol and throw it at him.

He falls instantly and cries. I kick him.

Shane punches me.

Robin stands and begins boxing Shane's face.

Carol pushes himself up from the ground, abandons Shane. I see his head bobbing up and down through a swath of pussy willows.

Laura sits where she stood and continues crying.

Robin grabs Shane by his neck and wrestles him to the ground. He struggles with her, but she pins him on his back by sitting on his chest and digging her knees into his inner biceps. He tries to break her pin by bucking up and down, but she won't let him go.

"Get a rock!" she says.

Quickly, I find one, one bigger than both my hands, and run to her side.

She looks at me.

"If he moves anymore, crack his head with it."

Shane becomes very still.

I begin thinking of the rules my father gave us for fighting. At first they had been simple, with a lot a room for interpretation. "If someone hits you, you hit them back. Don't let anyone pick on you." Then, I accidentally broke a boy's arm in a school fight and our father changed the rules. "Don't go overboard," he said to Robin and me (not to Laura because she never fights). "Only use necessary force." The way he said this, as if it were of the utmost importance, made me feel like a student in a karate movie. I vowed never to forget and always obey his new sacred rules. I can almost hear his voice.

Robin shouts.

"Hit him in the head!"

I drop the rock.

Shane bucks but remains under Robin's control.

"Get the rock. Hit him!"

I bend, grab the rock, then stand above Shane's head.

He quits bucking, stares at me, begins to stutter.

"Wu,wu,wu . . . wut . . . wut you gonna do?"

He sounds like he's going to cry.

Robin juts her face toward me.

"Stay where you are, Santi'."

Then she looks at Laura sitting by the pond, whimpering.

"Come here, Laura."

Laura looks at Robin, confused.

Robin motions with her head.

"Now!"

Laura stands up, shaking, makes her way over.

Shane looks at all of us, puzzled.

I keep thinking of my father's fighting rules and wonder if Robin remembers them. She clears the phlegm in her throat and spits into Shane's face. He starts to cry. She speaks. Softly. At first.

"You said you fucked my sister. How come? Why did you say that? Suckassfucker! Laura, stomp on his face!"

Laura doesn't move.

"Laura!"

Laura whines.

"Why? I don't want to."

My mind returns to my father's rules. I don't want to be punished for "going overboard."

Robin shouts as loud as she can.

"Stomp his face!"

Then her voice softens.

"He said he fucked you, Laura. He lied about you. Stomp his face, and he'll never do it again."

Shane's not very intelligent. The odds are against him. Robin on top of him, me with my rock, and Laura, an unknown in the equation, should tell him to keep quiet. Instead, he glares at Laura and speaks with a laugh in his voice.

"I told everyone you have a lot of pussy hair."

Laura lifts her foot and stomps his face.

Robin gets off of him. I'm not sure why, maybe to give him a fair chance.

He struggles to his feet and grabs Laura by her hair which hangs past her butt.

Laura begins punching and kicking.

I start toward the two to help Laura, but Robin stops me with one of her looks.

All I do is watch.

A bloody fight.

Shane's a good fighter but he's tired from fighting with Robin and me.

Laura stands about as tall as Shane, weighs at least 15 pounds less, and has never fought in her life. She's a quiet girl, uncertain of herself. She usually walks around with bad posture, a slightly hunched back. And she's always crying. About something.

But when she fights Shane, the Laura I know disappears.

I can't see her anywhere.

Instead, I see an animal fighting for its life.

With grunts and groans, she kicks Shane, punches him, claws his face, bites him and spits on him.

He gets in a couple of licks that I know would floor me but they have little effect on Laura.

If Robin and I don't stop her, I think she'll hurt Shane badly.

We pull her off of him.

Shane stays where he is, stretched out on the ground bleeding. His eyes look like the eyes of Wile E. Coyote after he's been hit by a train. Slowly, he gets up and limps away; disappears into the pussy willows.

I look at Laura.

She looks . . . like someone sprinkled her with magic. Even though she's bloody and bruised, she's not crying, she's not hunched over and her eyes have a bright intensity I've never seen before.

I think she'll never be the same.

I look at Robin.

She looks as though she's thinking big important thoughts. Then she smiles, a slight and brief smile, barely noticeable, and orders us to begin our walk home.

I obey immediately, because today I know she is some kind of magic person, and I worship her.

* * *

We're pulling into the hospital parking lot, and Adam spots my dad. He's wearing greasy cover alls and has grease smudges on his cheeks, forehead and chin. I figure he was restoring one of his old cars when I called him. Restoration is his passion. He sees us and waits for us to park.

When we reach him, he asks me what the fuck is going on. He clenches his dirty muscular hands and hits a parked car.

We go to the emergency area and find out that the doctors put Kootie in the intensive care unit on the third floor. They tell us she's going to live; her situation is not life threatening.

The three of us walk to the elevators in silence.

In the elevator, I stare at my dad. He looks how I hope to look when I'm his age. He has all of his hair, and it's still black. His wrinkles complement his face instead of destroy it. They make him look rugged. And his body still looks solid, like he could probably take out two guys half his age in a fight.

I notice Adam using the elevator mirror to stare

at me. I get an urge to laugh at his bald head and round spectacles. He looks like a well-fed Ghandi. I think of where we're going and my urge dies. The elevator doors open and, in silence, we follow arrows on the floor to the intensive care unit.

When we reach intensive care, I look for Laura but don't see her. Before I can think about her absence, I notice Tony. He's hunched over with his eyes closed, sitting on a chair. He smells like booze—cheap beer. He has on dirty jeans and a shirt too small for his fat body. His long hair glows with grease and his face looks as though he hasn't shaved it for three or more days.

I want to kick him in his face.

I scan the room and see Robin in a far corner. She's talking to a woman with a note pad, who's nodding seriously and exchanging glances with a tired-looking cop a few feet away.

My dad looks at Tony and hisses.

"What the fucking hell happened?"

The question assumes Tony's guilt. My dad bases the assumption on a suspicion, a suspicion that all of my family—from my teen-aged cousins to my 99-year-old great grandmother—has had for some time and has never bothered to prove or disprove. Ever. Everyone has always wanted to mind their own business. But we've all suspected. We've all entertained the idea that Tony is a fucked up sonofabitch and beats the shit out of my sister and does weird shit, crazy shit, to his kids. We've all suspected and none of us ever done a damn thing about it.

The thought lingers in my brain, and I want to kill Tony.

Tony looks at my dad and says nothing.

My dad kicks Tony's feet.

"Goddammit, I asked you a question!"

Tony sighs.

The cop crosses the room, hurries to my dad, and squeezes his body in between Tony's chair and my dad.

"Sir, would you please sit over there?"

My dad doesn't like cops.

"Sure, yeah. Are you going to arrest this piece of shit?"

The cop puts his hands on his hips.

"Sir, if you don't sit down, I'm going to arrest *you*."

My dad snorts, then walks slowly to a chair on the other side of the room.

Tony closes his eyes, leans back in his chair and sighs.

I think, *if only I can catch the fat bastard in the act. I'll eat the motherfucker for lunch. Nobody fucks with my god. Nobody.*

* * *

On the drive back from the hospital, I can feel Adam staring at me.

"What the hell you looking at?" I say.

"I'm trying to read your face. How do you feel?"

"Read my face."

"You need to tell me."

Adam's the brother I never had. There's something between us, a connection hard to understand, hard to believe, but I know it's there.

"Read my face," I say.

Adam says nothing for about three minutes. Then he clears his throat.

"Uh . . . Santiago, you gotta tell me what you're thinking."

"I'm not thinking about anything. That's what I'm thinking about."

"But what about Robin? What are you thinking about all that?"

"Well, I wasn't thinking about it, but thanks to you, now I am."

"That's what you should talk about, how you feel

about that."

"Okay. This is what I think. I think if I ever had the opportunity, I'd kill Tony. If I could get away with it, he'd be dead. If I ever see him do anything to Robin, I won't care if I can get away with it or not. I'll try to kill him on the spot. I hate him. He's a piece of shit. His life doesn't mean shit."

Adam says nothing until I pull in front of his apartment.

"We'll work on your paper tomorrow in my office," I say. "Right now I'm gonna go get fucked up at Mile-Hi Saloon. Maybe snag one of those ripe kitties. Tell Brandy hi for me."

He looks at the ground.

I wait for him to say good-bye.

"Be careful," he says.

* * *

I'm sitting at my table where less than a month ago I helped Adam write about starving Somalians. I'm shaking, staring at the phone.

I want to call Adam.

I need to talk.

But I just stare at the phone and think.

About the incident in the hospital that happened not more than a month ago. About how social services stopped their investigation of Robin's family because she convinced them it was an accident. About a news story I read not too long ago that stated that each social worker in Denver has a case load of 100 per day. About how none of us who know about the unspoken ugliness in Robin's life did a damn thing when given the opportunity at the hospital.

About how my father, despite the intensity of his soul, seeming to forget about it all, disappeared in his garage, his heaven of restoration. About how Laura has changed, become an adult version of the child she was before her rebirth at the pond. About how I keep teaching and getting fucked up every night.

About how I said I'd try to kill Tony if I ever saw him do anything.

About how, less than an hour ago, I picked up Robin from her house and took her to Safeway because she doesn't know how to drive. About how Tony can't drive with all his DUIs. About how I asked Robin on the way why Tony doesn't take the bus and shop for her and her kids. About how she changed the subject.

About how when I dropped her off, Tony, looking pissed, opened the door to the house and said, "What the fuck took you so long?"

About how Robin cowered before him.

About how I thought of Robin fighting and winning near the pond.

About how I worshipped her.

About how Tony said, "I'm talking to you goddamn it. Answer me!"

About how I didn't want to look at him when he said that.

About how, as I was staring at my feet, I heard the crack of a slap and a scream.

About how I looked up and saw that Robin's eye was all puffy.

About how I froze; did nothing.

About how Robin looked at me and I could tell by the brevity of her look, her unwillingness to make real eye contact, that she no longer believes in herself, nor in me, and is ashamed of both of us.

Esteban Martinez is an appellate attorney in the criminal justice section of the Colorado Attorney General's office. He says: "I write and practice law, because I love to do so. Writing fiction and poetry gives me an opportunity to play with the logic—or is it antilogic?—of art. Law practice, par-

ticularly legal writing, allows me to believe that I can impose sense on the very complicated mess of the human condition."

Close to Home

by Janie Breggin

My grandmother died on a cold, grey day in November. We didn't know until the next day, when old Mr. Parson, who lives down the lane, went to check on her and found her dead in the yard with her boots on.

When Mom called, the first thing I thought was how much I would miss Thanksgiving dinner at my grandmother's house. I grew up in my grandmother's kitchen, Thanksgivings and summers, in boots or barefoot. We were close the way women get when they've been through hard times together. Losing my grandmother was like losing a piece of me.

The second thing I thought was Oh, my God, how am I going to manage three children in the car for the four-hour drive over the Colorado Rockies, a stay in a strange hotel, their first funeral, one where they would surely cry because I would be crying, and then four hours in the car back again the next day.

"When is the funeral?" I asked.

Mom's voice was quiet but steady. She had already told me she didn't intend to cry. "Saturday, I expect." Grandma always said women in our family are supposed to be tougher than boot leather, stronger than grief. Often we are stronger than the men we choose and that can be a problem. Grandma was a widow for 28 years, Mom raised my sister and me by herself, and I was raising my three girls since their father decided he was tired of being a family man three years ago last August.

"Friday would be a good day to travel," I said. Tia's kindergarten class got out at noon. If I took Katie and Sarah out of school at lunch, and the weather held, we'd be down off of narrow twisty Rabbit Ears Pass and checked into the Holiday Inn in Craig before dusk. If the weather didn't hold, the driving could get seriously bad. Friday was also good because I knew Matt could get the afternoon off, if he asked. Yes, Friday would be good.

I knew Matt was home, so I waited the six and a half rings it took him to answer. "How was your day?" I asked. Matt always listened better when he'd already had his say, and today I wanted him to listen. After he went on for awhile, I thought it was time enough to change the subject.

"My grandmother died yesterday."

"Ahh." Matt dragged it out, slow and soothing. I was glad I had called, glad I wasn't going to be alone with my grief and my girls. "Jody, I'm sorry."

I didn't intend to cry, at least not until later. "The funeral's on Saturday," I said. "I thought we could drive over on Friday." Unasked, I let the question float out like a wisp of cloud.

"You're going then?"

Idiot, like I'm not going to go to my grandmother's funeral. She had always been there for me, when Katie and Sarah and Tia were born, and when I ran out of money in college, one semester short of the degree that would get me a job better than any my mother ever had a chance for. And when I tried to fall apart when my ex-husband walked out on the girls and me, she was there to remind me that I had children to take care of and that the women in my family have more staying power than most any man any of us had ever seen or were likely to see. "Yes," I said. "I'm going."

"Will your ex keep the kids for you or what?"

"I'm not going to ask."

"Don't you think he'll do it?"

After 18 months of hearing me tell stories, Matt didn't much care for my ex-husband, but then again neither did I, so I let that go by.

"I want the girls with me." They had never stayed at my grandmother's house, that was my only regret, that they had all been born after my grandmother decided the farm wasn't a safe place for city kids. I wanted them to see it before it was sold out of the family. I wish I'd had the money to buy it. "This is their family, too."

"So, you'll leave on Friday, then," he said. "What time?"

Last year on my birthday, my sister had kept the girls so Matt and I could go out to dinner. He said I deserved wine and candlelight on my birthday, and he was going to make sure I got both. He gave me a small wooden box, a box he had made and painted with sea shells and gulls. When I opened it, there was a gold sand dollar on a chain, nestled in red tissue paper. Next birthday, I thought, it might be a ring. I twisted the chain around my finger and asked, "Matt, would you go with us, help me drive?"

I heard his lighter snap. He inhaled deeply, then let it out. I could just see the smoke curl up to the ceiling, dingy yellow from all the years Matt had meant to but hadn't quit smoking, and I knew it wouldn't matter when I decided to leave. I waited to hear how he would tell me that.

"I don't think that's a good idea, Jody."

Once I get started, I can be a lot like my grandmother and my mother are with men, stubborn and unforgiving, sometimes hurting no one but myself. I knew he wasn't going to help me, but I wasn't going to let him get away without saying it.

"Why not?"

"It's just not a good idea."

"You could help me drive. It's a four-hour trip." I choked the whine out of my voice. Each way. And you're going to make me drive it alone.

"It's just not a good idea," he said again.

Maybe I couldn't quite believe he was really going to let me go alone. Or maybe all that sorrow, all that loss I was holding inside, holding until after all the arrangements had been made, all the things that needed taking care of were taken care of, maybe all that had gotten inside the boot leather, had softened me up a bit, made me stupid, but I asked again. "Matt, please." Please help me do this hard thing. Please come with me and drive so I can tell stories to my daughters about their great grandmother, so I don't have to be the only grownup with three tired, hungry, confused little girls, so I can get ready to see my mother cry. So I don't have to be alone at night with my grief in a strange bed in a hotel room so far from home. So I can start to believe that not all men are like my ex-husband. I could hear all of that in my voice. I don't think Matt could and I don't think it would have made any difference, at least not in how it turned out, even if he had.

"Jody, no!" He should have left it at that. I might have forgiven him for the sake of peace, for the sake of our future together I thought about, for the sake of not sleeping alone. But he said, "I don't want to intrude on your family."

Intrude on my family. My family that he'd managed for 18 months to avoid meeting. My family who had been there, in Grandma's kitchen for Thanksgiving, on the front porch in summer, year after year. My mom, my sister, my aunt and cousins. My family.

"Matt— "

He talked over the top of me. "I don't see what the big deal is. It's not like you were close to her or anything. You haven't visited her once, not one time, since I've known you, so how close could you be?"

* * *

The drive west out of Denver, through the Eisenhower Tunnel, then north to Kremmling, was long, but the weather and the roads were clear for the first three hours.

Tia sat next to me in the front seat, keeping me company by keeping quiet. Katie and Sarah read and talked and were bored in the back seat, but they didn't fight and they only asked once, just as we passed through Dillon, to stop for ice cream and to go to the bathroom.

The rain started after we were down off the pass; it didn't turn to sleet until we cleared Steamboat Springs, 45 miles shy of my grandmother's house. Suddenly, in this weather, it was another hour-and-a-half away.

After we checked in, the girls went down to the hotel game room with a fistful of quarters among them and a promise from me that we would all go in the pool together later, once we were settled.

I unpacked my black sweater and the long black skirt I'd brought, shook them out, and hung the skirt in the closet, on one of those weird wooden hangars, the kind you can't steal because they come apart into two pieces, leaving the ring on the rod and in your hand a worthless triangle of wood, sort of a boomerang that never gets thrown, so it never needs to come back around. I put the sweater in a drawer, hid the remote control to the TV (that would have been more than I could stand), and looked at the phone. My sister was staying out at the house with my mother and my aunt. My cousins, both coming with husbands and children, hadn't checked into the hotel yet.

I wanted to just sit and cry, those great heaving sobs I'd been holding back since Mom called, the kind where you want someone to hold you and to hand you Kleenex when you're done, but I still had to deal with dinner, room service or the dining room, or something. I didn't think I could face fast food, even though the girls would be begging for burgers and fries. Being alone filled the hotel room, spreading out over the chenille spread, the rough woven curtains, the standard issue white towels that looked soft but weren't. I twisted the sand dollar chain around one finger, picked up the phone and dialed 8 for an outside, long distance line.

* * *

I didn't cry until the funeral started. After, I stopped long enough to drive, headlights on, to the cemetery for the graveside service. My grandmother's casket sat low to the ground, next to my grandfather's grave, which was obscured by the mound of sod that would be rolled out by the cemetery workers after the family and other mourners left.

Sweet Tia sat with my mother and my aunt on a folding aluminum riser whose legs sank into the soggy ground. The sky began to spit little bits of wet that couldn't decide if they wanted to be rain or snow. I started to cry again when Tia leaned her head against my mother's shoulder.

* * *

Matt had picked up the phone on the third ring.

"How was your day?" I asked.

"Fine," he said. "How was the drive?"

"Long," I said. "Lonely." Underneath this I'm thinking please, please, please—

"Jody," he said. "I don't do funerals."

Something inside me shifted, and I let go of the sand dollar chain. "What do you mean, you don't do funerals?"

"I mean I don't do funerals. Not since my mother died."

Right. Matt's sainted mother had been dead for over 10 years. In the time I'd known him, his days were always harder than mine, and insults and slights cut him deeper. That was bad enough, but now his grief was going to be bigger and grander than mine as well.

"Goddamned doctors," he said. "If I had been there it never would have happened." Matt told everyone, whether they wanted to hear or not, whether they had heard the story before or not, that it was the doctors' fault, giving her too high a dose of the wrong drug. "They killed her," he said. Matt's sister told me once it was alcohol and cigarettes that killed her, just like it would kill Matt if he didn't quit. She said Matt and his mother fought like cats and dogs over her drinking, so bad that she didn't even want him there at the hospital toward the end, all because he just wouldn't let up on her. His voice, rough from the cigarettes, broke into a righteous cough. "And we were close. We were so close."

* * *

Katie and Sarah, unbearably beautiful in the drizzling rain, stood with me after the graveside service.

Tia walked with my mom back to the long black limousine. I could just see her boots dangling out the door, swinging back and forth. I knew she'd wait for me to come fetch her, that she'd want to ride with me out to the house, where my grandmother's friends and neighbors would come to eat cold cuts and cake and swap stories. Tia wore the sand dollar chain, which now held the tiny shamrock charm Mom gave her to remember her great grandmother by. I had left the sand dollar next to the phone in the hotel room.

I turned back to my grandmother's casket and my grandfather's grave to say goodbye. I was ready to go now, out to the house, where I would have plenty of stories of my own to add to the telling of my grandmother's life.

Sarah and Katie walked with me all the way back to the car, their small hands soft and warm and comforting in mine. Although I didn't feel it now, I knew I wasn't done with being lonely. But I was done with Matt, and that was fine with me. After all, it's not like we were close.

Prize-winning poet Janie Breggin lives and writes in Denver, Colo. Her day job as a real estate and environmental lawyer pays the bills and provides her with unlimited material for her fiction. Life with her soon-to-be husband and their combined four teenagers provides her with great joy and continuing challenges.

Coming Home

by Charles A. Riccio, Jr.

The luggage appeared on the carousel only a moment after he arrived. He secured it and went out to the taxi stand. There was a cold rain falling. It was just as well. It matched his mood. This was not a vacation or a business trip. He would have been hard pressed for an answer if he had been asked why he had come here at all. He told himself it was "something he had to do," knowing full well that was no explanation at all.

The cool drops and the tock-tock-tocking of the taxi's windshield wipers were soothing after the uncomfortable eight-hour flight.

There were office buildings and high rises where previously there had been open fields and sheep grazing. The residences of the Spanish nobility (many were palaces) had been razed to be replaced by apartment complexes and shops. They drove down the Castellana. There was the statue of the Marquess de Duero mounted on his charger pointing his sword at the Hotel Hilton, there was the Embassy Tea Room, the editorial offices of *ABC*, the monarchist newspaper that had been publishing for 100 years or more. There was the wedding cake building, the post office, called by everyone the Palacio de Comunicaciones because it resembled the palace of some titled nobleman more than a place where anyone could mail a letter, and, of course, there was Cibeles, the monument to the Goddess of the Earth, a sculpture that was old when the American Revolution was new, smiling with benign maternalism on the Bank of Spain and on the Calle Alcala. Regally, she sat in her lion drawn chariot surrounded by her attendants while fountains threw silver water into the air.

Up the Calle Alcala the taxi flew, and then it darted onto the Gran Via, Madrid's Great White Way, no longer called the Avenida de Jose Antonio as it had been called during the Franco years, and then down the hill on the cobblestones that the International Brigades had marched on a cold November day to save the city from the advancing nationalist army. And, at last, the taxi stopped in front of his hotel on the Plaza de España.

There was a bit of a mix-up when he opened the door to his room and saw that he had a view of the air shaft rather than of the plaza as he had requested. But that was straightened out by an obsequious desk clerk who had hoped that the gentleman would not wish to make an issue of the incorrect room assignment.

From his 17th floor window he looked out onto the Plaza de España. Don Quixote, astride Rocinante, and faithful Sancho on his mule, were still there gazing westward in all their cement and concrete dignity. He could see the spot where the Montaña Barracks had stood, the military cuartel, which had been attacked by the citizen army of Madrid on the day of "The Rising." It had been razed and now there stood a garden, a park, peaceful and quiet, with no sign of the desperate but brief and fratricidal battle that had been fought there so many years ago.

He unpacked—he had carried only one bag—and then took a brief nap. Showered and dressed he stepped out onto the plaza. It had stopped raining and though the sun was high, the air was fresh and cool. The teeming street was much as he remembered it, though many of the buildings had been renovated. There was the Hotel

Emperador; the Telefónica, the telephone building that had been the tallest building in Madrid during the war and that had been an observation tower for the Republican army; Sepu's, the department store, which had been the children's favorite because their small weekly allowance of a few pesetas went so far there; Chicote's bar, a favorite hangout of the war correspondents and soldiers of the International Brigades and the ladies who might be persuaded to provide consolation between battles. Plaza Callao boasted a large new department store, the Corte Inglés. He didn't remember what building it had replaced. He continued his stroll until he came to the Plaza of the Gate of the Sun, the Puerta del Sol. There was the bronze bear, the symbol of Madrid, gnawing the branches of the madrona tree, and there were the public buildings surrounding the Plaza. He continued up the hill, winding his way aimlessly through the maze of streets, the Street of the Hat Makers, the Street of Health, the Street of the Morning Star, the Street of the Foot Washers, the Street of Disillusionment, the Street of Dangers, the Street of Bitterness, (what poet had named these streets?) and the Street of the Rivers of the Roses.

In many ways, it was not the city he had known. The men had lost that seedy look. The one good suit (so-called even though it had become threadbare) that every man wore through all the seasons of the year had been replaced by fashionable and well-tailored clothing. And the quiet city had been infested by a plague of large metal insects that choked the streets, inhaling the clean air and exhaling carbon monoxide, polluting the atmosphere with poison and noise, and threatening the lives of anyone who carelessly stepped into the street.

The blind lottery ticket sellers no longer thronged the streets chanting, "*Para hoy . . .,* " in their attempts to sell the key to a better life. The tickets were now sold in newspaper kiosks scattered around the city by sellers who were not at all physically challenged. And the gypsy beggars were gone. Each had carried a milk bottle wrapped in a blanket to simulate a child, as she held out her hand to every possible benefactor who, in his haste, might not notice the deception.

He strolled amidst the press of pedestrians and through the streets redolent of garlic and olive oil and of frying fish until he came at last to Plaza Santa Ana. And it was there, as it had been since Madrid was little more than a collection of mud huts. He sat on the bench he had sat on the first day he discovered the Plaza (and he felt that, notwithstanding its ancient pedigree, he and he alone had discovered the Plaza Santa Ana). It seemed so long ago.

He went into the Cerveceria Alemana, the bar on the corner, and ordered a cold beer. It was exactly as it had been on that first day so long ago. The zinc bar, the sink filled with water, the hams and chorizo sausages hanging from hooks in the window. Framed pictures of celebrities, movie stars and bullfighters, some long gone, hanging on the walls.

He took his foaming glass to a table, and when the waiter came up, he ordered a dish of *gambas a la plancha*. He examined the other patrons. A few tourists, some young people, a couple of old men reading their newspaper, and two nuns. It might very well have been 30 years ago.

When the shrimp were brought, he ate them slowly, one at a time, and drank the beer. It was good to sit in the Cerveceria Alemana and eat *gambas a la plancha* as he and his wife had done, so many years ago.

Later, outside, as the sun was setting, children were still playing in the plaza, kicking and chasing a ball. Three filthy, disreputable looking men were discussing something very emphatically and then, quite unexpectedly, one of them, the one with the long hair, instead of pulling a knife and killing someone as you might expect, burst into a song, singing lustily. The other two began clapping in time with his singing. It was flamenco, at 5 p.m. on a sunny afternoon in the Plaza Santa Ana in Madrid, a city he had always thought of as the capital of the world.

In the twilight, he walked up the Street of the Orchards past Plaza Angel and past the Hotel Victoria to the Plaza Mayor.

The plaza, in its long history, had seen bull fights, *autos-da-fé*, the burning of heretics and lapsed Christians, parades and demonstrations. Now, in the evening hours, it was quiet, with couples strolling, going to restaurants and glancing idly in the shop windows.

Down past el Pulpito, past the Caves of Luis Candelas, past Botin's, along the calle Cava Baja, and at last to Plaza de La Puerta Cerrada to Casa Paco. The restaurant was as it had been. The brightly colored Talavera tiles on the wall, the tiny bar, a few patrons eating *tapas* before the dining room opened. He sat on a bench in a corner watching the patrons and waiting for 8:30 p.m.

When the dining room opened, he was shown to a table. It was the same room where they had dined so many years ago.

The waiter came and took his order and, later, when he brought to the table *pollo al ajillo,* and that good Spanish *pan* and *vino de la casa* the man said, "Good evening, Javier. Do you remember me?" It was not a fair question. But the waiter, startled by the sound of his name and knowing that the man must have once been a patron, smiled and said quickly, "Ah yes, of course, you look very familiar."

"We lived here many years ago. I lived in Madrid with my wife and children. I was with the United States Forces."

"Ah!" exclaimed the waiter. "Yes, there were many in those days."

"And the daughter of Paco—is she the *gerente* still?"

"Ah, yes, she is upstairs now in the office. She will be down presently."

"I remember her well. A charming lady."

"She remains the same." The waiter smiled, remembering when so many of the Americans who patronized the restaurant were residents of Madrid rather than merely tourists.

Soon, Paco's daughter arrived and the waiter told her who the man was. She was remarkably unchanged. A little stouter, a little grayer, but charming as always, still unable to speak a word of English all these years. They chatted amiably for a few moments. She asked, "And the children, are they with you?"

"Oh, no" he laughed, "They have families of their own now. They remain in the United States."

"And your wife, is she with you?"

"No" he answered. He hesitated. "She is not here, she is . . . not with me." And again the sharp, painful memory of a dimly lighted hospital waiting room and the surgeon's announcement that had destroyed his life.

The woman noticed the change in the man's tone of voice and the look of, what was it, resignation on his face.

"It is good to see you again," she remarked quite sincerely, and the man replied, "And I am happy to see you so well."

Later, he paid his check, tipped too much, and, as he left, he embraced the waiter. "Goodbye," he said and for a moment it was difficult to see through the mist in his eyes.

Next day, he walked up the Calle Princesa to the Plaza Moncloa to the Spanish Air Ministry. From the sidewalk he looked up at the third floor to the window behind what had been his office. The building showed some signs of age and there was a lawn in front of the building where there had been none before, and there were benches where people were resting.

There was now a metro stop there. He disappeared into the ground and bought a ticket. He thought he would ride, perhaps to the end of the line, to see how far it went and what was at the end.

He stayed on the metro longer than he had intended. He saw that he was at the Estrecho stop, and he left the train and walked up the steps to the street. This was the metro stop closest to their apartment, and he had come out of the station every evening in the busy bustling district of the city that had always seemed the most alive to him. It seemed to have changed not at all. The shops were all open, fruit and vegetables displayed openly on the sidewalks, newsstands draped with newspapers and magazines. People, people, people. There was the kiosk where he bought the evening paper, unchanged in all these years. The old man who had stood there silently was gone these many years, but a girl in her 20s now went about the serious business of selling newspapers, collecting money, and making change. The coffee bars, the barber shops, the clothing stores—nothing seemed to have changed. He saw a blind lottery ticket seller and he was chanting in the old familiar way, "*Una tira . . . para hoy.*" "A ticket . . . for today."

So, progress had not made its way this far up from the Gran Via. It was a comforting thought and he felt a twinge of the nostalgia he had hoped he would not feel in returning to this magical, captivating city, the city they had always considered their home town.

He walked slowly up the street. Traffic was much lighter here than it was anywhere else in the city. He remembered their first days in Madrid. There was no traffic at all to speak of. Anywhere. And then the motor scooters, the Vespas, came, and then the automobiles.

He hesitated at the corner. To the right was the Calle General Yague the street that led to the apartment.

This is why he had come. He knew if he walked down that street there would be no turning back. But perhaps it wouldn't be so bad. Perhaps it would not pain him merely to look. He would simply stand across the street and glance up at the windows of the apartment and the terraza, the balcony, from where so often they had looked out at the city and to the mountains beyond.

He heard a familiar whistle as he approached the apartment. He couldn't quite place it in his memory and then he saw the knife sharpener. He was pushing his bicycle that had on its handlebars two whetstones that he used to sharpen the knives of the occupants of the apartment houses. He blew on his pipes of Pan whistle to inform the housewives of his approach. The man thought the knife sharpener would have gone the way of the lottery ticket sellers and the boot blacks and the gypsy beggars and the lamplighters, the lamplighters who had added so much to the charm of the city.

In front of his apartment building a whole city block had lain vacant the whole time they had lived there. He supposed it had been built up by now. Another apartment building had undoubtedly been built there, and it would block his view, but as he approached the building, he saw with surprise that the empty area had not been built up at all, and while standing at some distance he could see the entire front of his apartment building remarkably unchanged. There were the shops that fronted on the street, the beauty parlor, the travel agency, the florist's shop. He glanced up at the seventh floor. The orange awnings, though rolled up, were still there. The white terraza railing was still there, unchanged.

He leaned against a building and stared up at the apartment. I wonder if I could go up and visit, he thought. But that would be foolish. How could he explain who he was. The occupants would be suspicious or embarrassed. He would become tongue tied as he tried to explain his wish merely to look once more at the place that had been their home. And for what. What good would it do. Everything would be different. It wouldn't be the same. How could it be?

The sun was setting and he saw lights go on in the apartments. Lights went on in his apartment, too. He wondered if he might get a glimpse of one or two of the occupants. A man, perhaps, a woman, a child. He stood and stared for a long time, but he saw no one and, after a time, he turned and went back to the metro station.

He felt relieved. He hadn't known what effect seeing the old place would have on him. But he felt refreshed somehow. It hadn't been so bad after all.

He spent the next day at the Retiro walking along the paths beneath the leafy canopies, watching the young men and women rowing on the lake, the children with their nannies watching. The day was spent idly but pleasantly. The apprehension that had dogged him from the start of the trip seemed to have left. Perhaps this visit would be a good thing for him as he had hoped. He had lunch at a small restaurant and then a siesta at the hotel.

Toward evening, he found himself at the apartment again. It was foolish to try to convince himself that he had simply wandered there aimlessly. He felt drawn to it, but he did not feel the trepidation he had felt the day before.

He wanted to see the lights go on again. Surely there would be someone in the apartment passing a window or stepping out onto the terraza. A child, perhaps, or . . . a woman.

After a half hour of staring up at the windows and hoping for some sign of the slightest movement, he saw a shadow pass in front of the window. He couldn't tell whether it was a man or woman. But he saw movement there. He waited, but it was too far for him to see behind the drapes that covered the living room windows.

He felt a strong desire to go up to the apartment and introduce himself. To go in and tell the people who he was. To ask their permission to spend a few minutes there, to see again the familiar rooms. But his resolve evaporated and he was seized with the realization of how awkward his request would sound to the people who lived there now.

But then he saw the glass door from the dining room to the terraza open, and someone came out. It was a woman. Her figure was indistinct. The potted plants in the terraza obscured his view. He watched in the hope that she would turn her face toward him. She was doing something with the plants and then he saw that she was watering them with a watering can. Her head was bent to her task and he could not distinguish her features but then as she finished watering she stood straight and for an instant he saw her face. He drew a quick breath. The woman turned and went back into the apartment. He had seen her for only an instant but she had seemed . . . familiar. He stood stiffly watching the terraza and the windows, but she did not come out again. Eventually he tired, and now, strangely disturbed, he went back to his hotel.

The next day he rented a car and drove out to Toledo, the city on the Tagus. The traffic was so much more dense than it had ever been when they lived in Spain. But once in the Zocodover, the main plaza, he remembered the pleasant visits in happier times to the Alcazar and the cathedral.

That evening, he stood in front of the apartment building again, drawn there as he knew he would be. After a brief spell, the woman he had seen previously stepped onto the terraza. This time she apparently had no task to perform. She stepped to the railing and looked out toward the mountains. He remembered how they both had enjoyed, in the late afternoon, watching the sun set behind the mountains. How peaceful it was. It was a time of quiet for both of them, and they stood and held hands like lovers as they had done before they were married. Now, the woman's glance fell upon him, and she stared at him intently. He felt a tightness in his chest. It seemed that she was startled. They stared at each other. Her resemblance—it was uncanny. She stood motionless as did he. And then, in a moment of decision, he walked quickly across the lot and into the lobby of the building. The *portero* was sitting behind his desk reading a newspaper.

"Pardon me," he began, "If it is not a bother, the people above in 7D, how are they called? Can you tell me their name?" The suddenness of his appearance and his rapidly asked question startled the portero. He stared at the man.

"I'm sorry," he began again, "I am an American, and I believe I know the people who live in 7D, and I wonder if you could give me their name."

The portero was, of course, instantly suspicious. The only people who asked questions about tenants were the police, and he had learned long since in a country that still had memories of fascism that ignorance, real or feigned, was the only safe response to questions. He shrugged his shoulders, shook his head and went back to his paper.

"I beg your pardon," said the man, his irritation showing, "I used to live in this building in 7D, and I believe I know the people who are living there now. Can you tell me their name? It would be a kindness."

The portero folded his paper and stood up. He was afraid of this strange man who asked questions.

"I know no one. You are mistaken." He had turned pale.

"Very well," said the man, "I'm sorry, many thanks." He had started out all wrong. It was too late to start over. The *portero's* guard was up. He was afraid of this questioning stranger. He displayed the xenophobia of all Spaniards who remembered the Franco years. He would never give any reply to this stranger. And although a small bribe was known to get things done in Spain, it wouldn't work now because the *portero* was frightened. He would have to try something else.

He considered simply walking past the *portero* and using the elevator. That would only cause the *portero* to show the famous Spanish temper, and there would be the police and an arrest. It would be best to remain calm.

He went out again and crossed the street and looked back. The woman was gone. The door to the dining room was open but he could see no one.

He saw that the *portero* had come out of the building and was standing near the front door and was watching him. He would have to come back again when the portero was occupied elsewhere. He wandered about the city that evening, unmindful of the traffic and the people. Had the woman stared at him or had it been his imagination? But perhaps she had only been curious. Her resemblance . . . it was his imagination, of course. How could it be? What he was thinking was impossible. Could wishing so badly for something make it happen? Had he lost his mind? She was a stranger to him, just as he was to her. She had made no sign of recognition. Why was he tormenting himself so. Why had he come? What had he hoped to find here after so many years. Peace? An end? Some kind of conclusion? All he had found so far was confusion. All he had done was to create false hopes.

He spent the next day walking all over the city in the hope of tiring himself sufficiently to sleep away the afternoon. He dozed fitfully during the siesta hour. Nervously, he showered and dressed and then took the metro to the familiar street, determined to settle the thing once and for all, to discover the identity of the woman even if he had to force his way into the apartment.

As he approached the apartment, he saw her

standing on the terraza pacing up and down in the small space. She glanced from time to time to the street below. And then, as he came into view, she saw him and stopped suddenly. She faced him. She pressed her hands to her chest. She stared at him and squinted as though trying to focus her eyes. And then she began to cry. And then she waved her hand and called something that might have been his name.

It was she. Yes, yes, incredibly, impossibly, it . . . was . . . she.

And then, gasping for breath, he was running along the sidewalk. He burst into the lobby. There was no one there. He flew into the elevator and began the slow ascent to the seventh floor.

He stood in the vestibule catching his breath, his mind a torrent of thoughts. At last, his hand trembling, he knocked on the door three times—and waited. Again he knocked and listened. Did he hear a footstep? He knocked again. And again. He knocked until he was pounding on the door, unaware of the hysterical look in his eyes and the ghastly, tortured sound of his breathing. He pounded on the door with broken and bleeding knuckles while the sound of his pounding echoed and reechoed in the dark and silent, vacant rooms behind the door. . .

Next morning, they found him slumped on the floor. His head lay pressed against the door as though he had been listening there. The blood had dried on his broken, swollen hands and on his face there was a look of peace.

And so, perhaps, contrary to all logic and human understanding, they were together again . . . at last.

Charles A. Riccio, Jr., is a graduate of Boston University and a retired US Air Force Lt. Colonel. He is a municipal court judge, novelist, ("Falsehood and Foolishness"), short-story writer and a long-time resident of Europe. He lives in Denver with his wife of 50 years, Grace, at the home of their beautiful, spoiled-rotten, blue-point Birman cat, Dalila.

Something Animal

by Robert Baldwin

Many nights Hrabl recalled the voice of Talia, the Kurdish girl, her British English almost an echo as if from the bottom of a pit he himself had dug. He remembered this, too—the images of falling children—always the awful shots ringing out, and how bad dreams lied to him in the worst way.

"They are killing the children," Talia would say. "They are killing us. Are you killing us, too?"

Hrabl sat up in the middle of the night, his back wet with sweat, the image of falling children now no more than forms of light and darkness moving about the room. He searched the shadows for something familiar. All he recognized were the outlines against the wall, the shadow of tree limbs cast by moonlight. The faint light struck a mirror reflecting his face, the whiskers from a week of not shaving, the nose slightly bent to the left, the eyes round as a crow's. A cool wind blew through the open window, making him shiver. He touched the scar just below his collarbone and considered the other scar, the one not marked as a red welt across flesh.

His line of sight angled from the mirror to a map on the wall. The map bore the topography of the Korak Mountains and a yellow hand-drawn star, circled in red. He rose and tore the map from the wall, letting it drift to the floor. But the map disappeared. He looked at his bare feet and could not find it. Nothing appeared on the floor except his bare white feet. He remembered that now. There never really was a map. It was only part of the dream.

He shook himself back to his senses and walked down the moonlit hallway into the splayed shadows of the kitchen. He cupped his hand under the faucet and splashed cold water on his face, the back of his neck, across his bare chest, then drank from the pool of water in his hand, soothing his throat. He recalled his Hungarian grandfather, and the way his grandfather remarked, "How clear this water is. How simple. You see right through it. Can you imagine not having such a simple thing?"

Hrabl remembered the story of the war in which the Russians took his grandfather prisoner and chained him to a gang of men digging graves—how the Russians whipped him for digging too slow, then left him for dead. His grandfather crawled into the underbrush of the forest and curled up like a wounded animal in the warm spots of grass matted by deer spooked by his approach. His back oozed the pus and blood of sores from the whip. He ran to catch a slow-moving train, ended up in Gdansk, Poland, and worked his way across the Atlantic shoveling coal in the rusted belly of a steamer. In New York, he discovered the torch of the Statute of Liberty welcomed him to the stinking warrens of New York tenements.

He escaped to the pine forest of the North where he timbered trees, burned stumps and plowed dirt. In the furrows, he planted corn, potatoes, wheat and hay. In the grassy fields, he raised a few head of cattle, hogs and chickens, including a prize rooster that won a blue ribbon at the Gratiot County Fair.

Hrabl remembered how his grandfather took off his shirt, showing the muscles of his back, the welts from the Russian whip raised like lines of rope running from his shoulders to his waist. His grandfather slapped his knee, as if it were the best joke in the world. “Looks like our flag without the stars,” he said. “It’s nothing as long as you are alive. As long as you are free.”

Hrabl focused on the idea. He stepped outside, the damp ground beneath his feet, and squinted at the light of the stars faded by the waxing moon. Breathing was one thing, he thought. Being alive was another. The question of freedom brought his grandfather’s words back to him. “You think you are free?” his grandfather once asked. “When you see clearly, you are, just as clear as water in a glass.” Hrabl wondered how, in a mere two generations, such clarity had so completely lost itself in life’s continual accretions.

He went back inside, paced about the cabin in the dark, shadows split by moonlight. He lit a kerosene lamp, then retrieved his father’s .32 Winchester, the one his father had won in a raffle after returning from fighting the Germans in World War II. Hrabl cleaned the rifle, oiled it, sighted down the barrel. The problem, he considered, was not the lack of clarity. It was too much clarity, the way the forest draws a man forward with a steady tugging at his gut.

He knew the moon would soon rise fat and full and red. It would climb the sky and wash the dark night with milky seams of mystery and clarity. It would be a hunter’s moon; he would hunt again. A nerve in the back of his neck cinched like instinct, isolated and compelled, burning down the length of his spine—something akin to latent preservation, something animal, like the first cold rush of autumn.

He fixed his eyes on the corridor of darkness outside the open door, his angle of vision a tunnel he could not escape. He hung the rifle back on the wall and went back to bed and stretched a blanket over his legs and across his chest. His heart beat slow. He fell half asleep, dreaming of deer running in the moonlight. Shadows of the deer bounded across a meadow and into the darkness of the forest. The eyes of the deer glowed distantly like ice-green lanterns. The dream moved as its own dream and tore itself into the tatters of a relentless memory. With the memory came Talia's voice. "You kill the peshmerga," she said. "Do you now kill the children?"

The deer became Kurdish children in the crosshairs of his rifle sights. The dream fixed him to a spot from which he could not move; could not reach out with either hand to knock the rifle away, the rifle firing as if by itself. He turned his face away because it was a lie, all a lie. It had never happened, he knew, and it never could happen. Still it came at him, like metal to a magnet, and the rifle fired again and again as the children fell, one-by-one, into the dirt.

Talia whispered something to him again—something he could not comprehend. Her voice vanished in a hot sulphurous mist. A shot rang out, he fell to the ground, and something moist ran beneath his chest. Abstractly, he counted tiny red threads braided together, flowing from his gut. Quick heat filled the vacuum that surrounded him. With his weapon not two feet away, he could not move, could not reach out for it, even as the soft but deadly sure voices of the peshmerga rose below him on a slope of the Korak Mountains. He was no longer the hunter. The peshmerga were.

Now, his universe tilted on its axis again, until he found himself tracking a shot deer into the brush in Gratiot County, Michigan. He followed the trail of blood to the deer lying on its side, unable to move—the deer's eyes glazed with impending death. The heart of the deer pounded in his chest.

Another round bursting from an AK-47 brought him back to the Korak Mountains. The voices of the peshmerga echoed in his ears. The sound of felt boots gently kneaded the ground like a faint tremor of the earth. Hrabl did the only thing he could do. He lay upon the stony land as still as death and did not breathe, his chest did not rise or fall, and his heart stopped.

Hot mist like gas rose from the valley below, settled upon the side of the mountain, and fell across his face as his eyes rolled back into his head and peered into nothing, as if discovering the invisible side of another planet.

And then he woke.

He lay in his bed in his cabin in Gratiot County, Michigan. His hands quivered. He waited for the glimmer of daylight, for the light to burn the dream back into darkness.

* * *

The Pentagon still denied his nausea, his dizzy spells, the rash in his groin. It was no different than the story his father told of Nixon lying to the country on TV. It was expected; no different than had what happened to Talia. It was all worthless and nothing. It was like the red moon that would rise at sunset. It rose whether you wanted it to or not. The same was true of his camouflage trousers and shirt, his rubber-soled moccasins, his two fingers painting streaks of green and black on his forehead, down the crest of his bent nose, across his cheekbones. It was also true of the quiver of arrows he strapped over his shoulder, the compound bow in his hand, the way he walked deep into the woods.

A gust of wind swirled leaves around his feet. Branches reached for the sky like black arms of stone. He came upon a stream, where water seeped beneath the bank. He stopped long enough to breathe the moist air before crossing over a log. On the other side, a stand of poplars crowded one another for space and light. He was not envious.

In a mossy spot, the imprint of deertracks led

south, a direction he followed until he stood beneath an old oak with branches swaying white and bare in a lessening wind. Across a low marsh, a single redwinged blackbird swooped and dove. "You should have gone south by now," he said to the bird.

From the top of the old oak, a squirrel cackled with what sounded like the voice of an old Kurdish woman. He buried the thought and followed the deer-tracks instead. They petered out just before he came upon the remnant of a homestead, where a windmill rose haphazardly, as if ready to teeter over, crashing onto the ground in the next windstorm.

Scattered about the house lay a rusted cultivator, a stained watertank, a pile of boards once forming the walls of a shed. Ragged junipers surrounded the house, its windows absent any glass. He stood in the doorway and considered what kind of man and woman built and broke their lives on this place. "*Talia,*" he whispered. "*Oh, Talia.*"

From inside the house rose the scent of ashes mingling with the angle of autumn sunlight. Against one wall lay charred pieces of floorboards ripped up and burnt by other hunters. He despised the thought of other humans, other hunters, and turned away when his eye caught bare and rusted bedsprings lying on the bedroom floor, the long indentation in the middle of the springs.

Sweat warmed the back of his neck, his forehead, his face, and he retreated outside into the shade of the woods, where a cricket sang, a wren called, and wind blew cool on his face, a rush of air unlike anything any woman had ever been able to do. "You've never had it like this, have you?" Talia had asked. And when she brushed her hand along his side, her hand warm, her skin like brown cream, her eyes dark as obsidian, he melted between what he had to do and what he wanted to do.

Now he climbed a gradual slope through the trees.

The slope rose steeper, rising to a hill, where his shadow crawled up before him. He knew what waited at the top. With each step he came closer, not making any sound, his breath measured and quiet. He edged over a line of rusted barbed wire. A breeze blew in his hair. He held up the palm of his hand, feeling the play and heave of its currents, making sure he was downwind.

A buck snort startled him.

His moccasins touched the side of the hill quieter than the step before. Gradually, moving like a ghost, carefully planting his feet, as if not touching the soil at all, with the sound of buck snorts growing near, he reached the top of the hill, where he lay down on his belly in a stand of sumac.

Before him pranced young bucks in rut, digging at the earth with their hooves, furrowing the ground with their antlers. They scraped the bark from the trees with their horns. They charged one another and bashed skulls. They locked horns, twisted from side to side, kicked dirt with their hind hooves.

Hrabl placed an arrow to the string of his bow and sighted past the feathers, down the length of the graphite shaft, past the razor tip and aimed for the heart of the biggest buck.

The breeze shifted, stirred upward and down, circled, and came now from behind. Hrabl held his breath.

Immediately several whitetails flicked up like flags as each deer, except the biggest buck, leaped away through the trees. The eyes of the big buck locked with Hrabl, as if a dark corridor filled with a shot of light, until all of Hrabl's breath seeped from his lungs.

He had let the arrow fly before. Each time it had sunk deep into the buck's chest. And the buck bounded up, as if hit by lightning, and ran thirty yards, then dropped dead.

Hrabl released the tension. He took the arrow from the bow. He stood and waved his arms and gasped for air to shout. His voice sounded distant, like the voice of another. "Run, you silly animal! Run into the trees with the rest of them!"

The buck tossed his head, antlers flashing in the sunlight. Still, he stood there, watching Hrabl watch him.

"Go," Hrabl whispered. "Before it's too late."

The buck leaped away through the brush with his tail flashing white.

Hrabl turned and descended the hill. At the bottom he fired the arrow into the air, the bow string twanged, the feathers of the arrow whistled, and the arrow disappeared above the trees into the sky. Dusty sunlight surrounded the homestead. He sat in the light and buried his face in his hands. He knew the nightmare about the children in his crosshairs was a lie, that it had never happened, that he would have killed himself before killing children. Yet the image remained, as if invented by his conscience to torment him for what he could have done to save Talia. Better to be dead than not save her, he thought.

But he didn't know. He never really would know. He lifted his face from his hands and discovered the green and black camouflage smeared onto his palms. He stared at his hands and laughed, then laughed again. The echo of his laugh resounded through the trees like a madman, like Talia laughing deep in the mountains half a world away—the sweet crazy sound of her voice as she escaped Hrabl's grip to warn away the old woman down the valley.

Once again, Hrabl stood from behind the rocks in the Korak Mountains where he and his unit had once hid. He yelled for Talia to come back, to not run away, to save herself. Then the old woman was not a woman but a disguised member of the peshmerga who flung aside his robe and sprayed a round from his Kalishnikov up the slope, against the rocks, riddling Talia with bloody red holes. Immediately, Hrabl's unit opened up on him and cut him in half with their machine guns. Then the peshmerga were everywhere—above them, below them, beside them—their guns blasting away, the American soldiers falling among the rocks, and Hrabl and the survivors fleeing for their lives.

Hrabl blinked. The day had turned to dusk. He leaned his bow against the open door of the old abandoned homestead, dropped his quiver to the ground. He positioned the rusty bedsprings in the doorway. He lay down on the springs, where the weight of another man, another woman, had left their indentation.

He lay there, barely breathing, and remembered the one night in the Korak Mountains when he had lain down with Talia beneath the stars. She touched him soft and breathed low and smelled faintly of woodsmoke in her hair. Now, to the west, the sun sank red behind the horizon. Above the hill to the east, the moon rose as if a reflection, round and red and painful to see.

Soon the deer drifted off the hill, out of the trees, into the opening, where they became the Kurdish children, dancing in circles of moonlight.

Robert Baldwin is a Denver attorney and founding member of Baldwin & Brown, P.C. His novella, "Door of Water," was a Denver best seller. His novel, "The Water Thief," is forthcoming from GreyCore Press in the fall of 2002 and was a finalist for the Ariadne Fiction Prize.

Opening Day

by Henry J. Rickelman

It was early morning in late October, still dark, the opening day of elk hunting season. My hunting partner and I were camped on the northern boundary of Eagles Nest Wilderness Area in the high country of central Colorado. It was cold, well below freezing. I knew if there were any light in our tent, I would see my breath—big clouds of it.

I had slept only fitfully, the excitement accompanying the arrival of hunting season having prevented sound sleep. I was bundled up in my down sleeping bag, hopeful that Jim would get up and start the coffee.

Our routine hasn't changed much over the years. The wind-up alarm clock sounds off at 4:30 a.m. I lie there, feigning sleep, while Jim, still in his sleeping bag, leans over and fires up the propane heater. We wait for the tent to warm up a bit. Jim is usually the first one up and dressed, and this morning was no exception.

"You goin' huntin', or are you just gonna lay there?" he asked, as he finished lacing up his well-worn hiking boots. I mumbled something unintelligible.

I listened to Jim rustling around for a few minutes, gathering his gear, then heard him opening the tentflap.

"I'm gonna go fill my elk tag now," Jim

announced. "I'll come fetch you later to help me drag it out."

I lay there as Jim tinkered around outside in the camp kitchen heard the hiss of gas from the propane stove and the "whuumphh" as it ignited. The smell of coffee brewing finally prompted me to rise. Grudgingly, I climbed out of my sleeping bag. It was then that I noticed how truly cold it was. Shivering in my longjohns, I decided to antagonize Jim a bit.

"Isn't that coffee ready yet?"

Jim grumbled under his breath.

Sitting on the edge of my army surplus cot, I turned the propane heater toward me and, as I shivered, surveyed my clothes and gear.

"Hey, Jim! What's the thermometer say?" I yelled.

"Nine!" came the reply. I knew it was cold, but nine?

"Clouds?"

"Not a one." That explained why it was so cold.

Although nine degrees is downright frigid, it could warm up considerably, maybe even up to 50 or 60 degrees. The weather in the Colorado high country is quite unpredictable and the temperature can vary 40 or 50 degrees in a day. As all high country hunters know, this requires a layered dress system. The trick is to wear enough to stay warm and dry, yet not so much that you can't carry the layers of clothing you inevitably shed as the day warms up.

I dressed, stuffed the extra gear in the back of my blaze hunting vest, and was ready to go. As I exited the tent, Jim greeted me with a steaming cup of coffee.

"Have a cup," he said. Helluva hunting partner, that Jim. I eagerly accepted the steaming coffee and offered to cook breakfast.

"I'll have two over-easy and four links," said Jim.

As I heated up the iron skillet and retrieved the eggs and sausage, I asked, "What's the plan? Do we head up Gore Trail or down to 'Bull Run'?"

Jim and I have been coming to Eagles Nest for eight years now and have given names to many parts of the wilderness area. After each day's hunt, we sit around the campfire and share our hunting tales. If the other deems the story worthy of honor, he appoints a name for the area where the hunting deed occurred. We then put these names on our topographical maps, which makes for easier reference. Every year the goal is to have at least one hunting story worthy of earning a name.

"Bull Run" got its name two years ago when, like a man obsessed, Jim ran about a mile up and over three ridges, trying to get ahead of some elk he saw traversing the mountainside below and parallel to him. After topping the third ridge, he headed down into a gulley, chest heaving, and there, squatted at the base of a large lodgepole pine with his Remington Model 700 across his lap. He scanned the woods below. Minutes passed. Just when he was sure the elk had disappeared, not one, but two bull elk emerged from the timber not ten yards away, heading directly toward him.

Jim held his breath, heart pounding in his chest. He sat there, frozen, afraid even to blink or move his eyes, while the first bull, a young spike, passed him so close Jim swears he could have poked him with his rifle. The second bull was legal, with an unusually large four-point rack. It, too, walked right past him and stopped about 20 yards away, facing uphill toward the other younger bull and giving Jim a broadside view of the impressive beast. He decided to take the second bull.

It would be a difficult shot. Jim was in a squatting position with his back against a tree, facing downhill, perpendicular to the bull. His rifle was lying across his bent knees, pointed away from his target. As long as he didn't move, he was invisible—for the moment. However, to get off the shot, he would have to move his legs, pivot and bring the rifle around toward the bull.

Jim would have to be quick; once he moved, the bull would sense him and it could bolt, making any shot risky. After his "bull run," Jim didn't relish the thought of tracking a wounded bull across several miles of high country. If he couldn't get off a clean kill shot, he would take no shot at all.

Jim was winded. After his long run and squatting for so long, he wasn't sure he could trust his legs to respond. But he had to try. In one quick motion, he pushed up on his legs, pivoted and dropped to one knee. Simultaneously, he swung his rifle around, brought the scope up to his eye, and put the crosshairs just behind the elk's right shoulder. He squeezed the trigger. The rifle bucked, its report echoing across the mountain. Jim immediately chambered another round.

The bull didn't move. It simply stood there, from all appearances unscathed. Jim watched intently, his pulse racing, wondering if, perhaps, he had missed. He waited for the bull to fall, willed it to fall. Instead, the bull started slowly up the hill. Jim set the crosshairs again, but a second shot was unnecessary. The bull stumbled and, as it struggled to stay on its feet, snorted loudly. It stumbled again, then lost its balance and fell to the ground.

Unknown to Jim at the time, his "bull run" had ended just 30 yards shy of an old Forest Service logging road. This made packing out the bull ridiculously easy. After we field-dressed the animal, we backed Jim's four-wheel drive pickup the short distance up the hill through the trees. Then, with no small amount of effort, we heaved/pushed/pulled the bull into the back of the pickup and drove back to camp where we hung the beast whole on our game pole.

That night, around the campfire, we sipped single malt Scotch and smoked expensive cigars, and Jim related his hunting-tale-of-the-day with great flourish. Deeming the story worthy of commemoration, I ceremoniously dubbed the area “Bull Run.”

“I say let’s take Gore Trail over to ‘Bull Meadow.’ If we don’t have any luck at first light, we’ll hit the timber at ‘Jack’s Glen’ and work our way down the ridge to ‘Headless Doe Gulch,’” Jim said.

It was a good plan. The meadows are a great place to start the morning—elk and mule deer often spend the night feeding in them, then head into the timber after first light to find a safe place to bed down for the day.

We finished our eggs and sausage and gulped down the remainder of the coffee. Dawn was not far off, and we wanted to be in place at first light. As we headed out into the dark, I wondered what adventures lay in store for us. I hoped that, by day’s end, I would have a tale worthy of telling.

We headed south on Gore Trail, which meanders southward over several ridges and drainages below Mount Powell, a “thirteener” towering over the sprawling forest of Eagles Nest Wilderness Area. After about an hour of hiking, we crossed the first ridge and began our descent into the next drainage. “Bull Meadow,” our destination, was a large grassy meadow tucked away in the dark timber, about a quarter-mile above the trail at the bottom of the drainage. A couple of years ago, some hunters in a neighboring camp had spooked several bulls in this particular meadow before there was enough light to shoot; hence the name “Bull Meadow.” We hoped to find elk grazing there at first light.

About half-way down into the drainage, we left the trail and skirted our way across the slope so we could come in from above. With our small flashlights, we negotiated our way through the timber and held up when we estimated we were about a hundred yards above the upper west edge of the meadow.

“Which side you want?” I whispered to Jim.

Jim just pointed south. I nodded and we split up

to take our respective positions. After a few yards, I stopped, clicked off my flashlight and closed my eyes for a couple of minutes to get my night vision. When I opened my eyes, I could see fairly well and began slowly negotiating my way through the forest deadfall to the north side of the meadow, concentrating on not making any sound. The last thing I wanted to do was crack a tree limb underfoot and spook any elk that might be in the area. It was slow going, and I began to worry that I wouldn't make the meadow by first light.

Eventually, I reached the upper north side of the meadow. It was still dark and the wind was perfect—a gentle, if cold, breeze rose up from the meadow below. I snuck up to a tree at the meadow's edge and stood up against it, waiting, trying to make out any shapes that might be moving down in the grassy open. The sky began to lighten, and I focused my eyes intently on the meadow, hoping an elk would materialize out of the thinning darkness. Soon it was light enough to confirm there were no elk standing in the meadow waiting to be harvested.

I looked across the meadow and saw Jim on the other side. He, too, was standing against a tree at the edge of the timber. I watched him for a couple of minutes and he was as still as the tree. His only sign of life was an intermittent cloud of breath in the frigid air.

I returned my gaze to the meadow and scanned the edges, looking into the surrounding timber. I listened to the many sounds emanating from the forest, trying to identify that sound which might betray the presence of an elk. I breathed the cold air slowly in through my nose, gathering the various smells, trying to catch a whiff of any nearby elk. I saw nothing, heard nothing, smelled nothing.

After about an hour, it was fully light. I could peer more deeply into the timber surrounding the meadow, but still saw nothing. I began to concentrate on an elk appearing, as if by sheer force of thought I could will an elk to step out into the meadow. Still nothing.

Then, out of the corner of my eye, I detected movement—Jim had started toward me. Our meadow watch was at an end. Just in time, too. My feet were starting to get cold.

"Well, there must be tastier grass somewhere else," Jim said, after he crossed over, "Let's backtrack on the trail and hit the timber at 'Jack's Glen.'"

Jim led the way back to the trail. As we hiked toward the ridge we had crossed earlier in the dark, we went through a small clearing and, as the trail took us back into the timber, I began scanning the forest on each side for any movement. About 50 yards in, we came upon a small dribbling creek. After we stone-stepped across, I looked to the right, down the gulch into which the stream flowed, and saw a dark form lurking in the trees about 40 yards away. I stopped and stared hard, abruptly realizing that the dark form was an elk, staring equally hard right back at me. I quickly raised my rifle and, through my 3.5 x 10 scope, observed the elk's head, and the large rack of antlers above. Several tree limbs effectively camouflauged the rack and I couldn't count points. However, I discerned four large browtines, confirming a legal bull. I put the crosshairs between his front legs, raised my rifle to his vitals, and squeezed the trigger.

My Winchester Model 70 bucked, discharging the 180-grain Nosler partition bullet. As the gun went off, I saw Jim, out of the corner of my eye, throwing his arms up and hitting the ground as if a bomb had just gone off over his head. He was ahead of me on the trail and had no way of knowing I was going to take a shot. He recovered quickly, though. Looking back at me and seeing my rifle leveled into the woods, he dropped to one knee, raised his rifle and began scanning the woods above the creek for any other elk that might have taken off through the woods at my shot.

As I chambered another round, the bull side-stepped and slowly began to turn. He took another step, faltered, then stumbled and fell to the ground. I stood my ground as Jim surveyed the woods for other elk. When he was satisfied that no other animals were going to show themselves, he lowered his rifle and started back down the trail toward me.

"Well?" he inquired as he approached.

"A bull," I replied. "He's down." Though I hadn't physically exerted myself, my heart was pounding and I felt out of breath. Adrenaline is a funny thing.

"Kill shot?" he asked.

I simply nodded.

"Well," Jim said. "Let's have a look-see."

I led the way through the trees toward the spot where the bull had been standing. I stopped when I saw the bull on the ground, about forty feet away. Jim came up to my side.

"He looks big," Jim said. "Let's give him a few minutes."

Many a hunter has been surprised when approaching a downed elk that they were certain was dead but that, when approached, came mysteriously, and sometimes violently, back to life. Neither of us relished the thought of being gored by an injured bull.

"I'm in no hurry," I said.

The bull didn't move for several minutes and we deemed it safe to approach. We walked over, unloaded our rifles, leaned them up against a tree and began examining the bull.

It was a large animal, probably 900 pounds or more. Its rack, while no trophy, was certainly respectable—five points per side, typically formed.

"Let's get to work," Jim said. As all experienced hunters know, the real work begins after you pull the trigger.

We stripped down to our shirts, hung our blaze orange vests conspicuously on a couple of tree limbs and began the arduous task of field dressing a large elk.

We saved the heart and liver, then skinned and quartered the elk, putting each quarter into a game bag. We cut off the backstraps and tenderloins and put them into a plastic garbage bag. Next, we used my Wyoming saw to take the rack. Finally, we hung the quarters from a tree so the cold air could better chill down the meat. Two hours after I had pulled the trigger, we were ready to head back to camp.

We reached camp by noon. After putting the backstraps and organs in a cooler, we grabbed some lunch, then headed back for the two front quarters. We returned to camp just before dark, dead tired. We would haul out the hind quarters the following morning.

That evening, we fried up some elk heart as an appetizer, then dined on elk steaks, cut from the backstraps, boiled potatoes and canned Veg-All. A better meal I cannot recall.

After supper, we built a fire and brought out the cigars and single-malt Scotch. Although the event of harvesting my bull took all of a few seconds, we talked about it for hours.

Late in the evening, we reached that point where we were beyond conversation, where each of us was lost in his own thoughts, staring into the campfire, content, warmed not only by the fire and the spirits in our bellies, but by the feeling of accomplishment, of a day well-spent in the wild, and by the comaraderie and kinship shared by hunting partners. At that moment Jim rose from his chair. He cleared his throat and raised his glass.

"Harry, the time for the naming has come. After much thought, deliberation and reflection, I hereby declare the following: Whereas, the bull elk you took this day did attempt to secrete itself during our passing by quietly standing still and hiding amongst the trees; and whereas said bull's behavior and deportment while attempting to conceal itself in said manner was sly, shifty, shrewd and devious; be it now known that I hereby designate and name the gulch wherein said bull was harvested 'Sneaky Bull Gulch,' and we shall refer to it as such henceforth." With that, Jim downed his drink with a grimace.

I smiled and followed suit.

"Sneaky Bull Gulch"—a new name for our maps.

I liked it.

Henry ("Harry") Rickelman moved to Colorado in 1987 and discovered a passion for hunting and fly-fishing in the Colorado high country. Harry writes stories about his outdoor exploits and "Opening Day" chronicles certain of his elk-hunting experiences. When he's not hunting or fishing, Harry practices civil litigation and family law.

Big Wind

by John P. Frey

For 20 years, Peter Randle had been riding bicycles and camping all over the country. He could count on one hand the number of times he had cut a day short because of weather or for any other reason. It was just a matter of pride and self-respect.

"Kelly, you have to just keep riding and try to forget about the stupid wind," he said.

At the height of a particularly strong gust she shouted back at him, "Peter, I just don't understand what is so frigging important about an extra five miles. Let's just flag down a pickup truck, give the driver 10 bucks, toss the bikes in the back, and head for Overton. We know there's a motel out there by the interstate, with air conditioning, cold beer and empty beds. We have credit cards and three graduate degrees between us. Why can't we just hang it up for today?"

He knew he could never really make her understand. Quitting and checking into a motel was something you did in your regular life or on some organized bike tour where they carried your gear and did everything else for you except pat the Johnson's Baby Powder on your butt in the morning.

He was ready to admit that Kelly was getting a real taste of wind on a bike today. Wind hadn't really had a place in his life until he developed his bicycle passion. Before that, wind just rustled the trees, blew hot dog wrappers at ballgames, knocked wobbly tee shots into the rough, and was sometimes the precursor of a bit of rain. All that changed on a bicycle. The wind is the enemy, giving voice to your fears. It comes at you silently at first, and never from behind. As it rises, you first hope that it is just the gritty wash from a passing truck, and that it will settle down. Soon it is upon you, either steadily or in gusts, and always in your face. The road may turn, but you know the wind will turn with it. It is resourceful and relentless. It makes downhill stretches flat, and flat stretches climbs. On a hot day, a zephyr becomes a desert sirocco, draining the moisture from your skin. On a cold, wet day it drives the rain through layers of GORE-TEX to your very soul. He wondered how many times over the years he had lowered his head into the wind, looked down at his slowly turning pedals and muttered, "Fuckin' wind."

Kelly was no rider, but in the dark of the previous winter she had agreed to this trip. She signed on for a number of reasons, only some of which she would admit to. Mostly, it was because she was lonely. Both of their girls were in college, and there was a void in their lives as big as the old house they rambled around in.

On all of his previous trips, Peter had been accompanied by two buddies, both lawyers like him. They always camped, carried all their gear, and set impossible daily goals in mileage and elevation gain. They exhausted themselves during the day and then drank and ate too much in camp at night.

When he suggested a bike trip for the two of them he was surprised by her reaction. She was hesitant but admitted that she was curious about all his years of bicycle adventures. Besides, she needed something new. Anything new. She'd only recently learned to hate her job, something he had been able to accomplish after only four or five years of practicing law.

They sealed the deal on a Friday night in the middle of February over burritos and Dos Equis at their favorite Mexican restaurant. They had first eaten there just after they met, nearly 28 years before. The menu was still the same and some of the help was, too, and they found that comforting in a town that was beginning to look like everything had been built in the last twenty minutes.

They compromised on distance, agreeing to a few 40- or 50-mile days in exchange for one or two of 70-plus. But they were stuck on the wind. He knew of nowhere on earth where he could guarantee her no headwinds, and she wasn't budging unless he did.

They finally settled on a ride across Nebraska on US Highway 30, the old Lincoln Highway. It looked to be six days of riding, covering about 370 miles. Highway 30 follows the Platte River across Nebraska and for much of the way is the mirror image of Interstate 80. The interstate is on the south side of the river, while Highway 30 is on the north, a mile or two away. The maps showed plenty of little towns on the Lincoln Highway, and he assumed that what they lacked by way of accommodations could easily be found at interstate interchanges, a short ride away. Nebraska was flat, on that they could certainly agree. They could drive from their home in Fort Collins to Julesburg, just a few miles from the western border of Nebraska the first morning, and leave the car there. He was sure they could find a couple of high school or college kids to drive it to Blair on the Missouri River, the eastern border of the state. And the wind? It would blow, that was for sure, but by riding in the middle of June they could start their days early enough to miss a good deal of it, and what they did get should be at their backs.

They left Fort Collins for Julesburg early on a Saturday morning. He loved the eastern plains of Colorado any time of year, but an early morning in May or June was the best. The prairie grasses were up, turning the empty, rolling hills an emerald green. When a perfect sunrise caught those hills in the springtime, the expanse looked as much like a restless ocean as a blooming prairie. They drove on with the quiet anticipation of new adventure. They were both bound up with fear of failure but they didn't talk about that. They never talked about that.

They got to Julesburg at mid-morning, took the bikes off the top of the Durango and began loading them with their bags and camping gear. All of their stuff added about 40 pounds to each bike and made them handle more like mules than bicycles.

They parked near the town water tower where they had planned to meet the two boys who were going to ferry their car to Blair. They were both sophomores at University of Colorado, and friends of their oldest daughter. They drove up in a old GMC pickup about 20 minutes late, looking as if they had spent the night trying to prove to themselves that night life in Julesburg in the summer was every bit a match for Boulder. If possible, the truck looked worse than they did. It had to make it to Blair and back, and that seemed problematic to him, but apparently not to them. He longed for the days when he felt like that—when running out of gas was just a part of life and not a crisis.

They agreed with the boys that they would leave the Durango in the parking lot of the courthouse in Blair. They would get it there no later than Thursday afternoon. With that, Peter and Kelly said their goodbyes to the boys and began pedaling east toward Big Springs, Nebraska, and their intersection with the Lincoln Highway. That was only two days ago; he could hardly believe it.

Their first day on the road was Julesburg to Ogallala, only about 35 miles. They pedaled out of town on Highway 138 and followed the South Platte River across the Nebraska border, covering the 10-mile distance to Big Springs in less than an hour. The road surface was fine, the weather was perfect, and save a tractor or two, there was no traffic at all. Most important, it was flat, and they had a tailwind.

They had stopped for a moment at the Nebraska border just two miles from Julesburg, and taken pictures of each other and the bikes in front of an oversized billboard with peeling red paint on a dull white background that proclaimed, "WELCOME TO NEBRASKA, THE GOOD LIFE."

"This is OK," said Kelly with some degree of satisfaction. "When do we eat and where do we camp?"

He was excited to see how relaxed she seemed. "Kelly, you have only ridden two miles, let's talk about eating in Big Springs and worry about camping when we get to Ogallala."

"Don't lecture me big boy; I'm starting to get the hang of this touring stuff," she said, and he believed it. He was delighted that the trip had started out so well, but he was also a bit jealous of what he knew awaited her down the road. She was about to learn just how extraordinary it was to see the world at 12 miles an hour. He thought about his first bike trip in Colorado years before, and how he had been hooked by that sensation. It spoils car trips forever.

They bought sandwich makings and fruit at the only store in Big Springs and headed for the city park. The park was notable only for the presence of a retired Union Pacific steam locomotive and a historical marker that told the story of Sam Bass. Sam was an obscure outlaw who robbed his first train in Big Springs in the mid 1880s. In western Nebraska you didn't mess with the Union Pacific Railroad. The marker made a particular point of explaining that Sam got what was coming to him a few years later at the hands of the Texas Rangers. Peter knew that the UP was a lifeline in Nebraska and that the UP tracks followed Highway 30 closely all the way across the state. The thundering roar of the coal and freight trains would be with them day and night, all the way to the Missouri River.

They met Highway 30 a bit north and east of Big

Springs and followed it to Ogallala. They set up their tent at a campground just south of town, hard by the interstate. They swam in the campground pool, cooked dinner, and then went to sleep listening to the constant sound of the big rigs passing by on I-80. Modern-day prairie schooners.

The weather held on Sunday, and with an early start they easily made the 53 miles to North Platte by mid-afternoon. They visited the Buffalo Bill Cody Homestead and then pitched their tents at the Lincoln County Fairgrounds. They treated themselves to dinner out, courtesy of Colonel Sanders.

They wanted to get to Overton, a distance of about 76 miles, on the third day. They had a simple breakfast in North Platte and hit the road early. It was hot, but clear and calm, and they made satisfactory time to Gothenburg and through Cozad. They stopped in Lexington to pick up groceries for dinner and breakfast since they didn't expect much by way of accommodations in Overton. They left Lexington late on Monday afternoon. They only had eleven miles to go to finish the day. The wind came up at as they reached the half-way mark.

It came at them from the west and then the north. Each gust pushed them to the very edge of the road shoulder, then relented, causing them to veer back into the eastbound traffic lane. With five miles left and nearly an hour of daylight, he was pretty sure they could struggle into Overton and find a motel. He'd prefer the tent, but he knew Kelly was ready for a little civilization after two nights on the ground.

"God, Peter, I really can't stand this," she screamed at him, "I'm not sure I can ride another foot."

Any distance over 70 miles in a day is bad enough on a bike, but when you add the wind, it can be impossible.

"I'm with you," he said. "This is awful, but we are damn close to out of choices. It's farther back to Lexington than on to Overton, and I don't think there's anything in between. I know we can find a motel by the interstate in Overton. We just have to try and make it."

She covered her face from the next gust, which carried its own special blend of stinging wind-borne dirt and grit. "OK," she mumbled, "If my choices are setting up a tent in a gully next to the railroad tracks and listening to those iron horses rumble by every half hour, or giving up my life trying to fight my way to a half-clean motel bathtub, I'll go for the tub and keep riding. But no pictures. I don't want to be a subject in one of your show-and-tell adventure stories at the next Christmas party."

"We'll make it," he said with an uncertain grin, and looked back over his shoulder to check for traffic before starting out again. What he saw brought him to full alert. The dark rain clouds that had been chasing the wind had turned black. The entire western horizon seemed to be a monster thunderstorm rolling east down Highway 30. It looked like it was going to arrive fast and in a mighty angry mood. Within minutes they were being pelted by random raindrops and occasional hailstones, which resounded convincingly off their helmets.

"We gotta find some kind of shelter right now," he said. "This sucker is coming for us, and we need to be under a roof, even if it's an old pole barn. Stay close in behind me and draft a little if you can. As soon as I see any sign of shelter I'm going to pull off."

"I don't care what or where," she said. "I just gotta get off of this bike and out of this goddamned wind."

He saw the abandoned motor court on the north side of the highway before she did. He quickly made the decision that broken down and overgrown or not, this was their best chance of avoiding the consequences of a huge storm.

Motor courts like this one dotted the Lincoln Highway for its full distance across the United States. They had been a staple of travel along the highway in the

'30s, '40s and early '50s. They were all pretty much the same. Located on the outskirts of small towns, they had nine or 10 separate, but very small cabins and a larger house out front that the proprietors called home. A metal double bed, a sink, a hot plate, an ice box and a kerosene heater for a bit of warmth was all you got for your 10 bucks, but they were a welcome stop for tired tourists. As surely as the Oregon Trail and Pony Express routes in Nebraska gave way to the Lincoln Highway and the Union Pacific mainline, so had the highway given way to Interstate 80, causing the sudden death of the motor court.

This one was set back quite away from the north side of the road, with only some big cottonwood trees left to announce its existence. A line of overgrown hedges in front blocked most the view from the road of the main house and the cabins. The court looked as if it had been standing alone and unattended for at least 20 years. The wood remaining on the buildings was a rotting shade of brown.

As Kelly and Peter turned into the rutted, weed-covered driveway, the storm arrived in full fury. They grabbed their gear, hid the bikes in a large clump of the overgrown hedge, and ran for the only cabin that looked like it still had a roof.

They pushed their way through the half-opened door and were greeted by a waterfall of leaks from the roof. Along one wall there was tangled plumbing, which had at one time been connected to a sink that now lay smashed on the filthy, wooden floor. There were three windows, one in front by the door and one on each side of the tiny cabin. They were all broken out and the glass from the panes mixed on the floor with the porcelain from the smashed sink and the droppings from a thousand mice. The only furniture was a rusted old double bed, with only the springs remaining, covered by a moldy piece of plywood. In one corner was a crumpled pack of cigarettes, several empty beer cans and a sports page from the *Los Angeles Times* dated May 12, just about a month before. This puzzled him, but he said nothing to Kelly.

"Well, I'm glad they had a room, but after 27 years did we really need to splurge on the honeymoon suite? You might call the desk, and see if they can get the house carpenter over here to mount a ceiling mirror over that bed and hook up the hot tub."

He welcomed back her sense of humor.

His bike-touring friends regularly made fun of him for all the gear he carried on his bike. But when they needed something, he had it, and that usually shut them up. He had forced her to follow suit. Out of their panniers came a candle lantern, a back-packing cook stove, a Boy Scout cook kit complete with utensils, the grub they had purchased in Lexington, dry clothes and a little radio. Of course, they had their sleeping bags and pads, which he plunked down on the squeaky bed with some degree of satisfaction. He looked at her and smiled.

She was brushing aside debris on the floor to make a cooking space. "I know what you're thinking big boy, and you can keep on thinking it until we get ourselves dried off, warmed up and fed. Duty before sex, old timer."

"I was just planning ahead and trying to make a comfortable little nest for you that's all," he responded innocently. "I have a little bottle of wine tucked away in that left pannier, and I thought maybe we could listen to the farm reports on the radio during a romantic dinner by candle lantern light, and who knows where that might lead?"

She was peeling off her wet riding stuff. "Might lead you to separate quarters," she responded with a grin. "Anyhow, let's get dry, make dinner, get into that wine, and call it a day. Didn't you say that we could zip those mummy bags together? Sounds pretty good to me, to tell you the truth."

The storm had brought dusk early and as the light

disappeared, so did the wind and the rain. They had plenty of water in their water bottles to cook the pasta they had picked up in Lexington over the little stove. They added the fresh broccoli and topped the concoction off with Parmesan cheese from a plastic film canister he carried in his bags. They tuned in some vintage country tunes on his beat-up little old radio, shared the wine, and dined in a perfectly acceptable silence, originating in the physical exertion of the day and their successful struggle with the elements. As they finished the last of the wine, a full moon peaked in through one of the broken windows, outshining the candle lantern. She blew out the candle and without speaking, they zipped the sleeping bags together and climbed in.

Later, as they held each other and slowly drifted off to sleep, he wondered when they last had gone to bed without doing the dishes, and when the springs of that old bed had last squeaked with that much pure joy.

He came awake when the first car drove in. He saw the reflection of the headlights come very close to the cabin and then go dark. The engine idled in the darkness. He was damn glad they had hidden the bikes in the brush out front. He knew in his gut that right now they needed to be quiet and to go undiscovered. He didn't wake Kelly.

"Probably just kids from town drinking beer," he thought. But somehow he knew that it wasn't. After a minute or so the motor shut down, and there was absolute silence. Nothing but the crickets in the cottonwood trees and occasional drips of water from the leaks in the roof. The wind was coming up a bit again and there was distant thunder and lightning flashes that periodically exposed the inside of the tiny cabin. He lay in the stillness for nearly an hour, wondering what the hell he should do or shouldn't do.

The arrival of the second car in the same manner as the first struck so much fear in him that it caused his testicles to tingle.

He heard the first car door open shortly after the headlights of the second car went out and its engine silenced. Then a second door. He felt as much as saw the reflections from flashlights across the roof of the cabin.

"You fuckers are late. We've been sittin' in this shithole for an hour."

"We fuckin' got busted for goin' 95 some place in Wyoming. Dickhead cop even searched the trunk. He would have shit if he'd looked inside that suitcase. But we're here, we still got the shit, and it's cool if you got the money."

The first voice was quick to respond, "Look dude, this deal's been goin' down with you assholes every month for six months. You suppose we'd drive to this shithole from Chicago without the cash? We just need to make sure you really got the shit, and that you fuckers didn't do too much of it yourselves on the road from LA, before we give you nothin."

"It's cool; it's cool," said the second voice. "Let's go inside, get this deal done and get the fuck out of here."

They were so close to the cabin that Peter didn't even have time to wake Kelly. There were four of them, and they were in the door and on to Kelly and Peter in a second. The beams from flashlights as long as night sticks were full in their faces.

Voice two shouted, "Who the fuck are you and what the Christ are you doing here?"

For a moment nobody seemed in control of anything. Then, voice one, the Chicago accent, took over quickly by producing a .357 pistol from under his leather jacket. At the sign of the exposed firepower three other jacket zippers screamed and, in a moment, four guns were trained on Peter and Kelly.

"Well, looks like you two assholes have set up quite a little love nest here. How the hell did you get here anyway?"

"We rode in on bicycles," Peter said. "We got caught

in the storm and needed shelter."

Voice one remained in charge. "Well, Mom and Pop, you better figure you just rode your last bicycles and found your last shelter. We got a little business to do here and then we'll do a little business with you. Get the fuck out of that bag and over there on the floor. And shut the fuck up."

Kelly and Peter crawled out of the sleeping bag and sat against the wall next to the bed and under the window. Kelly had been sleeping in running shorts and a t-shirt and as she got up her form did not go unnoticed by the shadowed faces behind the four guns.

"Maybe we do a little more than just business with you mama," said a third voice behind one of the flashlights.

"Shut up asshole, we're here to score some shit, not fall in love," said voice one. "Now make sure that shit is the real thing and then we'll show the boys from LA the cash. I'll watch the bicycle dickhead and his sweety."

Peter was sure they meant to kill them both. He watched as the four went about a scene they had obviously played out before. They snorted the coke, weighed it on a little portable scale, and then counted out the money. He could see what they were doing through the beams of the flashlights, but because of the rising storm he could barely hear a word they said. The wind was back, pushing rain and hail through the open windows and pounding off what was left of the roof. The thunder and lightning were constant, and very close. At the height of the storm it looked like the deal was done. The four men started to argue and Peter was afraid it was about Kelly. He couldn't bring himself to think of what they might be deciding.

Two of the men got ready to leave the cabin. One had the cocaine bound for Chicago, the other with the cash headed back to LA. Voices one and two stayed behind with Kelly and Peter.

"Wait in the cars," voice one said to the two walking out, "me and California Dreamin' here are going to take care of Mom and Pop." They started for Peter and Kelly.

"Get up Pop," voice one said to Peter, "you and I are going to go singing in the rain over by them cottonwood trees."

Voice two grunted and then grabbed Kelly by the neck forcing her to her feet. "You're going singing in the rain out there too bitch, but not until you and I have done a little dancing in here."

Peter heard what he thought was a ridiculously loud freight train rushing through the raging storm. He heard it for just a moment or so before the explosion blew apart the cabin. In that moment he thought that it just didn't compute. How could somebody have moved the track from the south side of the Highway to the middle of the motor court?

* * *

When Peter came to it was still raining, but only lightly. The wind was down, and there was the redness of dawn in the eastern sky. He was lying face down in the mud. His attention was drawn to a beam of light. He was unable to stand, but he felt compelled to crawl toward the light. As he crawled his head cleared, and when he reached the light he found it to be a flashlight. It was abandoned and lying in a pool of water. His first rational thought was of Kelly. After what seemed like an eternity he was able to sit upright, pick up the light and scan a scene of total destruction. The tornado had flattened everything. Only one of the cars remained, and it had been crushed by a cottonwood, which had fallen directly on it. Peter's light shone on the lifeless heads of two passengers, the men who had left the cabin just in advance of the explosion.

Peter swung the light around to where the cabin had been. At first he saw nothing, nothing at all. Then his light reflected off the twisted sink pipes and a body clinging to them. Kelly was naked, and she was covered in blood, but Peter saw her eyes and knew she was alive. He forced himself to rise up and hobble toward her.

She looked up at him as he came forward.

"All those bicycle trips you took, and you never told me about this part," she said.

John P. Frey was born in England and raised in Philadelphia. He received his B.A. from Marietta College in 1968, and his J.D. from the University of Colorado in 1972. He has been in private practice in Fort Collins since 1972, and is currently a shareholder in Frey, Korb, Haggerty & Michaels, P.C. He developed a passion for self-contained, long-distance bicycle touring in the early 1980s. He has taken many such tours throughout the United States, culminating in a 48-day cross-country trip from Seattle to Washington, D.C., in 1998. He is the author of a self-published book about his cycling adventures entitled, "How Far Do You Guys Go In A Day? A History." Sales of this title have been brisk, now topping 10 since publication in 1996. He is married to Chris, and they are the parents of two grown daughters.

Non-Fiction

St. Patrick's Day

by Doug McQuiston

Two great, conflicting passions burn within the Irish: a rebel's heart, and a poet's soul. Both have smoldered so long they are by now imprinted into the DNA of anyone with a trace of Irish blood. They are both blessing and curse. The rebel's heart blesses the Celts with a cantankerous tenacity, steeling us to hang on through daunting adversity. But that heart also forbids complacency in the face of injustice. Thus are we cursed, because the world can be so unfair. The poet's soul blesses us with lyric sensitivity to all that comes our way. We cannot escape our Celtic wonder at what Yeats called, "*all things the delighted eyes now see*." But thus, too, are we cursed. We see so clearly the beauty, trust and love that can be in all things, only more keenly to lament when beauty, trust and love elude us.

Ireland tells its history in its rebellions. Every generation has had its tragic heroes. There was the Protestant aristocrat and lawyer Theobald Wolfe Tone. He rose from the aristocracy to become one of the most beloved patriots of Ireland, then met death in prison for his role in the 1798 "Rising." Bold Robert Emmet followed just a few years later, with his United Irish movement and another aborted Rising. He, too, met with the executioner in 1803. A generation later came the

Fenians, Irish-Americans who returned to the Emerald Isle cold-forged by service in the Civil War, to spark the 1867 Rising. They failed heroically, as had their fathers, betrayed by dwindling supplies and inadequate numbers. Charles Stuart Parnell rose later in the 19th century to speak again for Ireland's freedom, this time creating a wave that crested in 1916 in a way that changed Ireland's course forever.

Each of the Risings before 1916 failed tragically, poetically. The Irish grew to expect failure, yet clung to the hope that one day they would be free from the Saxon yoke. They had a saying back then, "A Rising Every Generation." And, of course, they had a song. In *Four Green Fields,* the singer recounts the pain of the long battles for independence, the Four Fields being the four Provinces of Ireland (Ulster, Munster, Leinster and Connaught). The history of the struggle, and the long Irish memory, sings to us in the final verse: "*But my sons had sons, as brave as were their fathers, so my Four Green Fields will bloom once again, said she . . .*" That is the Celtic legacy, to shoulder the fight borne by our fathers, and theirs before them.

In 1916, the sons again answered their fathers' call. They were Michael Collins, Padráic Pearse, Joseph Plunkett, Sean MacDíarmada, and the other heroes of the Easter rebellion. That Rising, like the others, failed heroically following a merciless artillery pounding at their doomed stronghold, the General Post Office in Dublin. But this time, the "Saxon foe" made a mistake. This time, those who hanged Ireland's heroes would not be the ones who wrote her history. They left a hero alive.

Saved by intense pressure from American, and even English, political figures of the day, Michael Collins' death sentence was commuted. In his three years in an English jail, he read, and he learned. One of the books he read was a biography of Gen. Francis Marion, the "Swamp Fox" of the American Revolution. He read of

Marion's tactics of using small, disconnected cells of fighting men who skirmished with the British then disappeared into the swamp. With this knowledge, Collins would change Ireland's Risings forever.

On his release in 1919, Collins gave the British who occupied Ireland what Marion had given their great-grandfathers a 130 years before: The Flying Columns, small, disconnected bands of men fighting a ruthless, unrelenting, guerilla war. When it was over in 1921, Ireland had what it had never had before: freedom from British rule in all but the six counties of the North. Collins' legacy survives today in the peaceful struggle of Ireland's new sons to free Ulster, the last of her Four Green Fields.

Ireland has always idolized her rebels. But the poet's half of the Irish heart beats right alongside its rebel half. Through it all, there have been the songs. Ireland makes statues not just of her heroes, but of her poets. After all, her soldiers have all been poets, and her poets soldiers. She has always sung their songs.

The Irish have not always been the most successful rebels. But they are surely the world's greatest balladeers. What each rebellion lacked in armed troops and successful battles, it made up in songs. They took the songs with them in the great Irish Diaspora, so we sing them today as they sang them hundreds of years ago. Here in America, usually around St. Patrick's Day (a far bigger event here than anywhere in Ireland), you'll hear them in pubs, homes, even on the street in the grand parades. Played on bagpipes or sung off-key to the accompaniment of a tin whistle or accordion, you'll hear them this St. Patrick's Day. You'll hear the old tunes like *The Minstrel Boy* and *The Wearin' of the Green*. You'll hear the Fenian tunes like *Bold Fenian Men* and *Men of the West*, along with tunes from the more recent past, like *Roddy McCorley*, *Four Green Fields,* and *A Nation Once Again*.

The songs are a test of your ancestry—every bit as accurate as could be gotten with a microscope. If you have a trace of Celtic blood, when you hear them the hair on the back of your neck will stand up, and you'll wish there was a barricade nearby to man. It is the Rebel's curse working on you.

The words sing of the bitter fruit of the Risings—dashed dreams, hopeless odds, certain death, and astoundingly foolish bravery. In *Foggy Dew*, we remember the Easter Rising and the war that followed:

Right proudly high o'er Dublin town, we
hung out the flag of war;
Twas better to die 'neath an Irish sky
than at Suvla or Sud-el-Bar...

The Irish soldier-poets who fought that Easter knew they were doomed, as the song cries, to "*Brittania's Huns with their long-range guns.*" Yet they fought anyway, because it was better to be buried "*where the Fenians sleep*" than to die in service to the Crown in far off World War I battlefields like Suvla in northern Europe, or Sud-el-Bar in the Middle East.

The Irish history is not just written. It is sung. The songs bind the generations together. The tidal wave of Irish emigration during the 19th and early 20th Centuries spread Erin's curse of rebels and poets throughout the world. When Ted Kennedy eulogized his brother Bobby, he spoke of the rebel's heart when he said, "*Some people see things as they are and say why. My brother dreamed things that never were, and said, why not?*"

As maddening and painful as it may sometimes be to live with this fire burning in us, would it not be unthinkable to anyone of Celtic descent to live without it? Yeats both lived and wrote about the Gaels' timeless struggle between the anguish and the beauty of their rebellious history. He gave voice to the Irish soul in his poem "*Easter, 1916:*"

I write it out in a verse—
MacDonagh and MacBride
And Connolly and Pearse
Now and in time to be,
Wherever green is worn,
Are changed, changed utterly:
A terrible beauty is born.

This year, when you raise your glass on St. Patrick's Day, you'll know why. So sing like no one's listening. You're a child of Ireland, and yours is a terrible beauty.

Doug McQuiston has practiced law in Denver for 20 years, because he can't make a living playing the bagpipes or fly-fishing. He is a writer and former chair of the Denver Bar Association Docket *committee, and pipe corporal of the Michael Collins Pipes and Drums Pipe Band.*

The War on Drugs: An Impossible Dream

by John L. Kane

—United States Senior District Judge December 2000

The heedless pursuit of folly is a condition of human nature that has been with us throughout the history of mankind. With a collective refusal to recognize the inevitable and the obvious, various societies have thrust themselves headlong toward failure and disaster. The horror of the Children's Crusade is easy to admit because time has made it remote. A nation half-slave and half-free marching inexorably to Civil War is closer in time and consequence, but memory dims the barbarity and conceals fratricide in illusions of glory. Only recently have we dared admit the cultural ignorance and rejection of previous military counsel that were responsible for the national disaster we call Vietnam.

A monster gnawing in the belly of the human spirit impels us to abandon both cherished values and common sense. Like Don Quixote, we depart from reality to pursue imagined demons and leave naught but carnage and confusion behind. The sated monster laughs at our folly and awaits the next imagined peril.

As Mark Twain observed, "What you know that isn't true will cause you more harm than what you don't know at all." What we know that *isn't* true and what we refuse to know that *is* true about drugs forms the bedrock of our current national, indeed international, folly.

It is *not* true that illegal drug use is the nation's most serious health problem. Voluntary obesity is. More death and economic loss are caused by the consumption of legal drugs, principally alcohol and tobacco, than all illegal drugs. Over 100 million Americans drank alcohol last month. Over 50 million smoked tobacco. Nine million Americans smoked marijuana last month; 1.2 million ingested cocaine during the same period and fewer than 6 million used it within the past year. The figures for heroin and nonprescribed amphetamine abuse are so small they are not even in the same statistical league, much less the same ballpark.

Not all people who drink alcohol or smoke tobacco are killed or seriously injured, as a result, nor are all voluntarily obese people fatalities. The same is true of those who take illegal drugs; not all, nor even most who use them are killed, seriously injured or addicted. Yet, it is our stated national policy to imprison all those who possess, sell or use illegal drugs. That policy is pure folly.

Drug prohibition doesn't work. In 1914, when drugs such as cocaine were available on grocery shelves, 1.3 percent of the population was addicted. In 1979, before the so-called "War on Drugs" crackdown, the addiction rate was still 1.3 percent. Today, while billions of dollars are being spent to reduce drug use, the addiction rate is still 1.3 percent. Yet, America imprisons 100,000 more persons for drug offenses than the entire European Union imprisons for all offenses. The European Union has 100 million more citizens than the U.S.

Drug prohibition is also a waste of money. Local, state and federal governments now spend over $9 billion per year to imprison 458,131 drug offenders.

Incarcerating all cocaine users for a year would cost $74 billion, but only after constructing 3.5 million more prison beds at an initial cost or $175 billion. It would cost $365 billion to jail everyone who smoked marijuana last year—five times the total state and local spending for all police, courts and prisons. We would need a cadre of guards and other prison employees larger than all of our military forces. This is a cost we cannot afford and a project we could never accomplish even if we had the money,

More costly than money, however, is the price we pay for this failed policy in terms of the decline in public safety, the breakdown of our criminal justice system, the erosion of our civil liberties, and the pervasive public disrespect of the law. Good citizens, who are otherwise law-abiding, ignore or evade drug laws. With literally tens of millions of people using illegal drugs or related to those who do, a large portion of the population has become cynical about all laws and our legal system and political process in particular.

Much like in the days of Prohibition, when citizens, politicians, children and gangsters met on common ground in speakeasies and paddy wagons, and when judges and prosecutors sought the flimsiest of reasons to dismiss cases against franchised populace, ordinary people today transact purchases with criminals in the black market. Hostility and scorn toward law and law enforcement are a natural consequence. When approximately half of the members of a high school graduating class have smoked marijuana or snorted cocaine, few, if any, or them or their parents are willing to regard them as criminals. Each year since 1989, more people have been sent to prison for drug offenses than for violent crime. At the same time, only one in five burglaries is reported and only one in twenty reported burglaries ends in arrest and yet detectives continue to be reassigned from burglary details to investigation of street sales of drugs.

On an even more practical level, the War on Drugs is doomed to failure. The most fundamental concept of economics is the law of demand, which says that all consumers buy less when the price rises.

Misunderstanding this basic rule, the drug warriors attempt to justify interdiction. They claim drug consumption can be ended by cutting off supply, thereby causing a price increase resulting in little or no demand. In other words, interdiction will cause prices to rise to such a high level that demand will cease.

A little knowledge is very dangerous. In fact, the law of demand applies to only one product at a time. Our sorry experience shows that when one illicit commodity becomes too expensive, another is selected. A 1994 National Bureau of Economic Research study found that when the price of marijuana rises, youth drink more beer and that directly correlates with an increase in traffic fatalities.

A National Institute of Justice study reported a precipitous increase in the use of methamphetamine during 1985-86, after a crop destruction program eviscerated the marijuana supply in Hawaii. Making marijuana more difficult to obtain also causes an increase in cocaine consumption. When efforts to interdict marijuana are successful, the danger to our youth is increased by a rising consumption of alcohol and cocaine. When the supply of beer is reduced, the consumption of hard liquor increases.

Moreover, interdiction increases production and consumption of drugs. A 1992 United States House Judiciary Crime Subcommittee reported that the massive effort to destroy the Medellin Cartel resulted in an increase of cocaine transshipment points from eleven to twenty-five and an expansion of cocaine processing to as many as thirteen more countries. Researchers have also found a statistically significant correlation between higher incarceration rates of drug offenders and greater, not less, drug use.

As Benson and Rasmussen observe, the failure of the War on Drugs makes legalization an attractive alternative in the eyes of conservative and liberal luminaries such as esteemed Nobel Laureate Milton Friedman, author and commentator William F. Buckley, and former Secretary of State George Shultz on the one side, and former Baltimore Mayor Kurt Scmoke, *New York Times* columnist Anthony Lewis, and ACLU President Nadine Strossen on the other. They all publicly advocate the legalization of drugs, treating them like alcohol and subjecting them to advertising restrictions, age limits, time and place restrictions and excise taxes. For many, legalization is the logical solution to the nation's drug problems. For some, it is not only logical, but a matter of fundamental freedom. People are responsible for themselves and should have the right to make their own decisions.

Prohibition has always failed and always will, but there is an alternative to outright legalization. We are not forced to make a Hobson's Choice. The drug problem will evaporate when the black market is eliminated, but the evaporation process will take time and effort.

The middle approach between the extremes of legalization and prohibition is to accept drug use as an undesirable part of the human condition and treat it as a health problem. A 1994 Rand Study shows that treatment of heavy cocaine users is seven times more effective than asset forfeitures, arrest and imprisonment. The same study shows that the cost of treatment is one-fourth that of police enforcement.

As Americans, our biggest fault is the overriding desire to solve any problem, "once and for all." To borrow from drug culture vernacular, our national psyche demands a "quick fix." Unfortunately, it isn't there. What we as a nation must do is learn to live with uncertainty and expect less than total success.

If our appraisal of American history is honest, we

must recognize that our country has succeeded when it has placed its faith and trust in the spirit of American enterprise and that we have failed when we have followed a puritanical path. Our highest purposes are achieved when we proceed with the consent of the governed. Our failures occur with force, the threat of force and the practice of fraud. American drug policy includes the use of military force in other countries and on our national borders, the threat of force to other nations, and the threat or severe economic and diplomatic sanctions even to long-standing allies. In furtherance of that policy, the dissemination of false and misleading data by the government has become commonplace. The same policy results in ignoring, deriding and distorting facts that would otherwise show more successful alternatives to the present practices of interdiction and criminal sanctions for drug consumption.

Police agencies still need to protect the public by holding those who cause accidents or commit crimes while under the influence of drugs and alcohol fully accountable for their acts, but we must get them out of the business of financing their operations through the seizure and forfeiture of private property. The costs of law enforcement should be funded from the public fisc, under direct legislative control. In other and harsher words, we need to terminate the symbiotic business relationship that law enforcement has with the illegal drug industry. Each scratches the other's back.

One of the longest and most cherished traditions of this nation is that the military is subservient to the civilian government, and that military might shall never be engaged in domestic matters. For as long as we have been free, we have disavowed the existence of an all-national police force. Law enforcement is the business of local police agencies.

Federal grants and financing of multi-governmental task forces, coupled with military assistance, seriously jeopardize local control of police action. The federal government must get out of domestic drug law enforcement for no reason less important than the freedom of all individuals.

State and local officials are responsible for domestic law and order. There is an understandable temptation for state officials to shape their policies and programs to conform to federal grant requirements, but state legislatures must ensure that control of state agencies is not abdicated in the grab for federal funds. Indeed, if legislators do not meet this responsibility, they can be defeated at the polls and replaced by those who will. Community safety and freedom must not be compromised in pursuit of the federal dollar.

Alexis de Tocqueville called our states and communities the "laboratories of democracy," where experiments in self-government could take place and the success of one could be substituted for the failure of another. Our federally directed drug control policy has closed these laboratories. The consequence is that as a free people we continue to pursue but one path—the path of folly.

In order to deal successfully with drug abuse, this nation must eliminate the black market and permit a regulated one. We must permit the several states to resume their role as laboratories of democracy, in which policies and programs suitable to their individual needs and conditions can be implemented. We must restore local authority and autonomy over police practices. Most important, we must confront drug abuse as a threat to health, treatable through science rather than superstition and hysteria.

Most of this research data can be found in The American Drug War: Anatomy or a Futile and Costly Police Action, *by Bruce Benson and David Rasmussen, The Independent Institute, July 10, 2000.*

The War on Drugs—John L. Kane

John Kane is a senior judge, U.S. District Court for the District of Colorado. As an undergraduate at the University of Colorado, he majored in both literature and philosophy, aspiring to become a drama critic (although a professor told him The New York Times *hardly ever had openings). He was editor of the student literary magazine, played parts in student productions and musical variety shows. While in law school, he acted with an amateur group and later directed a couple of community theater productions. "I write for two reasons: I enjoy writing and I think lawyers and litigants (and the court of appeals) are entitled to know the bases of my decisions. When it's at its best, the trial court is theater."*

Ghosts in the Writing Field

by Jacqueline St. Joan

When I was growing up, we had two magazine subscriptions in our house: *Reader's Digest* and *Arizona Highways*. We were not a literary family, yet my mother had been a country girl who'd taken pride in her perfect spelling, perfect penmanship and perfect attendance. She had memorized, perfectly, poem after poem after sing-song poem. *Shoot if you must this old gray head, but spare our country's flag,*" she would bellow dramatically, her right arm waving above her head. She sang it seriously and with such passion that I was sure that if she ever saw someone threaten to shoot Old Glory, she would happily re-direct a rifle to her brain and die a martyr to red, white and blue.

The gingham dog and calico cat, she'd begin, and a weird light would spark in her eye. To my mother, a poem was a workout: every poetic idea had a gesture to accompany it. I was only six, but I could see how she must have looked at my age, reciting the poem in the parlor on Sunday for company.

Half past twelve and what do you think!
Not one of them had slept a wink!

Her pointer finger was wagging in the air, and she was winking and rocking. It was a little embarrassing to see her bald effort, but I couldn't take my eyes off of her.

Her store of corny pone was always full:

Oatspeasbeans and barley grow
Oatspeasbeans and barley grow
or
Would you rather be a colonel with an eagle on his shoulder or a private with a chicken on his knee?

Her words would singsong here and singsong there, and they still do.

But even before I hear it, I have to feel it start and stop and start again. Robert Haas writes that, "rhythm has direct access to the unconscious; because it can hypnotize us, enter our bodies and make us move, it is a power." I hear the "powerful thing," and it makes me feel something. It makes me wiggle and want to move toward the paper and the pencil. It's not an emotion that has a name: not sad, bad, mad or glad. The urge to move is more neutral, both voluntary or involuntary, as with bowels. The trick is to get that far and then get out of the way. Follow it to the first words. then follow it right into the field.

That's it. It's a place. The words come into the body like a lump or a bump or a bad case of the mumps, but they also come around the periphery of the field of consciousness, what Joy Harjo calls the "field of miracles." The words are hiding near dreams. I often sense I am lying in that field in the morning. I believe I know without looking how many of my cats are still on my bed. I say all three cats are on the bed, then I see that one of them is not. She is sitting over there by the glass door licking her front paw. You can be wrong in the field; in fact, being wrong is an important part of it—you are joyfully encouraged to make mistakes. In this field of the periphery, it's right to be wrong. Here you are looking up between the cracks in the world from your spying station. Your assignment, should you choose to accept it, is to stay there quietly in the light where they can see you and just watch them in the shadows. Images from sounds come forth. Do nothing and a message will arrive. You have the rest of your life to wait for it. We are all waiting to die anyway. Lorca says that's where the poet's true fight is.

As a child, I sometimes wished my mother could go to school, too. She seemed to like it so much. She was especially excited when we were assigned to write compositions. She would traipse up the attic stairs and emerge with one or two volumes from the dusty corpse of an encyclopedia she stored up there. The books were dated 1908. The only thing I'd ever seen that old was a dime my grandfather once showed me. Somehow, mother would always find something useful in the old books, and I'd wipe the Formica table clean after dinner, pull out the red vinyl chairs, and we'd set to work. This went on for the first few years of grade school, until the day I had to put my foot down.

I was in fifth grade and the composition was a biography of Susan B. Anthony. I took scissors to the encyclopedia and cut a picture of Miss Anthony in the shape of an oval so it would look like the cameo at the throat of her high-necked shirt. I pasted it on the cover of my composition, and using Sheaffer's blue-black ink pen, I began my final draft. With great concentration, I copied the words proudly one by one. By the time I came to the final paragraph, I was falling in love with my own writing. I was lost in the scene that described Miss Anthony as an old woman, delivering a speech on the stage—something about justice and equality. She was standing alone at a podium in a shawl looking "frail," my composition said. "Frail?" The word "frail" was inserted in my earlier draft in my mother's neat hand. It was not my word. I had no idea what "frail" meant. But the paragraph was so beautiful, and I didn't know a better word, and I didn't want to call my mother's attention to the moral dilemma I now was in—especially since she had put me in it. So, I learned the compromises writers make, copied the word "frail" into my final version and finished the job. I was ashamed because it was fraud. The next time Mother had that "let-me-help-you-with-your-homework" sparkle in her eye, I turned her down.

"Oh, so now you're so smart you don't need my help," she accused me. I could see she was hurt. "It's 'mother, please-I'd-rather-do-it-myself' is it?" she mimicked the television commerical that featured an impatient teenage girl fronting off her mother. "Just like when you were little and wouldn't hold my hand crossing the street!" she continued, her mind going off somewhere in the wind without me.

I could hear something calling me from out in the field. Something was starting to die. It would take many years of waiting before I could tolerate the ongoing tension between what was calling to me and what was dying in me.

The writer's problem is that as soon as we start to wait attentively for the sound, the image or the beat, our minds start to spin somewhere else. We forget to remember to keep waiting. We lose our concentraion, and the inchoate sounds of poetry become instead the drone of the shopping list. Shifting images that resonate in timelessness become the familiar, dry pages of a calendar full of lists, planned activities jotted down next to the numbers we assign to time. This is what takes us away from making art—not the need for money, or for uninterrupted time, or for the right teacher, or for a publishing contract. (These do have important effects all their own.) Forgetfulness steals us away while the wind is looking for something to do—anything at all. Write it on your prayer flag: Remember!

My father was a music teacher. As a child, I could listen to the music lessons from the top of the basement stairs. His student's clarinet played slowly and deliberately while his loud, deep voice intoned the beat:

Baaa/BaBa Ba

Baaa/BaBa Ba
Baaa/BaBa Ba
Baaa!

The bass line of my writing today was born in that basement. The treble was trained by television.

My father was a union man—a working musician. Art and beauty were good—very good. But so were wages and reasonable hours. He worked at night. During the day he would teach students, attend union meetings, have dinner with us, then nap in front of the TV until it was time to get ready for work again. During the years I was in high school, my father was teaching himself to play the flute. With his busy schedule, he found no time to practice the flute, so he played during television commercials. He kept the instrument primed and laid across the mantel. Dinah Shore would start singing about Chevrolets, and he'd switch off the sound, pick up the silver tube, run a few scales, check his embrouchure in the mirror, adjust the position of his fingers and elbows, and finish all the variations in several keys before the horses and guns appeared again on the screen. Then he'd settle back down in his chair where Bret Maverick and Ben Cartwright were his kind of guys.

What keeps me from writing is a certain weakness of the mind and a little dread. I recoil from the mystery with a lingering sense stored in my body that writing is not a legitimate way to live. But in the field of the imagination, writing makes perfectly good sense—just like shamanism or infinity or the dual nature of light. In the field, time melts, but you must be brave.

From the time I was 10 or 11, I felt that something was terribly wrong. I polished my saddle shoes nightly, and had my homework ready on time. My mother stood on the speckled linoleum and ironed my blouses long past the age when I could have done it myself. Now I think she did it repeatedly to keep her sanity in those years when she was so unhappy and we couldn't talk or do anything about it. I'd rush home from spending the night at my friend's house in the cool, dark morning of winter with a growing sense of disaster that would be waiting for me. But there was not obvious disaster. Mother would be watching television or waitng. Or ironing and waiting. Always waiting.

My first short story was about a lonely little girl in the park with an imaginary playmate and a mother in a mental hospital. She was really a very angry little girl. I entitled the story in code, "Step on a Crack." Since everyone knew the rest of that verse, my outcry was complete; we could pretend the story was fiction, and since I never said my mother was crazy, I was still loyal to the woman I loved.

Meanwhile, my father kept playing his sax: *a-one and a-two and I love Paris in the springtime, I love Paris in the fall . . .* Because he was a music teacher, he knew about the importance of practice—that as long as you put in your time, your star would climb. You'd improve; you had to. His body, as much as his mind, was learning to play the flute. My body does the writing and my mind takes the hits. Phil Jackson, coach of the Los Angeles Lakers, says the key to success is being in continuous motion—repetitive drills that train the player on the experimental level to develop an intuitive feel for the connection between their own movements and the other players. Anyone who is open and receptive can have the ball in this place of total and profound realization.

It's the field again.

For example, whatever made me write about my father fitting music practice into his schedule? You think I sat down and tried to think of a good example to presuade you to squeeze writing in between Cosby and Star Trek? No way. I don't have that kind of control. I just was sitting here typing and feeling relaxed watching the cursor move across the screen, and I started hearing my father's voice—Ba/BaBa/Ba—and I could see his right shoe tapping, and the next thing, I'm telling you about how he was a teacher and then about how he learned to play the flute. I had no idea I was going there anymore than I knew I was going to describe my moral dilemma with my mother over the word "frail," and a page later tell you about her frailty. My point is that I didn't do it. The words did it; I just followed along.

My mother died this year. She slowly lost her mind. Her brain responded to the interrupted flow of oxygen with little bursts of electrical charge that zapped first her memory, then her energy and, finally, her life.

The day before she died, I visited her. She was all dressed up and her fine white hair was fixed. She slumped down in her wing-back chair. One side of her mouth dropped and she couldn't talk. She could make sounds, but her eyes were red and strained, flicking around her mind, searching for the word that would unlock the door to the world of words again.

I wasn't sure she understood the words I spoke, so I sat on the floor at the feet by the chair, and I wrote her a few:

Your name is Peggy.
You are my mother.
I love you.
You will feel better soon.

I handed her the little notebook as if to ask her to check my spelling. She turned it this way and that. I started to take it back to read it aloud to her, but she snapped it away from me with all of her strength. She kept turning the words this way and that, over and over, until finally, exhausted, she surrendered back into her chair. She looked so frail, I believed she would be dead soon.

Later that night, my sister and I helped her into bed. She was agitated, pulling her nightgown off, her underpants, too. She wanted to be naked. So she curled up on her side, pale and soft between the white sheets.

Ghosts in the Writing Field— Jackie St. Joan

She was the shape of a scoop, a slice of the moon, the line of an egg. We pulled up the sheet to cover her in the dim room and she pulled it right down, hard, squeezing the palm of her protective hand down in there between her legs.

Ten years before this, waiting outside the hospital room where my father would die, my mother and I sat in silence. We were tired from the ongoing strain of it all. She turned to me and said: "He told me to meet him at the pass. I could hardly hear him at all, so I leaned over and put my ear right to his lips. He said: 'Meet me at the pass.' He said, 'Come alone.'"

In the field of reverie, I am wise and wordless. The urge toward words is small and moves quietly, simultaneously with all else that cannot be named. The urge widens my world. In the field of ghosts, I dream of my grown children as if they were six and nine years old. I contact another galaxy where my father's foot is under the kitchen table, tapping the back beat, and my mother is out there with him, winking and wagging her finger in his direction. She picks up the iron and pushes words back and forth across the board. She is preparing it for me. She is ironing a clean, white shirt.

Jackie St. Joan is a Colorado attorney, law professor and former county judge. Her prose and poetry have appeared in literary and law journals, magazines, and several books and anthologies. She has won writing awards from the Colorado Council on the Arts, Rocky Mountain Women's Institute, University of Colorado, the Clinical Legal Education Association and the Denver Press Club.

Off the Record

by Leland Anderson

There are ways of moving through the world. I don't know. I watch how others move, and sometimes I believe in miracles. I don't know. This is the time of darkness and, in the time of darkness, I am not sure whether anything moves. If it does, it moves very slowly, an ancient winter-time rhythm; the tumbrel creaks toward another year's execution. The heart beats slower, the inevitability of things ending becomes more inevitable, and the sad parade moves toward complete stillness. Persephone calls her children to gather 'round her robes.

This was the time of year when Yankee died. A dog. Nothing more than a dog. Something that came into life and passed beyond life; an idea made essence and then idea again. The last we were together, I awakened at 4:00 to be with him. He was scheduled to depart our lives at 7:30. We rocked, we talked, we joined our hearts one last time. His spine was gone, his rear legs hung like useless dead weights on a scale. Even then he pulled himself forward to retrieve a rolled newspaper, a stick, a worn slipper. Chesapeake. The word will always mean something special to me. When it was over, I stayed with him. My children waited outside. My wife waited outside. This was my dog. It was a respected relationship. I needed space to be alone with what was, but was no more. It was winter, a dark time, and that which was inevitable was now fact.

Leaving the veterinarian's office, I was not sure how to move in this world. I did not feel as if I was present in this world. Oh, I understood how to place one foot ahead of the other, to shift weight, and to go through certain motions. There was still breakfast to do after all, and someone said something about one of the car tires being low. These are the things one must attend to when grieving. The automatic things. The little things. It was not a time for planning trips to Greece or purchasing beautiful paintings. It was a time for seeing things quite simply. Tighten the screw on the front-door lock, replace the bulb in the bedroom lamp, straighten the carpet in front of the fireplace. I don't know. It was the little things that had to be done, just the little things. All of the rest did not matter. Not at all. Not at all.

Oh, I could tell you stories, even after these nine years since I lost him. We were a fine pair. Saturday mornings at the duck pond above the house. The early morning sun gave his deadgrass coat a ruby sheen. At heel, the curly bristles along his spine twitched in anticipation, his forepaws stamped the ground. He was at the ready. The command, the huge thrust and leap—his entire body stretched muscular over the water, finally crashing into the blue stillness. Then, the violently bold strokes as he moved toward the prey. A few others saw these things. I mention these things now and then. They remember. They remember.

There are things you have once in a life, but perhaps only once. For a time, you move together with these things. Circumstances, people, old habits, dogs. Then, they are gone. That is the way with winter. It takes things. Despite the promise of spring, sometimes things never come back. That is what I know. Of this, I am sure. What does come back is the sadness. Things are lost. Things are removed. Things die. That is the way it is.

Why? That I don't know. I simply don't know.

There are other things this time of year. A short candle burns on top of the piano at this time of year. That's for John. He was 26 when he left. I called him Crazy Horse because he would say "Hoka Hey" before every surgery. The Lakotah saying means, "Today is a good day to die." The stuff was moving throughout his body. He traveled around a lot before he left. Houston, Tijuana, Los Angeles. These are places that promised miracles but did not deliver. In the end, he submitted to the surgeries. A great deal of cutting and probing. After all the surgeries, his torso looked like a practice post for Titans swinging broad-axes. He showed me the scars once. I did not want to see them again. He wanted to stay, but he could not. Crazy Horse is gone.

Steve is gone, too. He and Crazy Horse were my friends. Now I think they are together watching over Yankee. They all are waiting for me. Steve went much faster. When it hits different parts of the body, it can move very quickly. Perhaps a month or two at most. I don't know. Steve did not have much time to move. He turned down the surgery, chemo, and other heroic measures. That allowed things to move more quickly. Steve once told me that I was accompanied by an angel throughout my life who wanted me to be the best person I could be. I think Steve was the best person he could be, far more so than I have been. People danced at his funeral. He would have liked that. I watched his five-year-old daughter that day. She moved very slowly. She did not dance.

And so we move through the world, looking for the proper pace, the right rhythm as we go on our way. I once road a mountain bike down a steep logging road cut into the side of a mountain. What I understood was that I had to focus on things immediately in front of me. Things moved very quickly. It was intense. I did not have time to look into the far valley or into the broad sweep of the sky. If my attention strayed from things immediately at hand, I would be in something akin to peril. The way was strewn with rocks, ruts and runnels. Things happened very quickly, very unexpectedly. It was exhilarating. I felt defiant and invulnerable. At the bottom, I crashed and did not care. I enjoyed the fear, the race, the nonchalant disregard of disaster. So there are times when you move through the world with a white-knuckle grip. You can absorb a great deal of pain, ignore a great deal of fear, and be very much here and now without even knowing where here or now is.

At times, in the midst of a trial in court, it seems as though everyone is rushing headlong down a mountainside without applying the brakes. The objections rise like stones ready to burst the tires. Lawyers clench the sides of the podium, eyes fixed on the witness. Everything is focused on the next few yards of testimony. Ground is lost or seized in a matter of moments. Risky, exhilarating. Time speeds up. I have seen lawyers in the courtroom moving at that pace. I wonder about their lives, how much pain they are absorbing, and whether they will crash at the bottom.

There was another time not too long ago when I walked through a dark forest on a moonless night. I could not see the ground beneath my feet. The trail was there, to be sure. I simply could not see it, only feel it as I scuffled across root, rocks and rivulets. The only way I could find my way along the trail was to look upward toward the break in the trees overhead, keeping my eye on the litter of stars channeled between the dark silhouettes of the branches. I followed the narrow path of starlight. I walked slowly, cautiously, and the stars told the story of the trail. I eventually found a place I wanted to be. That is a different kind of moving through the world. In that kind of movement, you must let go of the cold grip. You must let go of the fear. Things cannot be held tightly. You must feel your way in the darkness and float across the fear. That is the way on dark trails without moonlight.

Often, I have looked across the courtroom at the many inquiring faces, and I simply do not know what to do. I hear the many problems, and I do not know what to do. I am, of course, required to do justice, but the search for justice can be as obscure as a dark trail through the forest on a moonless night. Where can I find the break in the branches, the faint trail of stars overhead, something that will lead me to the place I want to be? The expectations of others can be daunting. They expect us to be informed, to be intelligent, to act with wisdom. That is not always the case, and many times we know less, far less, than the many blank, staring faces we encounter during the course of every day. That is when we must move quietly in the dark and float over the fear, trusting the distant sparkle of something true to take us where we need to be.

Sometimes we look for signs in the heavens. In the early morning hours on the day of John's funeral, the Perseid meteor shower began. I arose in the hour the Scandinavians call "the hour of the wolf," the hour before the first light of dawn (the same hour I stood watch with Yankee), walked into the backyard and lay down on the grass to watch the torrent of meteors pulsing from the constellation Perseus. I waited for almost an hour but saw nothing. I felt discouraged and alone. I got up, brushed myself off, and walked toward the back door. Walking through the back door, I happened to glance over my shoulder. Suddenly across the eastern morning sky, I saw a meteor brighter than even the dawning rays of the sun. It literally screamed across the emptiness.

The Perseids remind me of St. Lawrence in 258 A.D. whom the prefect of Rome ordered to bring all of the treasures of the church and to turn them over to the court. When the time for turning over the church's treasures arrived, St. Lawrence presented himself with hundreds of lame, crippled, elderly and diseased people. "These," he said, "are the treasures of the church." For this act of defiance, St. Lawrence was burned to death by the Roman Emperor Valerian. That night, the Perseids burst forth across the black Roman skies. Those who understood concluded that even the heavens were crying. For many years thereafter, the Perseids were referred to as the tears of St. Lawrence. On John's day, I saw one great tear that streaked across the cheek of dawn and disappeared, just like John.

Many people celebrate with lights at this time of year. In some homes, the celebration of lights is private and very sacred. In others, the displays are more outward. Our home is usually crowned by hundreds of lights twinkling through the night. We have received anonymous notes from people who work late-shifts thanking us for the bright lights they pass on their way to work. Things are lost. Things die. That is the truth. But I also believe something gives light beyond the darkness, something unperishable, something readily available to guide our path if we are willing to look.

I choose to look for miracles. When I hear the stories I must listen to throughout the day, I have no other choice. Without miracles, the tumbrel would be all that we could hear. From the vast silence, there would be only more silence, and the branches of the trees overhead would close in. Does this mean ignoring the pain or pretending it is not there? Not at all. Miracles occur because of the darkness. Those who follow the tumbrel often stop at the well of sadness. The well is deep, but looking in, I see the sparkle of stars and meteors glancing across the surface of the water. I know there is something more than the cold water in the well. This much I know. Of this, I am sure.

Leland Anderson is a district court judge in Jefferson County who writes a quarterly column, "Off the Record," in

The Colorado Lawyer. *His column addresses philosophical, spiritual and lifestyle issues facing lawyers and judges in their daily lives and work.*

13 DEAD

by Scott Robinson

13 Dead. 23 Injured. Someone has to pay.

In the aftermath of the Columbine High School massacre, another dark shadow has fallen over the victims: a shadow cast by courthouses.

The rough beast that took form in the malevolent minds of Eric Harris and Dylan Klebold months ago is now slouching slowly toward courthouses to be borne, to enter into another phase of its useless, base existence: litigation.

The fledgling arms dealer who sold an assault pistol to the teen terrorists has been arrested and charged with a weapons violation, but that represents only the beginning of years of legal wrangling over criminal culpability and civil liability.

None can rest in peace until "responsibility" is assigned, prison terms meted out, and money changes hands: the American Way of Death.

It is all too often my job to counsel parents who have lost children to the violent or careless acts of others. So, what would I tell the Columbine families about what the law can do for them? Nothing very encouraging.

Unfortunately, while criminal prosecution may begin to satisfy their understandable human need for vengeance, legions of lawsuits will have the opposite effect: victimizing them again, but in agonizingly slow motion.

The criminal law is clear-cut and unequivocal: any accomplice is just as guilty of murder as were Harris and Klebold, young men who simultaneously lost sight of reality and humanity.

Anyone who helped them, knowing what they had in mind, deserves everything that the justice system can deal out. Knowledge that even one bomb could be planted, that a single bullet might be fired, is more than enough.

Simple justice arising like a phoenix out of complicated facts. If only the same were true in civil court.

So what does the competent lawyer who handles injury and death cases tell the parents of teenagers shot down like animated figures in a video game, left terrorized, paralyzed, or for dead? That insurmountable obstacles confront them: too many claimants, too little money, too many legal hurdles, and too few facts to work with, to make such suits even remotely worthwhile.

The principal perpetrators are dead, leaving less behind to satisfy creditors than did Romeo leave Juliet. The parents of the teens could be held liable, but only if it was reasonably foreseeable that the two young men would attack their schoolmates with firearms and pipe bombs, which was hardly presaged by their prior conduct.

Even the wretched Web site maintained by Eric Harris may not be enough, as there is no hard evidence that his parents knew of its hateful contents, and Eric Harris was an adult, not a minor, and thus responsible for his own actions.

Ironically, Dylan Klebold's parents are more likely civil lawsuit targets, because he was under 18 and living at home, rendering his parents strictly liable under an obscure state law for bodily injury and property damage maliciously, willfully, or knowingly caused. Liability is one thing; actually collecting meaningful damages is altogether another. The Klebolds' statutory liability is limited to $3,500 per claim. With 36 injury and death cases alone, coupled with property damage and investigative costs in the millions, $3,500 does not stretch very far, even assuming homeowners insurance and the Klebold's own assets are implicated.

There are simply too many dead, too many injured, too many medical bills, too much destroyed, and not enough to go around. All of this leaves little for the victims, even if creative attorneys work "downstream" from Harris and Klebold.

How about suing teachers and the school district for not blowing the whistle on Harris and Klebold after their sadistic videotape was shown in class, or for writing assignments full of murder and mayhem?

Or suing the SWAT team or the sheriffs' department for "mishandling" the shooting scene, or for failing to fully investigate prior warnings about Harris? Such claims ultimately will only escalate the anguish of the victims, because of one cruel word: immunity.

Under the Governmental Immunity Act, teachers and the school district are immune from suit except for "willful and wanton" conduct or "dangerous conditions" in the building itself. Even if not immune, the maximum exposure would be a measly $150,000 per person, $600,000 for the entire incident.

Small change indeed, considering the many meritorious claimants who would be placed in the horrendous position of fighting each other for the few dollars available.

So, too, the police agencies that responded to the shooting and the sheriff' department: immunity attaches to "discretionary" acts by them, conduct involving decision-making within the context of the job.

Reported accounts make it factually difficult to fault the responding officers, all of whom displayed heroism by risking their own lives in efforts to save as many students as they could. Yet, even had there been some SWAT team "negligence," no liability would attach.

In contrast, while factually the sheriff's department could have done more in following up on information previously provided to it that still does not create civil liability. Ordinarily there is no legal "duty" to predict and prevent future criminal conduct, viewed as "superseding intervening" acts.

No one can blame parents for wanting to do something. So why not just file suit and attack the Governmental Immunity Act as unconstitutional? Because lawsuits are not cost-free, and because it has been tried before to no avail, as recently as 1992, when the Colorado Supreme Court for the umpteenth time upheld the constitutionality of limitations on state liability, in a case arising out of the 1987 bus disaster on Berthoud Pass.

Sue in federal court under the Civil Rights Acts to get around state law immunity? Not very likely. It is one thing to file in federal court; it is altogether another to stay there and get to trial. Unless it can be shown that school officials or law enforcement personnel acted with "deliberate indifference," such suits will be unceremoniously thrown out of court.

So why not sue everybody, and throw in for good measure firearms manufacturers, gun dealers, film and recording industries, and video game creators, for "planting" violent thoughts in the minds of impressionable teenagers, and for supplying deadly instrumentalities that make mass mayhem possible? Appealing in theory, dismal in reality.

Notwithstanding the recent "Jenny Jones" liability verdict, our Colorado courts are very hostile to such exotic claims, scrupulously limiting legal "duty." In addition, any defendant named in such a suit can "designate" other people and entities as "responsible" non-parties, permitting jurors to weigh the comparative culpability of others. In other words, if you sue the manufacturer of the video game Doom, the jury will also compare the responsibility of Eric Harris, Dylan Klebold, their parents, the school district, law enforcement officers, gun manufacturers, and so on.

Like it or not, any jury hearing the case will assign most if not all responsibility to Eric Harris and Dylan Klebold, their parents, and to the immune entities, even in the unlikely event that some judge somewhere permits a trial to take place.

But shouldn't the parents of the young people brutally murdered in this insane incident be compensated? And how about the wounded? Why shouldn't they look to the civil justice system, if not for money, then to rid the world of readily-available semi-automatic weapons, sadistic video games, distracted teachers, and disinterested police officers?

Because such suits will only aggravate the pain already suffered, through years of failed litigation, stimulated by ambitious attorneys' unfulfilled promises of trials to be won and riches to be garnered, adding insult to injury no matter how noble the ultimate goal of bettering society.

And no matter how honorable the intent to help these poor people heal by letting them do something, so that death, dismemberment and disability do not go entirely for naught, unchallenged and unremedied. Above all else, our civil court system is just not very good at grief counseling.

So what do I tell a potential plaintiff in this case, or an attorney seeking my advice on how to proceed?

That the victims have suffered enough.

Scott Robinson is a trial lawyer who has been involved in a number of high-profile criminal and civil cases, including the defense of James King in the United Bank case and the prosecution of Denver police officers in the Jeffery Truax shooting. He is the legal analyst for KUSA Channel 9 and has provided legal commentary for the BBC, CBC, Court TV and KOA radio.

Some Philosophical Political Projections

by Walter L. Gerash

As one reaches three quarters of a millennium, the tendency is to look back rather than forward. On the other hand, as the great pitcher Satchel Paige once said, "Don't look back. Something might be gaining on you." When telling a history of experiences, a man can appear to be wise; when looking forward, as he continues the struggle in life, he can have the illusion of being younger.

While life carries sweetness and light, it's also bitter-sweet. Our law profession is filled with the crises and tragedies clients bring to us. Hence our profession has an aura of cynicism concerning people and their life processes and destiny. Clients come to us to cure, resolve or help them in their plight. Sometimes, in plunging into our adversarial, and hopefully helpful, role to solve problems, we live in the glory of the struggle for victory or solution.

Social movements, religious movements, martyrs, philosophers and revolutionaries have tried to spark a hope of a healthier existence and a better society. May this effort continue in the history of humanity on this planet.

Sadly, in the last 80 years, after two world wars, the rise of the nuclear age and the posturing of mutually assured destruction, one wonders if we will make it. We have bulging military budgets to target the destruction of humanity by first-strike weapons, which are poised underground, under the seas, in the air and in space. This terrible and useless anti-human burden contributes to the inability to feed, clothe and attend to the medical needs of the billions on our planet. In our existing global economy, 50 million people (17 million children among this staggering number) die each year of preventable diseases, malnutrition and starvation. Multi-national corporations, in the quest for greater profits, pollute our air, water and the earth. Their economic and political power controls the government, and it in turn refuses to adequately regulate excessive exploitation of labor and natural resources.

We still live under the threat of nuclear holocaust. Unfortunately, there's always the possibility of error, social pathology or a computer glitch to trigger the destruction of millions and billions with the awesome power of the fearsome foursome—underground Minute Man III missiles, underwater Trident submarines, Stealth bombers in the sky, and now reaching into space to provide a fourth dimension to kill our brothers, sisters and children on this planet. The corporate domination of the media now speaks in one voice to support this madness and glorify violence. The economic military complex that President Eisenhower warned us about is doing a massive brainwashing job from cradle to grave. Any effort to protest is met with informers, provocateurs, and local, state and federal enforcers.

Recently I have been retained to represent Rev. Carl Kabat. He has engaged in a symbolic struggle to alert us to the realities of the impending holocaust. His noble mission, as a "clown for Christ," is to preserve humanity and show that the emperor, although he has no clothes, is armed and dangerous.

In researching international law as one of Father Kabat's defenses, we found a 1996 decision of the World Court. It held that the threat or use of nuclear force with first-strike weapons of mass destruction could very well be a violation of the United Nations Charter and other international law that has been in place for 300 years. All lawyers should look at the writings of the Lawyers Committee on Nuclear Policy and then try to help enlist the rule of law to expose the aggressive Pentagon in its efforts to control every corner of the earth with force and threats of mass destruction. A good example of what's going on is the 78-day massive bombing of Belgrade without a declaration of war or any United Nations sanction.

Is our struggle hopeless? The Spanish philosopher George Santayana said, "Those who cannot remember the past are condemned to repeat it." Greece, Rome and Great Britain once dominated the world. Why do we have to shoulder that mantel?

During the '60s and '70s, a minority of Americans (which eventually grew to a majority) opposed the Vietnam War and waged a successful struggle for civil rights, voting rights and desegregation of the schools. Our law firm defended the D.U. students at Woodstock West, the *Currigan Hall Protesters vs. Vice President Spiro Agnew*, the Fort Collins Eight, the Crusade for Justice, the Black Panther Party and other deserving social struggles.

During these turbulent times, I met John Kane, who assisted me and Irving Andrews in some of our cases. I still remember him jumping out of his MG with a big smile. When he took a job as first county public defender in Adams County that began an experiment for the public defender system in Colorado. Later, he joined the Peace

Corps. My personal view at the time was that the Peace Corps was a hand-maiden of the military economic complex to control other people.

I was very upset with our government's intervention in Southeast Asia, which not only caused casualties to our sons and daughters but caused a million casualties to the Vietnamese who had just thrown off the yoke of French imperialism, which had gripped their country for 130 years. I learned that three times more bombs had been dropped on Vietnam than in the European Theatre of Operations in World War II. I was very disturbed about that situation. A number of friends got together and had a going-away party for John and his young wife. At that time, I was torn about whether he would help humanity more by being a public defender or by doing his thing with the Peace Corps. At the party, I penned this poem for John:

Adam Dove to the Eagle's Nest

I.

Out of the spine of America,
Out of the Rockies great,
The defender goes east,
to the lair of the Eagle Mars,
to the bully-great.

II.

Defender of the lumpen-poor,
Petty-cheat and psychopath,
The world of dog-eat-dog,
He was at their side,
With compassion, wit and well-honed writ,
He gave them all their day in court,
and walked them out to freedom—the jungle.

III.

He sprung the writs,
Wrung the jury's conscience,
And squeezed the court's equity,
He gave them the best of the worst,
But they kept coming.
The door to freedom or short sentence revolved.
Back came the same faces of the poor.

IV.

He tried love, friendship and psychiatry.
Jobs, sympathy and scorn for the system.
But they kept coming—
Yet he bridled the State of Adams.
He made the law less harsh.
He was our Defender—Adam Dove.

V.

He labored with pride of our people's greatness.
Out of the farmer's sweat and the bra ceros bent back came
the cornucopia of plenty.
From the miner, worker and scientists—
mountains of creature comforts—
From the iron worker, welder, laborer—
Levit Town, skyscraper and cities,
Freeways and freedom,
Great, lusty and creative,
They deliver the dream.
He loves this America.

VI.

Abroad other people's dream,
They want the same in their own way.

VII.

Come the killers of the dream,
In a five-cornered nest,
In a green beret—
Gendarme of the world.
Military economic complex—our other face.
Hatcher of plots, protector of petty kingdoms
—and dark dictatorships.
Batista, Chiang Kai Shek, Sigman Ree, Boa-Dai,
and Hitler-Ky.
Bomb the stone age into the dust age.
Spray gas, spread poison and devastate.
Make the world free from Communism,
Oh, Viet Nam, Oh, Viet Nam, Oh, Viet Nam.
Domingo, Cuba and Lebanon.

VIII.

Peace, Peace, and there is no peace.
Peace Corps, Voice of America, and there is no peace.
Muffle the sound of the naval guns,
Cover the napalm keloids on the baby's face.
Sing folk songs to drown the screams as the lazy dog tears
into flesh and bone.
Give medicine and a book so they can be strong to work
in our mines.
See our image gilded, not real.
See our sweet daughters and lean sons-they want peace.
They will teach you to sow, so others may reap.

IX.

But go great defender—you must learn in your own way.
Try to bridle war-mongers—and shade the rockets red glare,
Tell the people in the dung,

That out of the cradle endlessly rocking—
Out of the undulating eons of time.
There will be a change.
Tell them there will be a reckoning soon.
Tell them our love, not our hate.
Tell them there is another America.

—Walter L. Gerash, Denver, Colo., 1967

Walter L. Gerash has been a trial lawyer since 1956, specializing in personal injury and criminal law. He provides pro bono services for the poor, oppressed and people of color, trying to make the state and federal juries reflect a fair cross section of the community.

The Day I Flunked Out of Law School

by Sherman G. Finesilver

My father knew that something was amiss when he encountered me, late one afternoon, sitting on the stoop of our west Denver house. The dean of the University of Colorado School of Law, I said, decided I couldn't return to classes next fall. My grades were too low.

After listening calmly, my father then contacted Edward C. King, the law-school dean. But there was no changing the decision. Sherm is a terrific young man, Dean King said, but he'll never make a lawyer. He urged me to look for another career. In the meantime, he advised that I stay put in the grocery store where I worked on weekends. I wrote a note to the dean, and requested re-admission. It went unanswered.

Even today words cannot describe my upset. I'd never really failed at anything significant. In high school, I'd been a popular student and a highly regarded football player. I'd coasted through the University of Colorado at Boulder without working up a major sweat, and was duly admitted to its prestigious law school.

My dad's own schooling hadn't gone past the sixth grade, and he was a railway mail clerk for over forty years. But he loved learning, and he knew how much I wanted to become a lawyer. He suggested I look at

Westminster College of Law (now part of the University of Denver College of Law), where classes were held at night.

Dad's advice was perfectly practical. It also hurt like hell. The University of Colorado at Boulder was Taj Mahal—the door to judicial clerkships and prestigious law firms. Westminster was Tramway Tech—a poor man's school with no tenured professors or law review, whose students held down day jobs.

Visualizing myself at Westminster after Boulder was galling. And in truth, my self-confidence was badly shaken; maybe I wasn't cut out to study law. But in the end, I went to see Clifford Mills, Westminster's dean.

Mills read my college transcript, and I'll never forget him peering at me over the rim of his glasses. "Finesilver," he said bluntly, "the only thing you did well in at Boulder was athletics, a Spanish course and your fraternity."

He was right. I'd made it through, but lack of academic commitment and good study habits had finally caught up with me. Dean Mills let me enroll at Westminster, on one condition: that I repeat all my first-year classes, this time paying attention. "I'll be looking over your shoulder," he said.

One door had closed. But others opened.

Given a second chance, I worked much harder, becoming fascinated by the law of evidence. In my second year, the professor who taught the course passed away. I was asked to take over—inconceivable at a law school like Boulder. Evidence became a lifelong specialty, and for many years I taught classes on this subject for judges, law students and practicing lawyers throughout the country.

Meanwhile, I worked days in the Denver City Attorney's Office as a clerk. It was anything but glamorous. But it led to a job as an assistant city attorney after graduation.

I would become a county judge at age 28, one of Denver's youngest. Later, I was elected as a district judge, and then appointed by the President to the federal judiciary as a U.S. District Judge, and ultimately, I did return to Boulder—to receive the University of Colorado's George Norlin Award, and an honorary doctorate of law.

Sooner or later everyone will fall short at something important to them—whether it be a job, a dream or a relationship. Flunking out of law school, I believe, made me a better judge; it certainly taught me about the frailties of the human condition, and about the need to give people second chances.

But failure also taught me that life is a road with unpredictable forks and unexpected tomorrows. To take advantage of them, you can't let yourself be destroyed by defeat, or let others set the limits on your ability to achieve.

Sherman Finesilver is a retired chief judge of the U.S. District Court. He served as a federal judge for 24 years and a state judge for 16. He has been a leader in many judicial groups and served on numerous national judicial committees. He served on bar association committees, including Bill of Rights, Centennial, American Citizenship (chair for 20 years), Grievance and others. He pioneered courthouse visitations by students and has been a frequent motivational speaker in schools. He has lectured on legal medicine and society issues at law and medical schools. He has a national reading audience for articles and publications. He is now in private practice, specializing in arbitration and mediation.